Best Bike Rides
Washington, DC

D0877708

Help Us Keep This Guide Up to Date

Every effort has been made by the author and editors to make this guide as accurate and useful as possible. However, many things can change after a guide is published—roads are detoured, phone numbers change, facilities come under new management, etc.

We would love to hear from you concerning your experiences with this guide and how you feel it could be improved and kept up to date. While we may not be able to respond to all comments and suggestions, we'll take them to heart and we'll also make certain to share them with the author. Please send your comments and suggestions to the following address:

Globe Pequot Press
Reader Response/Editorial Department
P.O. Box 480
Guilford, CT 06437

Or you may e-mail us at:
editorial@GlobePequot .com

Thanks for your input, and happy riding!

BEST BIKE RIDES® SERIES

Best Bike Rides
Washington, DC

Great Recreational Rides
in the Metro Area

MARTIN FERNANDEZ

FALCONGUIDES

GUILFORD, CONNECTICUT
HELENA, MONTANA

AN IMPRINT OF GLOBE PEQUOT PRESS

FALCONGUIDES®

Copyright © 2013 Morris Book Publishing, LLC

FalconGuides is an imprint of Globe Pequot Press.
Falcon, FalconGuides, Outfit Your Mind, and Best Bike Rides are registered trademarks of Morris Book Publishing, LLC.

Maps by Trailhead Graphics Inc. © Morris Book Publishing, LLC

Photos by Martin Fernandez unless otherwise indicated

Text design: Sheryl Kober
Layout: Mary Ballachino
Project editor: Ellen Urban

Library of Congress Cataloging-in-Publication Data

Fernandez, Martin.
 Best bike rides Washington, DC : great recreational rides in the metro area / Martin Fernandez.
    pages cm
 Includes index.
 ISBN 978-0-7627-8081-5
 1. Cycling—Washington Metropolitan Area—Guidebooks. 2. Washington Metropolitan Area—Guidebooks. I. Title.
 GV1045.5.W18F47 2013
 796.6—dc23
                                                            2013012490

Printed in the United States of America
10 9 8 7 6 5 4 3 2 1

Contents

Acknowledgments. viii

Introduction ix

The Rides xi

Safety xiii

Equipment xvi

How to Use this Book xviii

Map Legend xx

Ride Finder xxi

🏔 Roads 🔄 Mountain Bike Trails 🚲 Paths

1. The Anacostia River Walk 🏔🚲. 1

2. The Capital Crescent Trail and Rock Creek Park 🏔🔄🚲. 9

3. The National Mall – L'Enfant's Grand Avenue 🏔🔄🚲. 18

4. The Four Bridges 🏔🚲. 27

5. The Tidal Basin and the Waterfront 🏔🚲. 36

6. The Alexandria Loop 🏔. 46

7. Burke Lake Park 🔄🚲. 56

8. The Arlington Beltway 🏔🔄🚲. 62

9. Laurel Hill 🔄 69

10. Prince William Forest Park 🏔🔄. 78

11. Arlington and the Pentagon 🏔🔄🚲. 87

12. Wakefield Park 🔄 96

13. Arlandia 🏔🚲. 103

14. Elizabeth Furnace 🔄 113

15. Loudoun County Roads 🏔 118

16. Meadowood Recreation Area 🔄. 124

17. Mount Vernon Loop 🏔🚲. 129

18. Prince William Road Ride, Brentsville and Manassas Loops 🔄 . . 137

19. The CCT, North to South 🚲 146

20. Fountainhead Regional Park 🔄. 158

21. Fairland 🏔🔄. 165

Overview

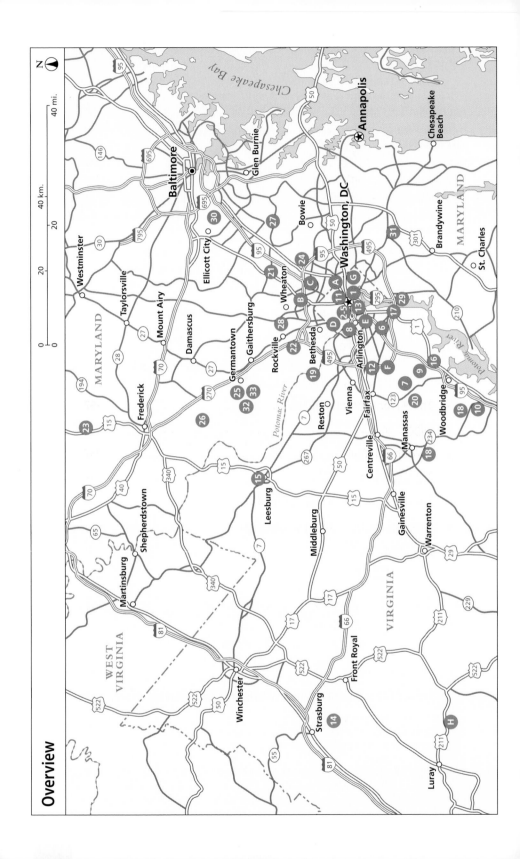

22. Cabin John Regional Park 175

23. Frederick Road Ride – The Covered Bridges 183

24. Agricultural Greenbelt 190

25. Montgomery County Back Roads 197

26. Sugarloaf Mountain Base Loop 203

27. The North Tract 208

28. Upper Rock Creek and Montgomery County 214

29. National Harbor 220

30. Avalon and Rockburn 227

31. Rosaryville State Park 236

32. Schaeffer Farms 242

33. Seneca Ridge Trail (SRT) 249

Honorable Mentions 257

A. The National Arboretum 257

B. Sligo Creek 257

C. N.W. Branch Trail 257

D. The C&O Canal 258

E. The Washington and Old Dominion Trail (W&OD) . . . 258

F. Lake Accotink MTB Trails 258

G. Fort Circle 259

H. Skyline Drive 259

Rides at a Glance 260

Regional Bicycle Clubs and Advocacy Groups 261

Ride Index 262

About the Author 263

Acknowledgments

This book is for Ari and all the rides ahead of us.

It's hard to imagine putting together a guidebook like this without help from others. And that is precisely the case with this one. I couldn't have done it alone. This book would not have happened unless I received both direct and indirect assistance from a multitude of individuals and organizations.

Every member of the Mid-Atlantic Off-Road Enthusiasts (MORE), without whom there wouldn't be any quality and sustainable off-road destinations in the Washington, DC metro area. Their tireless efforts and countless hours of volunteer work to ensure that there are a multitude of world-class off-road destinations for riders of all levels in our region is immeasurable.

The Washington Area Bicycle Authority (WABA) has spent countless hours lobbying for cyclists in this region. Thanks to them there are hundreds of miles of routes that can be enjoyed by everyone, and thanks to them, we have a voice that has helped turn Washington, DC into a Cycling City in less than a decade.

Without the tireless efforts and encouragement from some individuals this book would not have been possible either. Pete Beers, who really practices what so many preach, and is making a difference in the environment one pedal stroke at a time. "Uncle" Scott Scudamore, a true friend whose energy on and off the bike is intoxicating. Jason, who patiently led and followed me as I documented these rides; his companionship on the trail and road has been paramount to making this book happen. To all those strangers I asked and who graciously posed for a picture as you rode by, thank you!

To Courtita, my loving wife, without whom not a single word in this book would be possible, I love you two times, baby...

And, to you, for picking this book up and setting out to discover the joys that can be found on two wheels, keep the rubber side down, and see you on the trail, or the road...

Introduction

Despite mind-numbing traffic, and the ever-present elements of expansion and sprawl, one might think there are few recreational opportunities for the Washington, DC area's nearly 6 million residents and constant stream of visitors. The city itself is home to one of the most famous stretches of parkland in the nation, the National Mall, where everyone may enjoy not only our nation's treasures in one of the many museums that line its path, but also where you can take advantage of a variety of outdoor activities, the least of which is cycling.

To make sense of Washington, DC, you must first understand its very beginnings, tumultuous history, and recent revival. Shortly after Congress passed the Residence Act of 1790, President George Washington commissioned Pierre Charles L'Enfant to design what would later become the Nation's Capital at the intersections of the Potomac River and the Eastern Branch (Anacostia River). L'Enfant laid out a plan that consisted of a grid of streets traveling north to south and east to west, which were intersected by wide tree-lined diagonal avenues to honor the States. These "Grand Avenues" radiated out in a spoke fashion from what L'Enfant considered to be the most important structures in the new capital: the President's home and the seat of government—the Capitol.

L'Enfant envisioned grand avenues that would offer residents and visitors unobstructed vistas of landscaped parks and grand monuments dedicated to the young nation's heroes. Key to L'Enfant's design was a main avenue that would serve as a central axis for the Capital City. This back-bone would be a wide-open space lined with trees where people would feel a sense of harmony between the city and its natural environment. L'Enfant coupled this idea with the intention of designing a capital city that would rival its European counterparts, offering a sense of grandeur to the newly established nation. Today, that "Grand Avenue,"—the heart of Washington, DC—has evolved to become an inviting expanse of open space that welcomes all kinds of outdoor activities, including cycling.

What L'Enfant did not envision is the diversity and evolution of DC's neighborhoods. Long after the quirky architect of the nation's capital passed, the District of Columbia continued on a path of rapid growth. However, by the late 1960s and shortly after the assassination of the Rev. Martin Luther King, Jr. things turned sour. A series of racially provoked riots drove residents out of the city in hordes. That migration to the outskirts of Washington began a building boom that has yet to subside. Suburbs in neighboring Maryland and Virginia began to sprout all around, and the Capital City lost not only residents but also its sense of community.

H, I . . . K, L,

DC has no "J" street in any of its fourth quadrants. Urban legend states that Pierre L'Enfant omitted the letter J from the original design because of a dispute he had with the first Chief Justice of the Supreme Court, John Jay. The truth, however, is that in the 18th century the letters I and J were often interchangeable and often indistinguishable from each other when written, hence, no J Street.

Neighborhoods were clearly divided along racial lines, and for nearly four decades some of the city's more picturesque enclaves remained in decline and neglect.

Today, however, DC is experiencing a renaissance. Neighborhoods that had been neglected for decades have been rejuvenated by a new generation of residents, bringing energy and vibrancy back to the streets. L'Enfant's "Grand Avenues," such as the Pennsylvania Avenue corridor, are seeing rapid urban revitalization. Streets that were deserted even just a few years ago are now filled with activity late into the night. But what is most noteworthy—at least to this author—is the fact that the new generation of residents is influencing a movement that is transforming Washington into a Cycling City.

The emergence of DC's suburbs is also home to countless areas of open space where people can enjoy quality off-road or road cycling adventures. Thanks in large part to the tireless efforts of cycling organizations such as the Mid-Atlantic Off-Road Enthusiasts (MORE) and the Washington Area Bicycle Authority (WABA), the region has added an abundance of bike paths and trails, as well as designated bike lanes for both on- and off-road cycling. The efforts of these groups, along with the support of local governments, have truly transformed the greater Washington, DC metro area into a greener community that encourages cycling.

Locals and visitors may now enjoy many parts of the region from the unique view of a bicycle seat by utilizing the automated bike rental program, Capital Bikeshare, which allows them quick and easy access to get around the city on two wheels. Countless bike racks have been positioned throughout the area to ensure your ride is there when you return. To make things even more enticing, the Metropolitan Area Transit Authority (METRO) and other public transportation agencies now allow riders to take bikes on trains and buses.

Washington, DC has evolved to become a true cycling destination, and now, more than ever, it truly fulfills L'Enfant's vision of a city in which both residents and visitors can commune in social harmony with its surroundings.

The Rides

I chose the rides for this book for a variety of reasons, the most important factor being the relative proximity to the city. I have tried to keep the rides within a 40-mile (give or take) radius of the National Mall, with a couple a bit farther out because of their recreational and aesthetic "value." I have also considered length, historic and natural attractions, and traffic and road conditions, as well as the ability to do some of these with kids. I myself often bike with my (now 8-year-old) daughter and always want to make sure she has fun yet is always safe. In cases where I do recommend riding with your children, I have tried to minimize exposure to traffic, to make the day a bit more enjoyable and less stressful.

Most of the rides are between 9 and 20 miles long, with a few longer ones and a couple of shorter ones thrown in there for good measure. In many cases you'll have the opportunity to modify the rides to suit your needs. And in a couple I just point you to the trailhead, so that you can explore and enjoy the network of trails on your own. I, for example, often ride shorter versions of the routes outlined here when I take my daughter with me; at her age, even with as much fun as cycling is, she tends to get bored after 9 or so miles. I have also tried to select rides that can be pieced together to increase your riding distance. If you really are adventurous, you could combine two or even three of the routes to create an "epic" outing. I've indicated this on the specific rides should you choose to do so.

I have lived in the Washington, DC metropolitan area for nearly 25 years, and I'm happy to say that I have ridden every ride in this book multiple times and at different times of year. Cycling in DC can be a year-round activity. The availability of affordable winter cycling apparel should serve as an incentive to ride, even when the mercury drops. Who knows, you may find yourself enjoying cold-weather cycling more since Washington, DC summers can be quite brutal. Humidity levels can sometimes rival those of the Amazon. Cool weather also thins the crowd down; in the summer you may pass hundreds of other riders along the paths that line the city, but in the cooler months you could count encounters with the fingers on one hand.

Sometimes the weather conditions will force you to avoid, or at the very least reconsider, certain rides. Most of the off-road rides should be avoided during the late fall and winter months, when the thaw/freeze cycle is in effect. Early spring can also be problematic, especially when rains are plentiful and the trails remain wet and muddy. I have highlighted certain trails that are more susceptible to weather effects accordingly so that you are well informed about them. That way you can avoid them or hit them under optimum conditions accordingly.

I've discovered the majority of these rides through acquaintances, local cycling organizations, Internet posts, and my own exploration. The road rides in the city, specifically the ones through the neighborhoods, are courses I conceived myself. I present them only as a launching pad for your own adventures. There is nothing more rewarding for a cyclist than to discover a route on your own, especially if it starts and ends from your front door. I encourage you to explore the city and its suburbs and make riding a part of your daily life. One of the rides included is my local loop; while it may not be incredibly exciting, I share it with you to present the possibilities that exist out your door. It is my hope that you will share your loops with me as well.

I hope that you forgive me for including some of the off-road destinations that also appear in my other book, *Mountain Bike America, Baltimore/Washington*, but it was necessary. The DC region has one of the most successful and active mountain biking communities in the country. MORE, an International Mountain Biking Association (IMBA) flagship advocacy and recreation group, has lobbied extensively with various regional authorities to ensure cyclists have ample legal dirt to ride on. Thanks to MORE, the DC region is quickly becoming an off-road destination. You will find world-class off-road riding for all levels minutes from the Beltway. And if you find that dirt is your cup of tea, you'll be happy to know that to the west and north of Washington there are countless miles of amazing riding opportunities. I'll list some of these but won't go into too much detail simply because they are beyond my self-imposed distance radius, and I've written an entire other book detailing these.

I hope that the variety of rides featured in this book keeps you busy, entertained, and further whets your appetite to seek out other routes. In choosing road, path, and off-road rides, I also hope to introduce you to cycling as a whole. No one discipline is better than the other; fun can be had on slicks or knobbies. I know this firsthand.

My advice is to join one of the many cycling organizations in the region (listed elsewhere in this book). You will find that membership in one of the groups does have its advantages, and like me, you will likely make lifelong friends with whom to share your love and passion for cycling.

See you on the road—or the trail!

Safety

Safety is paramount when practicing any outdoor activity, and cycling is no exception to that rule. While there are risks involved in cycling, it is important to recognize that it is almost entirely up to you to eliminate, or at the very least minimize, the chances of suffering an injury or being involved in a cycling accident. As with any other activity, common sense always prevails. When in doubt, dismount. Risks do exist, and there is always the chance that someone else, no matter how in control or alert you are, may invade your space and cause a mishap, which is why you must always be vigilant and prepared.

Before setting out on any ride, on or off-road, I suggest you follow a set of simple rules: know your route, check your bike, check yourself, and always let someone else know where it is you're going and how long you plan to be gone for.

I'm confident that I have provided accurate descriptions in the ride guides that will allow you to anticipate what you will experience when you venture out on one of the routes. For on-road rides I've tried to minimize the exposure to traffic; unfortunately, in the DC area it is nearly impossible to completely avoid. In the majority of instances, the amount of traffic you encounter will be highly dependent on the time and day of the week that you head out the door. The DC metro area is notorious for its traffic jams, and while riding in the city, you may encounter backups in the least expected places and moments. Luckily, DC has a network of bike lanes that are often unaffected by these jams.

The most important thing to do while you are out on the road is to be pre-dictable and alert. If drivers can anticipate and have a good sense of what to expect from you, you will be safer. This means that making it a habit to obey the same laws drivers are subject to will ensure your safety. Staying alert will also reduce your exposure to situations when the ineptitude and carelessness of others puts you on the receiving end of a foolish act. The biggest on-road hazards comes from drivers who suddenly open their doors onto unsuspecting cyclists, or inattentive drivers who make left turns directly into your path. Make it a habit to ride far enough to the right of the road to allow motorists to safely pass while you, in turn, stay safely away from the zone where doors will swing open. If the road is too narrow to permit this, it is often acceptable to ride in the driving lane to ensure your safety. Common sense and following traffic patterns prevail here of course.

The next biggest hazard comes from drivers making left turns into your path. Never assume that an opposing driver sees you coming or that he/she will stop for you; you'd be surprised how "invisible" a cyclist is in these situations. Again, use your common sense. If you have any doubts, there is no shame in

IMBA Rules for the Trail

The International Mountain Biking association (IMBA) has set up six basic rules for the trail that will help you remain safe and ensure that the trails you enjoy remain open and accessible:

Ride Open Trails: Respect trail and road closures—ask a land manager for clarification if you are uncertain about the status of a trail. Do not trespass on private land. Obtain permits or other authorization as required. Be aware that bicycles are not permitted in areas protected as state or federal wilderness.

Leave No Trace: Be sensitive to the dirt beneath you. Wet and muddy trails are more vulnerable to damage than dry ones. When the trail is soft, consider other riding options. This also means staying on existing trails and not creating new ones. Don't cut switchbacks. Be sure to pack out at least as much as you pack in.

Control Your Bicycle: Inattention for even a moment could put yourself and others at risk. Obey all bicycle speed regulations and recommendations, and ride within your limits.

Yield Appropriately: Do your utmost to let your fellow trail users know you're coming—a friendly greeting or bell ring are good methods. Try to anticipate other trail users as you ride around corners. Bicyclists should yield to other nonmotorized trail users unless the trail is clearly signed for bike-only travel. Bicyclists traveling downhill should yield to ones headed uphill unless the trail is clearly signed for one-way or downhill-only traffic. In general, strive to make each pass a safe and courteous one.

Never Scare Animals: Animals are easily startled by an unannounced approach, a sudden movement, or a loud noise. Give animals enough room and time to adjust to you. When passing horses, use special care and follow directions from the horseback riders (ask if uncertain). Running cattle and disturbing wildlife are serious offenses.

Plan Ahead: Know your equipment, your ability, and the area in which you are riding and prepare accordingly. Strive to be self-sufficient: keep your equipment in good repair and carry necessary supplies for changes in weather or other conditions. Always wear a helmet and appropriate safety gear.

stopping and letting the two-ton vehicle pass before you. History proves that you will never win that argument.

Finally, while on the road, be aware of the other "obstacle" that rears its ugly head: people. It is not uncommon for an inattentive pedestrian hooked to an iPod or MP3 player to harmlessly walk directly into your path and wreak havoc on your day. In many cases, traffic-less situations, such as those you may encounter on the Mount Vernon or Rock Creek Park Trails, will provide bigger hurdles for you to overcome. The Mount Vernon Trail is notorious in this regard. On any given "pleasant" Sunday, you will encounter hoards of roadies on training rides alongside 5-year-olds on training wheels.

Off-road rides present a completely different set of challenges and hazards, yet the same commonsense rules apply. Mountain biking is not a "Mountain Dew commercial" and is only as "extreme" as you want it to be. I often enjoy off-road trails with my 8-year-old daughter more than on-road rides simply because they are safer. Still, like on the road, you must also be vigilant and alert. Again, common sense must prevail, and if you are ever in doubt, dismount. There is no shame in not trying to clear an obstacle that is beyond your ability. I suggest you tackle the easier trails outlined in this book and then progress to the more advanced ones.

Equipment

Chances are you've already purchased a bike, and the retailer you bought it from helped select the right size mount. If you have not yet bought a new bike, then take this as an opportunity to ensure you get the most for your money. A reputable cycling shop will ensure that you walk out of their show-room with a bike that fits you and the type of riding you want to pursue. If they push you to purchase a certain style, or a specific bike that's in stock, be wary. I personally will discourage you from purchasing a bike from a big box store. While you may save a few bucks initially, you will never get the level of service and attention that your local bike shop will deliver. I have listed several quality shops in this book that will be happy to help you out. Be sure to tell them who sent you!

It's always important to remember that the most critical safety feature of your bike is ultimately you. So, if you are not comfortable on your bike, you will be more likely to not ride well and be prone to accidents. Ensuring you are com-fortable when you ride is only achieved by having a frame size that fits your body. If the frame is too big, or too small, no amount of tweaking your saddle height or stem length will alleviate the issues presented by a poorly sized frame.

Before heading out on any ride you should always make sure your bike is in working order. Check your gears, brakes, tires, and air pressure. Also confirm that the hub/rim quick releases (if you have them) are tight and secure. I once saw a rider pop a wheelie in a parking lot only to see his front wheel fall out. The consequences were not pleasant, and the cyclist ended up taking a different ride that day . . . one to the emergency room. There's nothing worse than ending an outing on a bad note because you failed to check a minor issue that could have been avoided.

Always wear a helmet and be prepared. If you are venturing out for a long ride or to a remote place, bring enough water to last the outing. You should also carry along a snack or energy product. There are countless options of energy food products available for all tastes, and not just found in your bike shop either; also check your supermarket's shelves. Bring at the very least a CO_2 or compact pump, a spare tube, and a multitool, so you can fix a flat if necessary. Last, but not least, always check the local weather forecast to ensure that if need be you have a rain jacket or windbreaker for unexpected weather changes.

If you are a beginner, I highly encourage you to take an introductory cycling safety and skills class. Most bike shops offer some sort of clinic that can get you started. If they don't, local organizations such as WABA and MORE offer clinics that can get you headed in the right direction. WABA has a handful of free publications that can also introduce you to some basic cycling and safety concepts. The cities of Arlington, Alexandria, and DC also have free literature that can help you educate yourself on the rules of the road. Still, nothing beats putting rubber to the road or trail, and the more you ride, the more comfortable you'll be on two wheels. With every mile your skills will increase, and practicing safety will become second nature.

How to Use this Book

Unlike other cities, distance may not be the best gauge for you to use on how difficult or demanding a ride will be. The 9-mile Fountainhead loop, for example, will require considerable more energy than the 20-plus-mile Mount Vernon out-and-back outing. I highly suggest you read the quick introductions to each ride to give you an overall picture of what to expect.

When glancing at the "Rides at a Glance" section, you'll notice that most of the rides fall within the 9- to 20-mile range. I have not arbitrarily chosen this distance range, and know from experience that beginner to intermediate cyclists will feel comfortable riding these lengths. In many cases, the ride lengths are determined by the course themselves. For example, there really is no way to stretch the Meadowood Mountain bike trail any farther than 4 miles (there are plans to build additional trails there), but by riding two or three loops you can extend the ride to 8 or 12 miles. In many cases I have presented the rides with alternate starting points on how to increase or shorten their length, or how to make them more "kid friendly" if you wish to. And I have noted in each ride how you can combine them with another to make them longer. In Northern Virginia, for example, you could combine two popular local parks with the Cross County Trail to ride more than 50 miles.

The majority of on-road courses in the book are meant as launching pads for your own adventures. I highly recommend you purchase a copy of ADC's bike map of the Washington, DC metro area (available at most bike shops) since it will help you modify some of the rides in this book to make them your own. As I wrote earlier in this book, there is nothing more gratifying to a cyclist than coming up with his/her own route, especially if that route happens to begin from your front door.

My main goal with this book is for you to use it as inspiration for your very own adventures, and I welcome you to share your versions of the rides outlined here in our companion website, www.bestridesdc.com.

GPS Coordinates: Like most of you, my vehicle is equipped with a GPS unit that helps me find the quickest route to my destinations. Each ride in this book has been assigned a set of coordinates you can input into your unit (or Google maps) to get you to the starting point of the ride.

Mileage Markers: I also own a portable GPS unit that I use every time I head out on a ride and which I have used to chart all of the rides in this book. The GPS affords me the ability to accurately track how far I have ridden. Unfortunately, minor variations in specific units and bike computers will create slight deviations in between our measurements, and our markers may not match precisely. While I have tried to be as accurate as possible when charting the mile markers and cue points on each of the rides, there is a strong possibility that these may not match up with yours exactly, especially if you backtrack or take a short side trip on one of the routes. Most of the rides are well marked and you'll likely not need the unit at all, but for those where it is necessary, please use the markers as a general but not exact determination of how far you've traveled. I will also include specific landmarks as "markers" so that they may aid you during the ride in finding your way along the right path.

Map Legend

Transportation

Interstate/Divided Highway	═══════
Featured U.S. Highway	═══════
U.S. Highway	═══════
Featured State, County, or Local Road	━━━━━━
Primary Highway	────────
County/Local Road	────────
Featured Bike Route	▪▪▪▪▪▪▪▪▪▪
Bike Route	▪▪▪▪▪▪▪▪▪▪
Featured Trail	‑‑‑‑‑‑‑‑‑‑
Dirt Road/Trail	‑‑‑‑‑‑‑‑‑‑

Hydrology

Reservoir/Lake	⬭
River/Creek	～

Land Use

National Forest	▭
State/Local Park, Open Space	▭
State Line	─ ‑ ── ‑ ──

Symbols

Interstate	70
U.S. Highway	40
State Highway	74
Trailhead (Start)	10
Mileage Marker	17.1◆──
Small Park	♠
Visitor Center	❷
Point of Interest/ Structure	▪
Ranger Station	♦♠
Campground	▲
Airport	✛
University/College	☜
Boat Ramp	☲
Marina	✿
Bridge	⅄
Capitol	✪
Town	○
Mountain/Peak	▲
Direction Arrow	→

Ride Finder

BEST RIDES FOR GREAT VIEWS

1	The Anacostia River Walk
3	The National Mall—L'Enfant's Grand Avenue
4	The Four Bridges
5	The Tidal Basin and the Waterfront
8	The Arlington Beltway
11	Arlington and the Pentagon
13	Arlandia
23	Frederick Road Ride—The Covered Bridges
25	Montgomery County Back Roads
29	National Harbor
HM-A	The National Arboretum
HM-D	The C&O Canal
HM-H	Skyline Drive

BEST RIDES FOR RIVER LOVERS

1	The Anacostia River Walk
4	The Four Bridges
5	The Tidal Basin and the Waterfront
13	Arlandia
17	Mount Vernon Loop
29	National Harbor
HM-D	The C&O Canal

BEST RIDES FOR LAKE LOVERS

7	Burke Lake Park
24	Agricultural Greenbelt (Lake Loop)
28	Upper Rock Creek and Montgomery County
33	Seneca Ridge Trail (SRT)

BEST RIDES FOR FAMILIES WITH CHILDREN

7	Burke Lake Park
9	Laurel Hill
10	Prince William Forest Park (Out and Back)
12	Wakefield Park
16	Meadowood Recreation Area

17	Mount Vernon Loop (Fort Hunt Loop only)
24	Agricultural Greenbelt (Lake Loop)
27	The North Tract (MTB Loop)

BEST RIDES FOR NATURE LOVERS

2	The Capital Crescent Trail and Rock Creek Park
7	Burke Lake Park
9	Laurel Hill
10	Prince William Forest Park (All loops)
15	Loudoun County Roads
22	Cabin John Regional Park
30	Avalon and Rockburn
31	Rosaryville State Park
32	Schaeffer Farms
33	Seneca Ridge Trail (SRT)
HM-A	The National Arboretum
HM-D	The C&O Canal
HM-G	Fort Circle
HM-H	Skyline Drive

BEST RIDES IN THE CITY

1	The Anacostia River Walk
2	The Capital Crescent Trail and Rock Creek Park
3	The National Mall—L'Enfant's Grand Avenue
4	The Four Bridges
5	The Tidal Basin and the Waterfront
11	Arlington and the Pentagon
13	Arlandia
HM-D	The C&O Canal
HM-G	Fort Circle

BEST RIDES FOR HISTORY BUFFS

3	The National Mall—L'Enfant's Grand Avenue
4	The Four Bridges
5	The Tidal Basin and the Waterfront
9	Laurel Hill
11	Arlington and the Pentagon
15	Loudoun County Roads
17	Mount Vernon Loop

23   Frederick Road Ride—The Covered Bridges
29   National Harbor
HM-D   The C&O Canal

BEST RIDES WITH FAST SINGLETRACK

9   Laurel Hill
12   Wakefield Park
16   Meadowood Recreation Area
19   The CCT, North to South
20   Fountainhead Regional Park
21   Fairland (MTB Loop)
22   Cabin John Regional Park
26   Sugarloaf Mountain (MTB Loop)
30   Avalon and Rockburn
31   Rosaryville State Park
32   Schaeffer Farms
33   Seneca Ridge Trail (SRT)
HM-F   Lake Accotink MTB Trails

BEST RIDES WITH TECHNICAL TRAILS

12   Wakefield Park
14   Elizabeth Furnace
20   Fountainhead Regional Park
30   Avalon and Rockburn
31   Rosaryville State Park
32   Schaeffer Farms
HM-F   Lake Accotink MTB Trails

BEST RIDES FOR ROADIES

2   The Capital Crescent Trail and Rock Creek Park
10   Prince William Forest Park (Scenic Loop)
15   Loudoun County Roads
18   Prince William Road Ride, Brenstville and Manassas Loops
23   Frederick Road Ride—The Covered Bridges
24   Agricultural Greenbelt
25   Montgomery County Back Roads
26   Sugarloaf Mountain Base Loop
27   The North Tract (Road Out and Back)
HM-H   Skyline Drive

BEST ALL AROUND "BIKE PATH" RIDES, NO TRAFFIC...

6	The Alexandria Loop
7	Burke Lake Park
8	The Arlington Beltway
10	Prince William Forest Park (Out and Back and MTB Loop)
21	Fairland (Road Loop)
28	Upper Rock Creek and Montgomery County
HM-B	Sligo Creek
HM-C	N.W. Branch Trail
HM-D	The C&O Canal
HM-E	The Washington and Old Dominion Trail (W&OD)

The Anacostia River Walk

This ride will take you past one of the Capital's oldest stadiums and next to its newest. Along the way we'll get to see firsthand the revitalization of the Anacostia Riverfront, one of the region's most ambitious urban river renewal projects. We'll also ride past an old battleship and spin through one of the area's hippest neighborhoods, Capitol Hill.

Start: The intersection of 1st Street and East Capitol Street

Length: 10.7 miles

Approximate riding time: 1–2 hours

Best bike: Road bike

Terrain and trail surface: On road bike lanes and paved bike paths

Traffic and hazards: Other trail users, vehicle traffic in road portions

Things to see: The Capitol, Lincoln Park, Nationals Stadium, RFK Stadium, The Navy Yard, Capitol Hill, Eastern Market. Combine this ride with the Waterfront Ride to make it even longer.

Getting there: Keep in mind that there is limited off-street parking around the Capitol. There is metered street parking along the Mall west of the Capitol. Either take Metro or park your vehicle along the tidal basin and ride up the National Mall to the Capitol. You can also begin this ride on the Anacostia River Park, accessible from I-295.

    By Metro: The nearest stops to the Capitol are Union Station (1st NE and Mass Avenue) and Capitol South (1st SE between C & D). From Union Station take 1st Street south 4 blocks until you reach the intersection of 1st Street and East Capitol Street. From Capitol South take 1st north 3 blocks until you reach the intersection of 1st Street and East Capitol Street. GPS: 38.889764,-77.006006

Fees: None

THE RIDE

Two decades ago I would have thought twice before sending cyclists on a ride along a river that by all accounts many considered polluted, including by some of its most fervent advocates. Today, however, thanks to the tireless dedication and efforts of the local community, and a serious revitalization push from the city, as well as from various environmental organizations, riding next to the banks of the Anacostia is a pleasurable experience. From the seat of your bike, you will undoubtedly enjoy getting to know the east side of the city.

Long before it was nicknamed "the forgotten river," the Anacostia was home for many Native Americans and served as a valuable resource for the settlers who came after. The unfortunate "degradation" of the river began during those times. In the early 1600s settlers began clearing the forests along the Anacostia watershed to cultivate tobacco and other crops. The settlers also used the waterway as shipping lanes to the port in Bladensburg. For 200 years the practice went unchecked and the river became choked with toxic runoff from the cultivated lands.

Bike Shops

BicycleSPACE: 1019 7th St. NW, Washington, DC 20001; (202) 962-0123; www.bicyclespacedc.com
Capitol Hill Bikes: 719 8th St. SE, Washington, DC 20003; (202) 544-4234; www.capitolhillbikes.com

Over time, silt also built up along the bottom of the river, making ship passage to Bladensburg impossible. Once the river was rendered no longer shipworthy, or useful for business, it was abandoned.

Despite the health of the Anacostia River, the national capital's population grew exponentially and much of that growth happened along the watershed area. The forests that had been cleared for tobacco farms were replaced with other surfaces, and the damage to the natural hydrological system of the watershed compounded. The development practices of the late 19th and early 20th centuries along the nation's capital also contributed to the river's failing health. The dredging of the nearby Potomac had adverse effects on the river. The building of the combined sewer system (still in use today) often dumps a mixture of storm water and sewage into the river, and even the Navy Yard, through which we will ride, once dumped the toxic by-products of weapons manufacturing into the river. Today, though the lasting effects of that damage continues, clear efforts are under way to revitalize the river to its natural splendor. Some of the positive environmental strides that have been made are visible along our ride.

The river itself is not large; by all accounts it is considered a small river at only 8.5 miles in length, but its reach extends well beyond the nation's capital, and its confluence with DC's other river, the Potomac. The Anacostia River Water-

A family of cyclists makes its way toward the Navy Yard along the Anacostia River Walk Trail in Washington, DC.

shed reaches as far as Howard County to the north, and the eastern borders of Prince George's and Montgomery Counties to the east and west, respectively. But because of its generally short length—and location in a densely urban environment—the problems on the Anacostia are highly concentrated.

Symbolically, the Anacostia has served as a barrier that divided the city and region along economic, geographic, racial, and social boundaries. That said, over the past two decades individuals and nonprofit organizations have worked tirelessly to demystify the Anacostia so that it is seen for what it really is: a precious resource to be enjoyed by all.

The result of efforts to revitalize the river also hinge on the success of the Anacostia Waterfront Initiative's (AWI) vision. At its heart, the AWI wants to revitalize the waterfront district and transform the shores of the Anacostia River along DC's east side into a world-class waterfront. But a world-class waterfront is highly dependent on the river being clean, healthy, and safe. A solid effort to make it just that is clearly under way. Responsible development has begun

RFK, Home of Soccer in the Nation's Capital

Along the ride we roll past one of the capital's newest stadiums and along one of its oldest, **Robert F. Kennedy Stadium (RFK).** RFK has seen lots of tradition grace its field, including DC's original baseball team, the Washington Senators, as well as the Washington Redskins, and now DC United, the national capital's Major League Soccer (MLS) team. United was established in 1996, when the league formed, and to this day, despite a few bad seasons, remains the most decorated franchise in the league. The team has won a record four MLS Cups and has a trophy cabinet that's the envy of many storied clubs. Recently, the BicycleSPACE, mentioned in the Bike Shops section of this and other rides in the book, hosted a ride to a DC United match. Hundreds of cyclists rode together from the store's 7th Street location to RFK Stadium, where they enjoyed a match. Today, United is looking for a new home, and if they have their way, it'll be located not far from National's Stadium at Buzzard's point, also along the waterfront. Hopefully by the time you read this we can adjust this loop to include United's newest home as a destination and catch some of the country's best soccer athletes for a game to go along with our ride. In the meantime, as you ride past RFK and the auxiliary fields along C Street and Oklahoma Avenue, you can get a glimpse of the team training for their next match.

along the river. The construction of National's Stadium marked a significant milestone in the cleanup of the river. Environmental groups welcomed the development of the stadium simply because it would jump-start river cleanup, and it did. The stadium achieved a LEED Silver rating for its environmentally friendly elements, and the surrounding area has been considerably improved.

Part of the AWI's development project in the area also includes a system of trails that runs along the east and west banks of the river. For the most part these trails have been completed. In the process of the trail development, the Navy Yard, once an eyesore, transformed into a welcoming system of boardwalks. The trail also connected the west side of the city with the east, eliminating some of the symbolic barriers I mentioned before. Much work remains to be done though, and despite all of the efforts, the Anacostia continues to be one of the most degraded urban rivers in the nation, but solid progress is nevertheless being made. All the responsible development along its banks is transforming a once-abused river into a new urban landscape where "the forgotten river" may soon become "the rediscovered river."

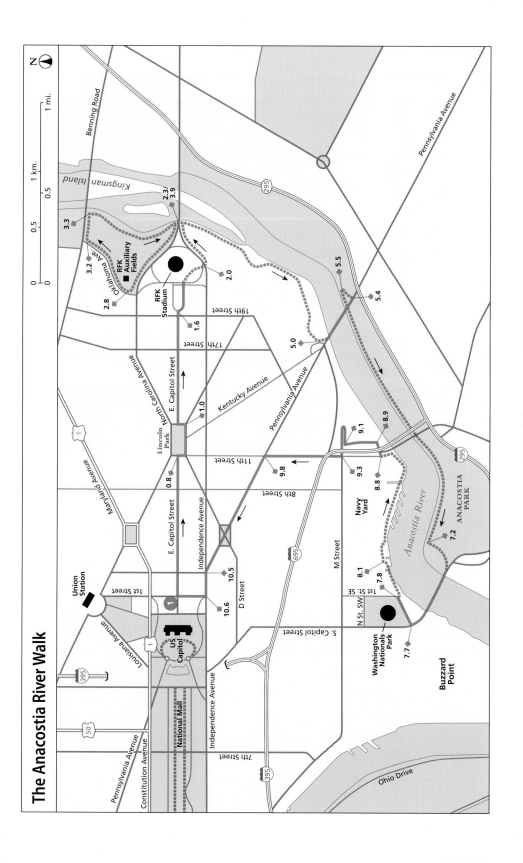

The Anacostia River Walk

0.0 Start at the intersection First Street and East Capitol Street. Head east on East Capitol until you reach RFK Stadium and the DC Armory. The Supreme Court will be to your left and the Library of Congress to the right.

0.8 Turn right onto 11th Street and then quickly left to continue on East Capitol Street. Alternatively, ride straight through Lincoln Park.

1.0 Turn left onto 13th Street and then immediately right to continue on East Capitol Street.

1.6 Continue straight and to the right on East Capitol toward the main entrance of the stadium. The Armory will be on your right.

1.8 Cross 22nd Street and head toward the stadium's main gate. The bike path will continue down and to the right into lot 5 of the stadium. Ride across lot 5 toward gate A and the underpass that will carry you under Independence Avenue.

2.0 Ride under Independence Avenue and then turn left immediately onto the bike path along the perimeter of lot 8.

2.3 Turn left at the T intersection and go under Independence Avenue again. Turn left immediately after the underpass to continue riding along the perimeter of the stadium.

2.7 Continue straight. The RFK Auxiliary Fields will be on your right. If you're lucky, you can catch a glimpse of DC United, Washington's professional soccer team, training.

2.8 Turn right onto Oklahoma Avenue. The trail continues along the edge of the fields.

3.2 Turn right onto Benning Road.

3.3 Turn right to follow the west bank of the Anacostia River Walk trail. This will take us back to mile marker 2.0.

3.5 Kingman Island Park is to the left. There is a short hiking loop and short bike path if you want to take a break.

3.9 Go under Independence Avenue again and continue straight through the next intersection and continue on the west bank section of the Anacostia River Walk. (Note: At the time I documented this ride, there was some construction along the banks of the Anacostia and the trail was slightly detoured.)

4.8 Stay to the right at this intersection. The left fork will take you over a new bridge to continue on the west bank of the trail. We will, however, go right to head toward the east bank of the river.

4.9 The trail turns right to cross the road and then left.

5.0 Cross the ramp and continue straight on the trail as it curves to the left to go over the Pennsylvania Avenue Bridge.

5.4 Immediately after crossing the bridge, turn left onto the trail and follow the signs for Anacostia Park.

5.5 Once you reach the bottom of the access trail, turn left to follow the east bank of the Anacostia River Walk trail. Stay on the trail and follow the signs to National's Park.

7.2 Turn left to head up toward the Douglas Bridge to cross the Anacostia toward National's Park.

7.7 Immediately after crossing the Douglas Bridge turn right onto Potomac Avenue. Detour: If you turn left and left again on First Street, you "may" get a glimpse of DC's first velodrome. At the time I wrote this, funds for the construction of the velodrome were an issue and hopefully have been resolved. Maybe take a fixie out for a spin on the banked track.

7.8 Turn right and then immediately left to ride on the boardwalk along the waterfront.

8.1 Turn right and go over the small metal bridge. You are now on Yards Park. Our goal here is to ride along the edge of the water toward the Navy Yard and the US Navy Museum.

8.3 Enter the Navy Yard.

8.5 Continue over the metal bridge just past the Swift boat.

8.7 Turn left to continue on the trail; you'll now be on 11th Street.

8.8 Turn right onto O/Water Street.

8.9 Turn left onto 12th Street. (Note: At the time I documented this ride, Water Street was under construction and closed. Once open you will be able to continue straight on Water Street to the intersection of M Street to continue on the Anacostia River Walk trail.)

9.1 Turn right onto M Street, then as you reach the traffic circle turn left and left again to hop onto the Anacostia River Walk Trail (Note: As with Water Street, this portion of M Street was also undergoing construction, hence the slight detour and right, left, left turns here.)

9.3 Turn right onto 11th Street.

9.8 Turn left onto Pennsylvania Avenue and you'll be treated to a nice view of the Capitol.

10.0 You've reached Eastern Market. This is probably a good area to lock up the bike and take a walk. To the left on 8th Street are several restaurants, two of which are recommended here, and to the right on 7th is the actual Eastern Market.

10.5 Make a slight left to ride on Independence Avenue. The Library of Congress will be to your right.

10.6 Turn right onto First Street.

10.7 Complete the loop.

RIDE INFORMATION

Local Events and Attractions
Eastern Market: Washington, DC's oldest continually operated fresh food public market is a community hub for the Capitol Hill neighborhood and a cultural visitor destination. It offers outdoor and indoor markets, and during the weekend local farmers and artists offer their products for sale. www.anacostiawaterfront.org

Restaurants
Zest American Bistro: 735 8th St. SE, Washington, DC 20003; (202) 544-7171; www.zestbistro.com
Matchbox Restaurant: 521 8th St. SE, Washington, DC 20003; (202) 548-0369; www.matchbox369.com
The Chesapeake Room: 501 8th St. SE, Washington, DC 20003; (202) 543-1445; www.thechesapeakeroom.com

Restrooms
Restrooms are available at various commercial establishments along the way near the Navy Yard and Capitol Hill. Some porta-potties are available in the RFK parking lots.

The Capital Crescent Trail and Rock Creek Park

This ride will start in a revitalized area of Georgetown, then move through the Capital Crescent Trail to hip Bethesda, Maryland, and then back down through Rock Creek Park. I offer you two options, one that uses most of Beach Drive along Rock Creek; the other makes use of the bike trails along the same area. Either one is great, but the "bike trail" version is a little more mellow (sans traffic) and scenic.

Start: 3255 K St. NW (in front of Cycle Life USA)—corner of K Street and Cecil Place

Length: 21 miles

Approximate riding time: 1.5–2 hours

Best bike: Road bike

Terrain and trail surface: Paved and dirt bike paths and asphalt roads

Traffic and hazards: Other trail users, including runners and cyclists. Vehicle traffic in sections of Rock Creek Park.

Things to see: Downtown Bethesda, Pierce Mill, the National Zoo

Getting there: From Maryland: Take Wisconsin Avenue South toward DC until it ends on Water/K Street. Turn right onto Water Street and proceed 1 block to the intersection of Cecil Place. There is ample street parking available along the waterfront and Water Street.

From northern Virginia: Take Route 66 east to exit 72 for Route 29 toward Rossyln/Key Bridge. Turn left onto Lynn Street and go over the Key Bridge into Washington, DC. Turn right onto M Street NW and then right onto Wisconsin Avenue. Turn right onto Water Street and proceed 1 block to the intersection of Cecil Place. There is ample street parking available along the waterfront and Water Street. GPS: 38.902723,-77.063974

Fees: None

THE RIDE

This is one of my favorite "new" rides in the region, and one I often do after work from my office in Arlington. I will take us along one of the newest and most popular trails in Bethesda, Maryland, then back to the city along one of the oldest routes—the canopied paths of Rock Creek Park. Until recently this loop was virtually impossible to complete, but thanks to the efforts of the Coalition for the Capital Crescent Trail, the route has become a reality.

The first half of our ride takes us along a major portion of the Capital Crescent Trail (CCT). The right-of-way for where the trail stands has in fact existed for quite some time, and like many of the other trails in the region, it was part of a rail bed that served the Baltimore and Ohio (B&O) Railroad. Part of the trail parallels The Chesapeake and Ohio (C&O) Canal, but unlike that trail, this one has been paved and offers a smooth, uninterrupted ride from DC to downtown Bethesda, Maryland, and then from there all the way to the border of downtown Silver Spring. Plans for the trail didn't become a reality until 1986, shortly after the last run of a train on the B&O in 1985.

Bike Shops

CycleLife USA (great smoothie bar in the shop): 3255 K St. NW, Washington, DC 20007; (202) 333-8883; www.cyclelifeusa.com

City Bikes: 8401 Connecticut Ave., Ste. 111, Chevy Chase, MD 20815; (301) 652-1777; www.citybikes.com

During its heyday in the late 1880s, the B&O Railroad operated a modest cargo line that ferried building materials and coal between Chevy Chase and DC. At the time B&O owners hoped to extend the line to Virginia via a new Potomac crossing west of the Chain Bridge to take advantage of economic opportunities to the south, but that never materialized. For most of its existence, the B&O terminated roughly in the area where our ride starts, but for a brief period of time the railroad was extended to fulfill an important role in the development of the city. In 1914 the line was extended beyond the Rock Creek to the site of the Lincoln Memorial to ferry limestone and other materials necessary for its construction.

Beyond that, the line succumbed to the times, and over the years it was less and less necessary. Ultimately it faded away and made its last run in 1985, giving way to cargo-ferrying trucks. The closing of the line prompted a group of individuals and groups to form the Coalition for the Capital Crescent Trail (www.cctrail.org). Its mission was "to convert the idle Georgetown Branch line into a high-quality, multiuse trail to be known as the Capital Crescent Trail." Other groups had their sights on the right-of-way as well, but ultimately, and after

A commuter heads toward DC along Beach Drive in Rock Creek Park.

years of hard work, the National Park Service secured the right-of-way from Georgetown to the DC line, and Montgomery County purchased the right-of-way from there through Bethesda to Silver Spring. Today, plans exist to extend the trail beyond Silver Spring and back to DC's Union Station, but funding and other obstacles—including the development of the purple light rail metro line—may defer its construction.

The second half of the ride will take us down one of DC's most protected areas and also one of its most beautiful, the Rock Creek Park Corridor and Beach Drive. But it wasn't always so beautiful. Several floods in the late 1800s, including the great flood of 1881, made the area an unhealthy and pestilent swamp. The hot and humid Washington summers further made it quite an unbearable place.

The quest to establish a park began on June 25, 1866, when the US Senate directed the Committee on Public Buildings and Grounds to find a suitable location to create a 100-acre park near the district. Rock Creek was identified, but it took nearly 25 years before it was established by an act of Congress in September of 1890—the same year Yosemite National Park was established. By then the 100 acres had turned into 2,000 acres. Much of it was the land north of the National Zoo and extended into what is now Montgomery County, Maryland. Later, with the creation of the Rock Creek and Potomac Parkway, the park was extended to the point where the creek emptied into the Potomac.

Aqueduct Bridge

Shortly after you enter the Capital Crescent Trail from Georgetown, you'll see the only remaining signs of one of the area's earliest Potomac crossings, the remaining abutment of the **Aqueduct Bridge.** The bridge was built in the mid-1800s to capitalize on the success of the C&O Canal and to ferry fully loaded barges across the Potomac from Georgetown to Virginia. The bridge consisted of abutments on the Maryland and Virginia sides and eight piers that suspended the span across the Potomac. The same piers supported three different bridges, the first a floating canal 7 feet deep with a corresponding towpath for mules pulling barges across the Potomac. The second included an upper deck that served as a roadway. Finally, a third, steel truss version was only used as a roadway. The Aqueduct saw its last days of service shortly after the Key Bridge was erected to the east in 1924, and was completely removed a decade later in 1934, with the exception of the abutment in Georgetown and a single pier on the Virginia side. Today, that abutment and arch serve as a welcoming entry point to the CCT from Georgetown, and a simple reminder of Washington's past.

Our ride follows the causeway of Rock Creek, all the way to Georgetown and K Street, where we will turn right to complete the ride along the Potomac Waterfront. Today, this section has become an integral artery in the DC traffic system, so if you do decide to ride on the road, you will encounter copious amounts of traffic. For that reason I have offered you the opportunity to ride along Rock Creek's bike paths and escape the vehicular traffic. Unfortunately you will have to ride on the road for a short portion as you enter the district from Maryland, but drivers are well accustomed to bicycle traffic and are more often than not courteous to riders.

As you travel south along the Rock Creek valley, you'll understand why this area has become a gem in the Capital region. The dense deciduous forest provides a buffer from the busy city that flanks it. Along the way you'll pass by Pierce Mill, which was built in the 1820s and operated commercially until 1897, shortly after the park was established. Though the mill no longer operates, plans are in the works to try to restore it to its original splendor.

Farther south you'll pass by the National Zoo. From here, you can enter the zoo and climb out of the Rock Creek toward Connecticut Avenue. Bikes are not allowed on zoo walkways, so if you plan to visit the zoological park, plan ahead and bring a lock. As you circumnavigate or ride through the Rock Creek Tunnel,

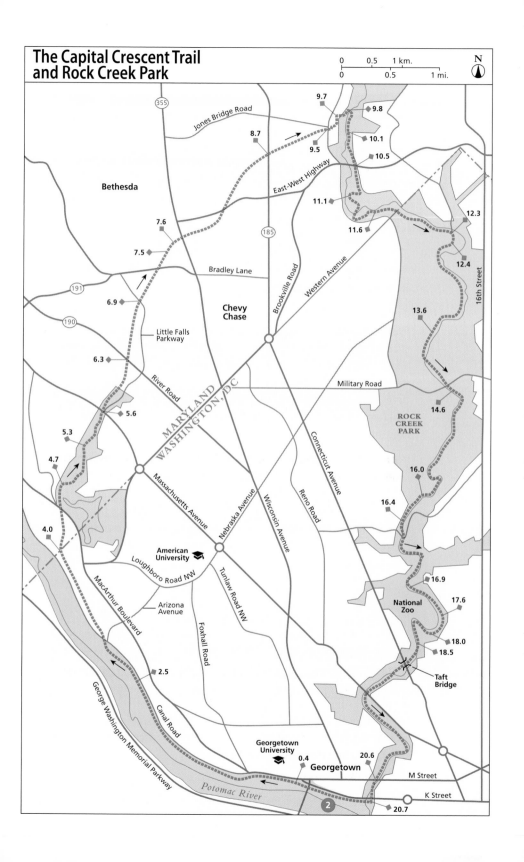

The Capital Crescent Trail
and Rock Creek Park

N

0   0.5   1 km.
0   0.5   1 mi.

355

Jones Bridge Road

9.7
9.8
8.7
9.5
10.1
10.5

East-West Highway

Bethesda

11.1

7.6

185

11.6

12.3

7.5

12.4

Bradley Lane

191

Chevy
Chase

Brookville Road

Western Avenue

16th Street

6.9

13.6

Little Falls
Parkway

190

6.3

River Road

MARYLAND
WASHINGTON, DC

Military Road

14.6

5.6

ROCK
CREEK
PARK

5.3

4.7

Massachusetts Avenue

Nebraska Avenue

Wisconsin Avenue

Reno Road

Connecticut Avenue

16.0

16.4

4.0

American
University

16.9

Loughboro Road NW

Tunlaw Road NW

National
Zoo

17.6

Arizona
Avenue

Foxhall Road

18.0
18.5

MacArthur Boulevard

Taft
Bridge

2.5

Canal Road

George Washington Memorial Parkway

Georgetown
University

0.4

20.6

Georgetown

M Street

2

Potomac River

K Street

20.7

you will come into view of the Taft Bridge (Connecticut Avenue Bridge), another example of Washington's monumental bridges. Built between 1897 and 1907, the bridge stands as one of the largest unreinforced concrete structures in the world. The ride will continue south along Beach Drive until you reach K Street, at which point you'll turn right and head past the revitalized Georgetown Waterfront (see Ride 5 The Tidal Basin and the Waterfronts for details) before taking you back to the starting point.

MILES & DIRECTIONS

0.0 The ride starts from 3255 K St. NW (in front of Cycle Life USA) by the Georgetown waterfront. Head West on K Street until you reach the entrance of the Capital Crescent Trail.

0.4 Enter the Capital Crescent Trail and the Chesapeake and Ohio Canal National Historic Park. You'll basically stay on the CCT for the next 10 miles, with one minor detour through the Little Falls Trail (which I find a little more interesting). Look to your left and you'll see the remnants of the original aqueduct bridge that spanned the Potomac from Virginia to Georgetown. The aqueduct abutment is one of the only remaining signs of the bridge that preceded the now-famous Key Bridge.

2.5 Fletcher's Cove. There is a snack bar to the left and restrooms to the right. Boat rentals and bike rentals are available here.

4.0 Welcome to Montgomery County, Maryland.

4.2 Water, anyone? You'll find a water fountain along the side of the trail where you can fill up. There are a few others along the way should you need to.

4.7 Turn right and then quickly left to grab the Little Falls Trail. You can continue straight here, but this section is a little more interesting and offers a nice view of the Little Falls Branch.

4.9 Veer to the left to continue on the Little Falls Trail.

5.3 Continue straight through this intersection; left will take you to the CCT. We're headed to Massachusetts Avenue.

5.6 Turn left onto the sidewalk along Massachusetts Avenue, and before reaching the tunnel, turn left and up to the CCT. Then turn right onto the CCT to ride over Massachusetts Avenue.

6.3 Cross over River Road. The bridge was opened in 1996.

6.5 Use caution when crossing Dorset Avenue.

6.9 Use caution when crossing Little Falls Parkway.

7.3 Water, anyone?

7.5 Reach the Bethesda Avenue and Woodmont intersection. The trail continues on the opposite side adjacent to the Cinema Row. Turn right onto Bethesda Avenue to cross Woodmont, then left to cross Bethesda Avenue and follow the signs for the Georgetown Branch Trail Tunnel (open 6 a.m. to 10 p.m.). This is the highest point of the ride; it is relatively all downhill from here.

7.6 Enter the tunnel.

8.7 Cross Connecticut Avenue. You'll have to turn right, then left to cross, then left again and right into the CCT. Capitol City Bikes will be on the right as you enter the CCT again if you need anything.

9.5 Turn left onto Jones Mill Road and then take an immediate right onto Susanna Lane. Follow the signs for Rock Creek Trail.

9.7 At the end of Susanna, turn right onto the Rock Creek Trail.

9.8 Turn right to head toward the DC line. To the left is Lake Needwood (see Ride 28, Upper Rock Creek and Montgomery County for details).

10.1 Go under the Rock Creek Trestle.

10.4 Water, anyone?

10.5 Cross East West Highway and follow the trail as it parallels Meadowbrook Road. The trail will then curve to the right around the Meadowbrook Stables and then to the left toward the baseball fields. The trail is well marked and easy to follow at this point.

11.1 Continue following the path to the left as it parallels Beach Drive.

11.6 The trail ends here. Cross the small parking area and continue in the same direction along Beach Drive.

12.3 Continue straight through this intersection.

12.4 Continue straight through this stop sign. On weekends Beach Drive is closed to vehicular traffic.

16.0 Stay to the left to continue on Beach Drive. (If you want to continue along the Rock Creek Path, see 13.6 below.)

17.6 Reach the entrance to the National Zoo. For safety reasons we'll hop on the trail to go through the tunnel and then under the high-arch Connecticut Avenue Bridge.

18.2 Cross the Rock Creek Ramp—use caution—to continue on the Rock Creek Trail. At this point riding on the road is impractical and dangerous; finish the ride off on the bike path.

19.5 Use caution at this intersection.

20.0 Cross the ramp that takes vehicles up Pennsylvania Avenue and continue straight on the Rock Creek rail over the K Street ramp.

20.1 Go under the Whitehurst Freeway and then turn right to follow the trail as it parallels K Street under the freeway toward the ride's starting point. The Georgetown Waterfront will be ahead to your left.

20.5 Complete the loop.

Path version:

13.6 The bike trail will pick up again to the right at the intersection of Beach Drive and Bingham Drive. Hop on it and continue riding parallel to Beach Drive.

14.6 The bike path ends again. You'll have to hop on Beach Drive once more for a little under 2 miles.

16.2 Turn right onto Broad Branch Road and then immediately left to pick up the Western Ridge Trail. Stay on the bike path as it parallels the Rock Creek virtually all the way to K Street and Georgetown.

16.4 Stay to the left to continue on the Western Ridge Trail. You'll pass Pierce Mill to your right.

16.9 Turn right to cross the bridge and then left to continue on the Western Ridge Trail.

17.2 Stay to the left at this intersection to ride under Klingle Road.

18.0 Stay to the right before the entrance to the tunnel and continue following the bike path. The path will meander around and continue on the opposite side of the tunnel. It is a much nicer alternative to riding through the tunnel.

18.5 Turn right to continue on the bike path, the Taft Bridge is right in front of you.

20.0 Use caution at this intersection.

20.6 Cross the ramp that takes vehicles up Pennsylvania Avenue and continue straight on the Rock Creek Trail over the K Street ramp.

20.7 Go under the Whitehurst Freeway and then turn right to follow the trail as it parallels K Street under the freeway toward the ride's starting point. The Georgetown Waterfront will be ahead to your left.

21.1 Complete the loop.

RIDE INFORMATION

Local Events and Attractions
For info on events and other attractions visit www.bethesda.org
Taste of Bethesda: www.bethesda.org/bethesda/taste-bethesda
The National Zoo: www.nationalzoo.si.edu

Restaurants
Quick Pita: 1210 Potomac St. NW, Washington, DC 20007; (202) 338-7482
Mussel Bar: 7262 Woodmont Ave., Bethesda, MD 20814; (301) 215-7817; www.musselbar.com

Restrooms
There are no public restrooms directly on the trail. There are public restrooms convenient to the trail at Fletcher's Cove, near mile 2.5.

The National Mall –
L'Enfant's Grand Avenue

This ride will take you by some of our nation's most iconic monuments and memorials, including the Jefferson Memorial, the Lincoln Memorial, the World War II Memorial, the Washington Monument, the Capitol, and the White House. I highly recommend you do this ride during the early morning hours, when crowds and the noise of autos en route to area offices are sparse. You might also consider doing this ride during any given weekday, when tourists and mall traffic are at a minimum.

Start: Lyndon B. Johnson Memorial Grove Parking Area along Boundary Channel Drive Pentagon North Parking

Length: 10.2 miles

Approximate riding time: 1–3 hours, highly dependent on your sightseeing

Best bike: Any bike

Terrain and trail surface: Paved bike paths and the gravel paths of the National Mall

Traffic and hazards: Other users, Segways!

Things to see: Monuments and memorials along the Mall

Getting there: From Springfield: Take I-395 north toward Washington and take exit 8B. Then merge onto Washington Boulevard toward the Pentagon/Arlington Cemetery/Rosslyn. Take the first exit toward VA 110/Pentagon North Parking. Turn left at the stop sign at Boundary Channel Drive. The Lyndon B. Johnson parking area will be on your left as the road curves right.

From the National Mall: Take 14th Street South to I-395 South. Take exit 10A for Boundary Channel Drive toward the Pentagon North Parking. Drive for approximately 0.5 mile on Boundary Channel Drive. The parking area will be on your right as the road curves to the left. GPS: 38.878197,-77.053385

Fees: None

The National Mall, or something closely resembling it, was part of what Washington's original architect, Pierre L'Enfant, envisioned for the capital city. In his plan, L'Enfant proposed several avenues that radiated from the capital's most important structures, among them the President's home and the Capitol building. A central "Grand Avenue, 400 feet in breadth, and about a mile in length, bordered by gardens," that would serve as an axis for the city, would anchor all of the avenues. The Grand Avenue would be a "place of general resort" and "public walks," a place that would represent the grandeur of the new nation and highlight the power of its people. L'Enfant's vision would never be fully implemented; however, his designs and ideas eventually took the form of the National Mall as we know it today.

When the cornerstone for the Washington Monument was laid in 1848, the area looked much different than it does today. The Washington Monument was erected on the waterfront at the confluence of the Potomac and the Washington City Canal. By 1875 the area had accumulated so much silt that it was called Potomac Flats. In 1881, after the great flood of Washington, which inundated much of what is now the Mall, including the White House, the US House Committee on the District of Columbia appropriated $1 million to reclaim the Potomac. Silt was laboriously dredged from the river by the Army Corps of Engineers, and then deposited west and south of the Washington Monument, creating nearly 700 additional acres of land.

Bike Shops

BicycleSPACE: 1019 7th St. NW, Washington, DC 20001; (202) 962-0123; www .bicyclespacedc.com
Capitol Hill Bikes: 719 8th St. SE, Washington, DC 20003; (202) 544-4234; www .capitolhillbikes.com

By the early 20th century, in 1901, Senator James McMillan and the Senate Committee for the District of Columbia established the Senate Park Commission. The commission's primary mission was to restore L'Enfant's original vision for the Mall. The McMillan Plan was to nearly double in size L'Enfant's original plan, taking advantage of the "new land" that had been created by the Army Corps of Engineers. The McMillan Plan laid out the foundation of what the Mall would become today, America's front yard. Despite that, there really is no clear definition of the exact boundaries of the National Mall.

L'Enfant's plans roughly outlined a rectangular area that extended from the west steps of the Capitol to a portion of land extending west of the Washington Monument—not quite reaching the grounds of what is now the reflecting pool—which was then the waterfront. McMillan's 20th-century plan extended

Riders in front of the Capitol on Capital Bikeshare bikes. The bikes are available in over 200 stations across DC, Arlington, and now Alexandria.

that vision to include the White House to the north, the Jefferson Memorial to the south, the Lincoln Memorial to the west, and the entire Capitol grounds to the east. McMillan's plan also took into account the surrounding areas, including parkways and other memorials and structures that would enhance the richness of the nation's capital and the Mall itself. Today, the National Park Service defines the Mall's boundaries from Constitution and Pennsylvania Avenues to the north, 1st Street NW on the east, 14th Street NW to the west, and Independence and Maryland Avenues to the south. As of 2003, however, a Congressional Research Service report states that there is "no statutory description or map of the Mall."

Our ride will take us roughly along the boundaries set forth by the McMillan plan, which I think serves as a basis for all the others and the one that mostly reflects L'Enfant's early vision for the Grand Avenue. Although we start in Virginia and do not quite go around the entire Capitol or White House, I've tried to take you over the new natural boundaries that the Senate Park Commission established in the early 20th century. Along the way you'll enjoy and visit some of the most iconic monuments on the Mall and travel through what may become future portions of the Mall.

Interested parties are still trying to define the boundaries of the National Mall, which has proved to be a key issue in the development of its future. In 1986, when Congress and the Ronald Reagan Administration identified the significance of the "Nation's Front Yard," it passed legislation to ensure the Mall's integrity was protected. President Reagan signed into law the

Washington Shakes

Having lived in the DC region for nearly 27 years, I have seen my share of strange occurrences: massive traffic jams, mega events, powerful storms, several record-breaking snowfalls, and even incomprehensible terrorist attacks. But what happened on August 23, 2011, shortly after noon took everyone in the DC region by surprise: a 5.8 earthquake hit Virginia, shaking foundations in Washington, DC. Having lived in Lima, Peru, for half of my life, I have felt my share of strong quakes, including an 8.1 magnitude monster in 1974 that will forever be stamped in my psyche. But this earthquake was different. In Lima people have learned to live with the possibility of an earthquake at any minute, and are somewhat mentally prepared for such occurrences. But here in Washington, DC, earthquakes are something you only read about, not feel. News coverage for the quake lasted for several days after the tremor, and to this day, DC residents are feeling its effects. Several buildings in the area that were never built to withstand the shocks of an earthquake—most notably the National Cathedral and the Washington Monument—continue to be structurally assessed and repaired to meet safety standards and, in the case of the Washington Monument, still remain closed to the public until they are properly repaired. Other buildings in the nation's capital, including the Smithsonian castle and the embassy of Ecuador, were also damaged but have since been repaired. Nerves may have settled down a little since that warm August afternoon, but the possibility remains that another earthquake will hit this region again. During one of your rides? I certainly hope not!

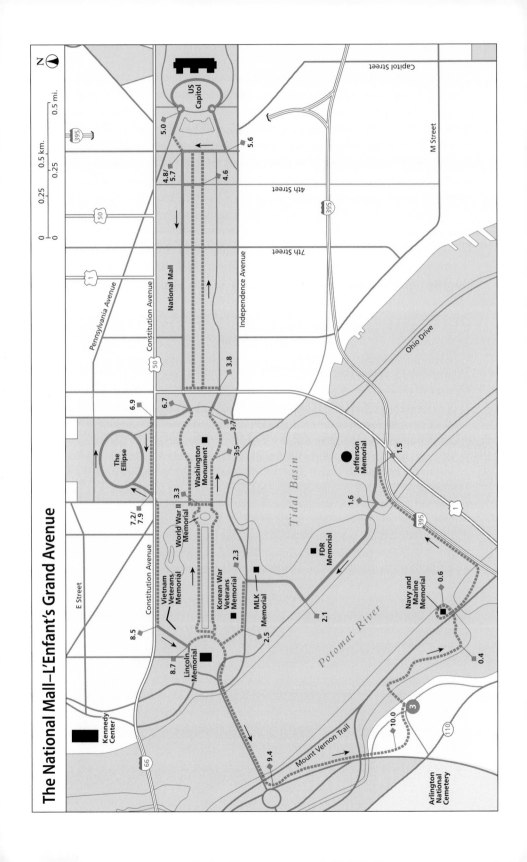

The National Mall–L'Enfant's Grand Avenue

N

0   0.25   0.5 km.

0   0.25   0.5 mi.

US Capitol

Capitol Street

M Street

4th Street

7th Street

Independence Avenue

National Mall

Constitution Avenue

Pennsylvania Avenue

E Street

The Ellipse

Washington Monument

World War II Memorial

Vietnam Veterans Memorial

Korean War Veterans Memorial

MLK Memorial

Lincoln Memorial

Kennedy Center

Tidal Basin

Jefferson Memorial

FDR Memorial

Navy and Marine Memorial

Potomac River

Mount Vernon Trail

Arlington National Cemetery

Ohio Drive

5.0

5.6

4.8/5.7

4.6

3.8

6.9

6.7

3.7

3.5

1.5

1.6

2.3

2.1

2.5

0.6

0.4

3

10.0

9.4

8.5

8.7

7.2/7.9

3.3

Commemorative Works Act "to preserve the integrity of the comprehensive designs of the L'Enfant and McMillan plans" and to "preserve, protect, and maintain the limited amount of open space and ensure that future commemorative works are appropriately designed, constructed, and located."

Despite the Act, exceptions have been made. Since the passage of that law, several new monuments and memorials have been erected. In 2003 the National Capital Commission amended the Act and imposed a temporary moratorium on building anything new on the Mall. That moratorium stands today, but increasing debate continues on what the future of the Mall will and should look like. Plans to preserve the Mall and expand it along East Capitol Street and East Potomac Park have been envisioned, and the National Mall 3rd Century Initiative has been established to create a master plan to ensure the integrity of the Mall's original boundaries is preserved and perhaps expanded beyond its current "vague" margins.

This ride will start on part of what that extended vision of the Mall encompasses. Combine it with the Waterfront ride to get a feeling for what the new proposed Mall boundaries would be like.

MILES & DIRECTIONS

0.0 From the ramp to enter the grove, turn right and head over the bridge. Immediately turn right and follow the stone path toward the Marina parking area.

0.1 Bear right away from the stone path and ride on the asphalt path. Continue to the right and enter the parking lot. There is a narrow path that travels along the parking area if you choose to ride that.

0.4 Turn left at the stop sign and then immediately right to enter the path that will take you toward the Mount Vernon Trail. Ride under the parkway (great views of the Jefferson Memorial and the Washington Monument).

0.6 Turn left at this intersection slightly past the Navy and Marine Memorial, then turn left at the T intersection to join the Mount Vernon Trail.

0.8 Continue past the first intersection then make a right to head up toward the 14th Street Bridge.

1.5 After crossing the bridge, make a left (almost U turn) at the Capital Bikeshare station and head west toward Ohio Drive on East Basin Drive.

1.6 Turn right to cross the small bridge that spans the basin waterway and continue north on Ohio Drive.

3

2.1 Turn right onto West Basin Drive to head toward the Mall and Independence Avenue.

2.3 Cross over Independence Avenue and turn left onto the sidewalk path that runs parallel to Independence Avenue.

2.5 Turn right onto Daniel C French Drive. The Korean Memorial will be to your right. Continue straight until you reach the Lincoln Memorial and ride in front of the Lincoln Memorial.

2.7 Turn right to ride east along the path that parallels the reflecting pool. The pool will be on your right. Restrooms are available to the left at mile marker 2.9.

3.3 Immediately after passing the World Word II Memorial, turn right onto 17th Street. You'll get treated to a great view of the WWII Memorial and the Lincoln Memorial. Immediately after passing the memorial, turn left to cross 17th Street and head up toward the Washington Monument.

3.5 Follow the path to the right to circle around the monument in a counterclockwise direction.

3.7 Follow the path to the right to cross 15th Street and head east toward the Capitol.

3.8 Cross 14th Street and then make a quick left and quick right to pick up one of the main gravel paths that parallels the mall. Continue east toward the Capitol.

4.6 Cross 4th Street and turn left toward the National Gallery of Art and then make an immediate right to continue east along Madison Street.

4.8 Cross 3rd Street. At this point we will head up and to the left along the path that will take us to the north corner of the Capitol.

5.0 Cross 1st Street and continue heading up to the left toward the north corner of the Capitol.

5.1 Follow the path to the right and ride directly in front of the Capitol. This is a great place to pause and take a few pictures.

5.3 Continue following the path past the Capitol facade to the right until you reach 1st Street again, then circle around the reflecting pool to return toward 3rd Street. The Botanic Gardens will be to your left. I highly recommend a visit to these.

One of the Mall's biggest "hazards" for cyclists: tourists on Segways.

5.6 Turn right onto 3rd Street and head back to the point where you crossed 3rd Street.

5.7 Turn left onto Madison. The entire lane is designated a bike lane. Head back toward the Washington Monument.

6.7 Turn right onto 15th Street.

6.9 Cross Constitution Avenue, and turn left immediately after you cross to ride on the path that parallels Constitution. The Ellipse and White House will be to your right as you head west toward 17th Street.

7.2 Shortly before reaching 17th Street, turn right onto the path that enters The Ellipse. You will follow this path in a clockwise direction around The Ellipse back to this exact spot. Along the way we'll pass directly in front of the White House's South Lawn.

7.9 Turn left to return toward Constitution Avenue and 17th Street. Cross Constitution and then immediately turn right to cross 17th Street to hop on the path that parallels Constitution Avenue. Continue heading west toward the Lincoln Memorial. The reflecting pool is visible to the left.

8.5 Turn left onto Henry Bacon Drive to head toward the Lincoln Memorial. The Vietnam Memorial will be to your left.

8.7 Turn left onto Lincoln Memorial Circle and follow the path clockwise.

8.8 Turn left at the crosswalk and then immediately right to cross 23rd Street to continue on the path to cross over the Memorial Bridge.

9.4 After crossing the bridge, stay to the left to follow the path over the ramp from the George Washington Memorial Parkway.

9.5 Stay to the right at this intersection and continue south to cross once more over a GW Parkway ramp. Continue south and toward the Pentagon.

10.0 Follow the path down the ramp toward the Pentagon's north parking and Boundary Channel Drive.

10.2 Your loop is complete.

RIDE INFORMATION

Local Events and Attractions
National Park Service: www.nps.gov/nama/planyourvisit/events.htm

Restaurants
National Gallery of Art: The Pavilion Cafe—Sculpture Garden, 7th St. and Constitution Ave. NW, Washington, DC 20565; (202) 737-4215; ww.nga.gov/ginfo/cafes.shtm
Museum of the American Indian: The Mitsitam Native Foods Cafe, 4th St. and Independence Ave. SW, Washington, DC 20560; (202) 633-1000; www.nmai.si.edu/visit/washington/mitsitam-cafe

Restrooms
Available in the Columbia Island Marina, the reflecting pool, the Lincoln Memorial, and inside the museums along the Mall.

The Four Bridges

From Virginia to DC, then back to Virginia and back to DC, and finally back to Virginia once again. Did you get that? This relatively short but entertaining ride will take you over four of the main bridges that span the Potomac River around the Capital DC region, two of which are National Registered Historic Landmarks.

Start: Roosevelt Island Parking Area

Length: 8.5 miles

Approximate riding time: 1–2 hours

Best bike: Road, hybrid, or cross bike

Terrain and trail surface: Mostly paved bike paths; one short section of road near the waterfront

Traffic and hazards: Other trail users and vehicles in the road section

Things to see: Historical landmarks, including the Key Bridge, Memorial Bridge, the Lincoln and Jefferson Memorials; DC waterfront restaurants in the SW Waterfront

Getting there: Theodore Roosevelt Island is accessible only from the northbound lanes of the George Washington Memorial Parkway. The entrance to the parking lot is located just north of the Roosevelt Bridge. Southbound traffic: take Theodore Roosevelt Bridge to Constitution Avenue. Take a right onto 23rd Street and cross Memorial Bridge. Once on the bridge, bear right to return to the G.W. Parkway. GPS: 38.89641,-77.066989

Fees: None

THE RIDE

This ride will take you from Theodore Roosevelt Island along the George Washington Memorial Parkway over four of the main bridges that span the Potomac River in the immediate vicinity of the nation's capital. We'll first cross the Francis Scott Key Bridge (Key Bridge), then the Theodore Roosevelt Memorial Bridge (Roosevelt Bridge), the Arlington Memorial Bridge (Memorial Bridge), and finally over one of the spans of the 14th Street Bridge. Each of these bridges has played an important role in the development and history of the nation's capital and each has a unique story to tell.

Named in honor of the author of "The Star Spangled Banner," the Key Bridge is the first of the four spans we will cross. The Key Bridge replaced the old Aqueduct Bridge that crossed the Potomac and extended the waters of the C&O Canal to the city of Alexandria. The bridge was designed by architect Nathan C. Wyeth and engineer Max C. Tyler and was built by the US Army Corps of Engineers between 1917 and 1923. As you ride its deck, you'll be treated to wonderful views of the Georgetown spires and the Potomac River below. While we won't get a close-up view of its eight arches from this particular spot (you will from the Roosevelt Bridge), you'll know that you are riding above one of the most impressive structures in the capital city.

After a quick ride through the waterfront and past the Kennedy Center, we'll hop on the Roosevelt Bridge, a complete contrast to the previous span. Completed in June 1964, the Roosevelt Bridge has been dubbed one of the "ugliest" spans in the nation's capital. I don't think anyone would argue that. The bridge serves no aesthetic purpose and provides only a utilitarian function in connecting Route 66 in Virginia with Constitution Avenue in DC. The bridge is often clogged with traffic during rush hour, despite its reversible center lane. I can't tell you how many times I've ridden the span and gazed into the eyes of the poor souls stuck in DC's abominable gridlock. Unfortunately, I myself have been in their place more than once. The bridge does offer some great views of the Georgetown Waterfront, the Key Bridge, and the Kennedy Center.

After exiting the bridge we'll hop on the Mount Vernon Trail and head south toward the city's most majestic span, the Memorial Bridge. When designing this loop, I took great care in ensuring that we rode this particular section of trail in the direction we are heading. As you exit the canopy of Roosevelt Island into the open sky of the Mount Vernon Trail, you'll get to see some of what I think are the best views of DC. Across the river you'll see the terminus of the Memorial Bridge, the Watergate steps below the Lincoln Memorial, the Lincoln Memorial and the Washington Monument in the distance. I urge you to do this ride at least twice, once as the sun sets so you can experience this view in the glow of the setting sun, and once

Bike Shops:

Bicycle Pro Shop: 3403 M St. NW, Washington, DC 20007; (202) 337-0311; www .bicycleproshop.com
Big Wheel Bikes: 1034 33rd St. NW, Washington, DC 20007; (202) 337-0254; www.bigwheelbikes.com

Three of DC's most iconic landmarks, The Arlington Memorial Bridge, The Lincoln Memorial, and the Washington Monument, as seen from the Mount Vernon Trail in Virginia.

Gwadzilla

If you ride long enough in DC, you are bound to run into Joel. "Gwadzilla" is one of Washington's bike culture documentarians. By the time you realize it's him, he'll have snapped a few pictures of you on your bike and posted them on his blog, gwadzilla.blogspot.com, a place where he "rants on cycling and life." Have a visit, it is highly entertaining. His words have also appeared on www.grist .org, an environmental blog that "dishes out environmental news and commentary with a wry twist." This is applicable for Joel. The tower of a man has been riding a bike since he can remember, he moved from doing his paper route on a bike to being a messenger in DC, which is why he knows the streets so well. He

Joel Gwadz out for a spin on the Mount Vernon Trail, camera around his neck and ready to shoot.

prefers the paths though, because "these trails can be a great escape from the car traffic." He has managed to combine his passion for riding with his love for photography. "Honestly," he says, "I would hate to try and figure how much time I have spent on this hobby of taking photographs of cyclists. Soon, I hope all of these will be compiled in a book." I sure hope so, because he has some gems in there, including a couple of me.

in the early morning, preferably as the sun rises, so you can witness the true monumental grandeur of Washington, DC.

These views were always intended, and we can thank Senator James McMillan and the Senate Park Commission for them. In 1902 when McMillan presented his plan for restoring Pierre L'Enfant's vision of the National Mall to Congress (see Ride 3, National Mall – L'Enfant's Grand Avenue for details), they also included a recommendation for parkways along the Virginia border of the river, a new monument on West Potomac Park, and a neo-classical bridge linking the two together. In the plan, it was emphasized that whatever was built needed to retain and preserve the views of West Potomac Park and Arlington House in Virginia. The plan's vision and forward thinking was remarkable. Not only are the views from the parkway outstanding, but also as you ride over the low deck of the Memorial Bridge, you'll be treated to one of the most iconic views of the capital city, if not the world.

Elsewhere in this book I've written that my love for cycling flourished when I moved to Arlington and lived at Fort Myer while in the Army. I often rode during the early morning hours through the cemetery and across this span and can't even begin to tell you in words how incredible the view of the city is as you approach it in the early morning from Virginia. Catch it at the right time and you will get a glimpse of early morning rowers slicing through the mist as it rises from the Potomac. In the distance you can make the shape of the Capitol Dome as it's lit by the rising sun, and the Washington Monument floats atop the majestic Lincoln Memorial in a bed of pink and orange streaks.

The bridge is highly symbolic, and although it was proposed by the McMillan Plan in 1902, its vision didn't become a reality until 30 years later when it was dedicated by President Herbert Hoover on January 16, 1932. Built in a straight line from the Lincoln Memorial to Arlington Circle, it serves a symbolic unification of North and South—it unites Lee with the Great Emancipator, Lincoln, and connects the Capital of the Union with the Capital of the South, Virginia.

As you enter the bridge from Virginia, you'll be greeted by a pair of sentry eagles atop large pylons, guards of the city. It's quite difficult to pay much attention to the bridge's details as you ride because of the view, and because despite being monumental, it was designed to be unobtrusive. Much of the details that are part of the bridge can only be seen from the river though; eagle reliefs carved by sculptor Carl Paul Jennewein decorate the sides of the pylons that support the bridge. As you exit the bridge into DC, turn back to get a good look at Sacrifice (the female figure) and Valor (the male figure), better known as the Arts of War. The two statues, created by American sculptor Leo Friedlander and cast in bronze donated by the Italian government, were completed and installed on the bridge in 1951. To the north, two similar statues, the Arts of Peace, flank the entrance of the Rock Creek and Potomac Parkway. The statues, created by American artist James Earle Fraser, represent Aspiration, Literature, Music, and Harvest.

As we continue our ride toward the final crossing, the 14th Street Bridge, we will ride along West Potomac Park. Along the way you'll pass by the John Ericsson Memorial, famous for designing the USS *Monitor*, the Union's first ironclad. Before reaching the Jefferson Memorial and the turn to the final span, you'll pass along the Washington Polo Grounds and the location (5.2) that marks the inaugural flight on May 15, 1918, of the world's first continuous mail delivery by air.

Like the Theodore Roosevelt Memorial Bridge, there is not much aesthetically pleasing about this crossing. The bridge, in reality, consists of five bridges that carry freight trains, metro rail, and vehicular traffic from Virginia into the city and vice versa. This span, however, marks the location of the second span that crossed the Potomac when the city was first built, the Long Bridge. That bridge served an important role in Washington's history and was twice burned to prevent troops from using it. It played a significant role in the Civil War and later served as a vital connector between Virginia and the District.

The 14th Street span was most recently in the news when in 1982 Air Florida Flight 90 crashed along its deck during a fierce snowstorm. Of the 74 passengers and 5 crewmembers, only 5 survived, and 4 motorists along the bridge were killed, raising the death toll to 78. WRC-TV's Chester Panzer captured much of the immediate aftermath of the accident on film. He and his crew happened to be stuck in traffic on the bridge when the accident occurred, and they were able to transmit the frantic efforts of rescue workers trying to pull survivors out of the Potomac's icy waters. The bridge was later renamed the Arland D. Williams Jr. Memorial Bridge in honor of a sixth surviving passenger of the ill-fated flight who gave up the rescue line in favor of other passengers in greater distress. Unfortunately he was unable to withstand the frigid waters and lost the battle with the icy river.

After completing the final cross, we'll head back to the starting point of the ride along the Mount Vernon Trail. To your right will be the Potomac River and the unobstructed views of the nation's capital as envisioned by the McMillan Plan.

MILES & DIRECTIONS

0.0 Start from the Roosevelt Island Parking Area where the Mount Vernon Trail intersects the entrance to the second parking area. Head north on the Mount Vernon Trail and go over the bridge that crosses the George Washington Memorial Parkway.

0.3 Turn right onto Lynn Street and cross over the Key Bridge toward Georgetown.

0.7 Immediately after crossing the bridge, make an immediate right (U turn) into the small park and head down toward the canal.

0.8 Continue straight at the bottom of the hill and ride through the alley on the cobble street. Leopold's and Big Wheel Bikes are on this street. Stop by Big Wheel Bikes and tell the manager, Patrice, I sent you.

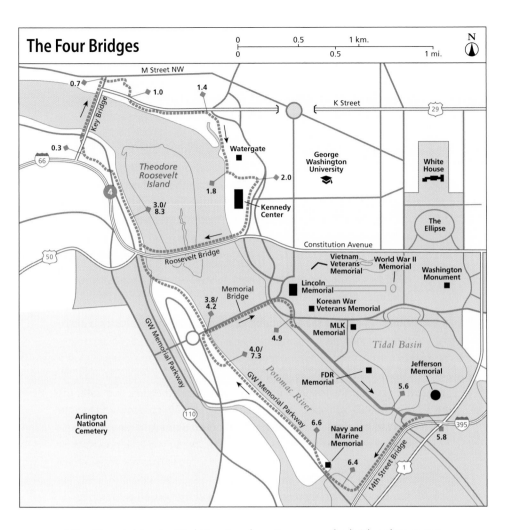

The Four Bridges

0.9 Turn right onto 33rd Street and continue over the bridge that spans the canal. After crossing the bridge, continue straight down 33rd toward the waterfront.

1.0 Turn left onto K Street or continue straight to follow the path along the waterfront. Either way you'll want to continue on K Street for 4 blocks until 29th Street. The waterfront is a nice area for a break or to soak in some views, but it is generally very crowded and difficult to navigate by bike, especially during warm weather months.

1.4 At the intersection of K and 29th, follow the path along the right side of the ramp toward Rock Creek.

1.5 Continue following the paved path to the right toward the Watergate Building and the Kennedy Center.

1.8 Turn left and cross the Parkway to ride between the Kennedy Center and the Watergate. Continue toward the right following F Street over New Hampshire Avenue and past the Saudi Embassy until F Street dead-ends at 25th Street.

2.0 Cross 25th Street and turn right onto the sidewalk/path along the edge.

2.1 Stay to the left at the fork to ride parallel to the road on the designated bike path. This will take you over the Roosevelt Bridge and will give you some great views of the Kennedy Center and the Georgetown waterfront to the north.

3.0 Make a U turn and head south on the Mount Vernon Trail along the boardwalk. You can also head back to your car at this point if you continue straight.

3.8 You'll ride under the Memorial Bridge; your goal is to turn back and over the bridge.

4.0 Turn right at this trail intersection and carefully cross over the George Washington Memorial Parkway. Continue heading back toward the bridge.

4.1 Stay to the right and cross the Washington Boulevard ramp to continue toward the bridge.

4.2 Stay right and go over the memorial bridge.

4.7 Continue bearing right and make a right at the second stop sign to head toward Ohio Drive. At this point you will be riding on the road. You can continue across this road and turn right on the path beyond it.

4.9 Go through the light and around the Ohio Drive circle and the John Ericsson Memorial to head south on Ohio Drive. You can hop on the bike path that runs parallel to Ohio Drive and the river at this point.

5.6 Go over the small bridge that spans the basin and turn left onto the opposite sidewalk; the Jefferson Memorial will be up ahead and to your left. The road here is one way, so you want to make sure to be on the path.

5.8 Make a sharp right (U turn) in front of the Capital Bikeshare Station to head over the 14th Street Bridge.

6.4 Turn left at the stop sign to ride north on the Mount Vernon Trail. The Navy Maritime Memorial will be up ahead and to your right.

6.6. Stay left to remain riding north on the Mount Vernon Trail. From now on you will remain on the Mount Vernon Trail for approximately 2 miles until you reach the starting point of the ride.

7.3 Stay to the right, you are now backtracking over what you rode earlier. There are some great views of the Memorial Bridge, the Lincoln Memorial and the Washington Monument along this portion of the ride.

8.3 Turn right at the stop sign. Left will take you back and over the Roosevelt Bridge.

8.5 Complete the loop.

RIDE INFORMATION

Local Events and Attractions
Kennedy Center for the Performing Arts (Millennium Stage): www.kennedy-center.org/programs/millennium/schedule.html
Roosevelt Island Marina: www.nps.gov/this/index.htm
SW DC Waterfront: www.swdcwaterfront.com/news
Georgetown Waterfront Events: www.georgetownwaterfrontpark.org

Restaurants
Phillips Seafood: 900 Water St. SW, Washington, DC 20024; (202) 488-8515; www.phillipsseafood.com
Sea Catch Restaurant: 1054 31st St. NW, Washington, DC 20007; (202) 337-8855
Cantina Marina: 600 Water St. SW, Washington, DC 20024; (202) 554-8396; www.cantinamarina.com

Restrooms
Restrooms are available in Roosevelt Island.

The Tidal Basin and the Waterfront

This ride takes you through some of DC's most prominent and popular "water-fronts." First you'll spin along the C&O Canal through Georgetown and then make your way along the Rock Creek Park Trail to the Tidal Basin. You'll then ride to the east side of the river along the Navy Yard. On your way back you'll ride along Haines Point, a favorite destination for "Roadies," before you make your way back to the starting point. This ride is enjoyed most during the early morning or late weekday afternoons when tourist traffic is down to a minimum. If you are going to do this ride during the weekend get ready to walk your bike along the Tidal Basin.

Start: Lyndon B. Johnson Memorial Grove Parking Area along Boundary Channel Drive; Pentagon North Parking

Length: 14.9 miles

Approximate riding time: 1–3 hours. Highly dependent on how long you hang out at the various memorials and sites.

Best bike: Road or hybrid bike

Terrain and trail surface: Paved bike paths and several paved road sections; boardwalks along the Navy Yard

Traffic and hazards: Other trail users. Avoid peak tourist hours.

Things to see: The Tidal Basin, the C&O Canal through Georgetown, the Kennedy Center, The Watergate, The Navy Yard, Nationals Stadium, and various monuments and memorials along the way.

Getting there: From Springfield: Take I-395 north toward Washington and take exit 8B. Then merge onto Washington Boulevard toward the Pentagon/Arlington Cemetery/Rosslyn. Take the first exit toward VA 110/Pentagon North Parking. Turn left at the stop sign at Boundary Channel Drive. The Lyndon B. Johnson parking area will be on your left as the road curves right.

    From the National Mall: Take 14th Street south to I-395 south. Take exit 10A for Boundary Channel Drive toward the Pentagon North

Parking. Drive for approximately 0.5 mile on Boundary Channel Drive. The parking area will be on your right as the road curves to the left. GPS: 38.877771,-77.052982

Fees: None

THE RIDE

Had you ridden this route at the turn of the 19th century, you would have needed a boat to complete most of its segments. Much of what encompassed the area we know today as the tidal basin and the waterfront once was under the waters of the Potomac River, the Anacostia, and the Washington City Canal. In 1848, when the cornerstone for the Washington Monument was set down, it was a stone's throw away from the waterfront. During that time only Pennsylvania Avenue and the Washington City Canal connected the President's House to the Capitol. The Washington Monument stood at the entrance of the Canal overlooking the mighty Potomac, the Long Bridge that connected the capital city to Virginia and the Potomac Flats, named so because of the great quantity of silt that had deposited along its banks.

It really wasn't until 1875 when the Army Corps of Engineers began dredging the Potomac that the waterfront we know today started to take shape. Charged with reclaiming the Potomac Flats from the river so that the waterway could be used for commerce, the Army Corps of Engineers began moving the silt from the Potomac Flats and depositing it to the south. Only a few years into the project, the devastating flood of 1881 inundated the White House and the Mall and virtually destroyed the Washington City Canal. What was left was a pestilent swamp that needed to be removed. So the US House Committee on the District of Columbia appropriated $1 million for the reclamation of the Potomac Flats and to rid the city of the rank swamp that was left in the wake of the flood and charged the Corps of Engineers to carry out the task.

Bike Shops

Bicycle Pro Shop: 3403 M St. NW, Washington, DC 20007; (202) 337-0311; www.bicycleproshop.com

Big Wheel Bikes: 1034 33rd St. NW, Washington, DC 20007; (202) 337-0254; www.bigwheelbikes.com

Revolution Cycles: 3411 M St. NW, Washington DC 20007; (202) 965-3601; www.revolutioncycles.com

By the end of the century, in 1897, the Army Corps of Engineers was close to completing its complex task and had reclaimed nearly 700 acres of land from the river. In the process they raised the grounds around Pennsylvania and Constitution Avenues by nearly 6 feet and pushed the mighty Potomac nearly 1 mile to the west, narrowing its banks considerably. They also established a new "island" park south of what is now the Jefferson Memorial, East Potomac Park. By 1911, when their task was fully completed, a road (Ohio Drive) had been built around the perimeter of East Potomac Park, and Japanese cherry trees had been planted along its perimeter. Although not part of the Mall today, East Potomac Park is part of a grander vision for the "Nation's Back Yard" and one day in the near future may very well be part of the National Mall complex.

Development of DC's waterfronts didn't end with the dredging of the Potomac and has continued over the years. The McMillan Plan included East Potomac Park, but much of what is now part of the Georgetown waterfront and the Anacostia waterfront was ignored, something that the National Mall 3rd Century Initiative hopes to avoid. Included in their National Mall Plan is a revitalized waterfront that includes East Potomac Park, portions along Georgetown, the Anacostia River, and along the banks of the Potomac in Virginia.

The Georgetown waterfront began its revitalization nearly 50 years ago. During the early days of the capital's history, the Georgetown waterfront served as an industrial seaport, but by the 1960s the area fell into disrepair and became an

A Perfect Addition

In 1885 Mrs. Eliza Ruhamah Scidmore inadvertently initiated the donation of cherry trees from Japan to the city of Washington, DC. Upon returning from a visit to Japan, Mrs. Scidmore proposed that Japanese cherry blossom trees would make a perfect addition to the newly reclaimed Potomac Waterfront. Her requests fell on deaf ears, and only after 24 years of persistence did her request get to the right person, First Lady Helen Taft. On April 7, 1907 the first lady agreed to plant the trees but not along the tidal basin. The next day word got to the Japanese Consul, Mr. Midzumo, that Washington was to have Japanese cherry trees, and he graciously offered to donate 2,000 more trees in the name of the city of Tokyo. The first lady agreed, and by 1910 the first shipment arrived in the United States. Unfortunately that first gift had to be destroyed because the trees were diseased and infested. The city of Tokyo took the news in stride and, two years later, donated 3,020 additional trees. On March 27, 1912, the First Lady and the Viscountess Chinda, wife of the Japanese ambassador, planted two trees (still standing) on the northern bank of the tidal basin and began what is now known as the Cherry Blossom Festival (www.nps .gov/cherry/cherry-blossom-history.htm).

Where are the riders? Enjoying the memorial of course. DC is best seen by bike—on two wheels you can hit most of the major monuments and memorials in a day.

eyesore. Plans for an interstate highway along the banks of the river forced the condemnation of the waterfront. The highway was never built and the area fell further in disrepair. It wasn't until the late 1970s that citizen groups began the effort to convert the dilapidated shores of the Potomac along Georgetown into a National Park. Their efforts moved slowly, and by 1985 the government of the District of Columbia transferred the land along the waterfront to the National Park Service. And in the early 1990s, the project finally began to move forward. It took awhile, but finally, in the fall of 2010, the park was opened for public use.

Having seen the revitalization of the area take place, I can attest to how different the waterfront is today. When I first arrived here in 1985, this area was

The Tidal Basin and the Waterfront

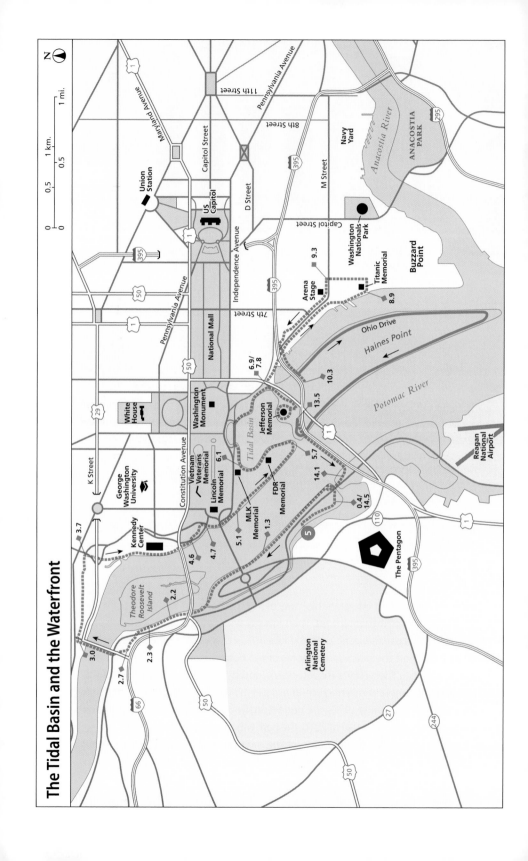

The Tidal Basin and the Waterfront

easily described with one word: dump. Today, there aren't enough adjectives to describe the transformation of the waterfront and how important citizen involvement is in converting a location. As you ride along Water Street, you'll appreciate the efforts made over the last five decades to transform this area into a recreational destination.

A similar transformation is taking place now along the east side of the city on the banks of the Anacostia River. Often referred to as the "forgotten river," the Anacostia has seen a resurgence of interest from citizen and environmental groups. No doubt that the success of the Georgetown waterfront transformation has had an impact on the efforts along the eastern side of the city. This ride will scratch the surface of that development (see Ride 1, The Anacostia River Walk for details).

Midway through the ride and before we enter East Potomac Park for the home stretch, we'll roll along the shores of the Washington Channel and what I think is the highlight of this spin: the Southwest Waterfront. Here is your perfect chance to stop for a bite to eat (try the ceviche at Captain White's) in one of the many establishments. The Southwest Waterfront, also known as the Wharf, is one of a few surviving open-air seafood markets on the East Coast and boasts the distinction of being the oldest continuously operating (since 1805) fish market in the United States. If you like seafood, this place will keep you satisfied. Blogger Lisa Shapiro of diningindc.net refers to it as "the red-light district of raw seafood. You'll find everything from rare fish to Maryland blue crabs." Rumor has it that Martha Washington herself shopped for seafood along the banks of the Wharf. Plans to also revitalize this area are under way. I'm unsure what development would do to this gem of a place though and hope that the character of the area remains intact.

MILES & DIRECTIONS

0.0 From the ramp to enter the grove, turn right and head over the bridge. Immediately turn right and follow the stone path toward the Marina parking area.

0.1 Bear right away from the stone path and ride on the asphalt path. Continue to the right and enter the parking lot. There is a narrow path that travels along the parking area if you choose to ride that.

0.4 Turn left at the stop sign and then immediately right to enter the path that will take you toward the Mount Vernon Trail. Ride under the parkway (great views of the Jefferson Memorial and the Washington Monument).

0.6 Stay straight and to the right at this intersection to join the Mount Vernon Trail.

0.7 Turn right at the T intersection to continue on the Mount Vernon Trail toward Roosevelt Island.

1.3 Continue straight.

2.2 Turn right at the stop sign and continue north on the Mount Vernon Trail toward Roosevelt Island.

2.3 Go through the Roosevelt Island parking area and head up the bridge that crosses the parkway and takes you to Rosslyn and the Key Bridge.

2.7 Turn right onto Lynn Street and go over the Key Bridge.

3.0 Immediately after crossing the Key Bridge, make a sharp right turn at Key Park and head down toward the C&O Canal.

3.1 When you reach the bottom, turn right to go down the steps to the bridge that crosses the Canal. Turn right before crossing the bridge to go down to the towpath and then make a U turn to head east along the canal. Continue on the towpath until it ends at the Rock Creek Trail. There is some construction going on in this area, so you may be forced to take a short detour (as I did) along the way.

3.5 Cross Thomas Jefferson Street. One block to the north on M Street (3501 M St.) is the Old Stone House, the oldest known private home in Washington. Along the Canal to the left is the C&O Canal Visitor Center.

3.7 Turn right onto the Rock Creek Park Trail. We'll follow this path until we reach the tidal basin.

4.6 Shortly after riding under the Roosevelt Bridge, take the crosswalk to the left and continue on the Rock Creek Trail through the volleyball courts.

4.7 The path will curve right and go under the Memorial Bridge. Before riding under the Memorial Bridge, pass by the Watergate Steps. The steps were originally built to welcome important dignitaries into the city from the Potomac, but that plan never materialized. Then they were used to host concerts on parked river barges, but those were abandoned when the noise of National Airport-bound jets drowned the sound of the music. As you reach the steps you'll now be on Ohio Drive.

5.1 Enter West Potomac Park. Continue along the road or path that parallels the river.

5.3 West Basin Drive is to your left; this is an access point to both the FDR and MLK Memorials. We'll ride past these shortly though. Also to the left are the Washington Polo Grounds. The location marks the inaugural flight on May 15, 1918 of the world's first continuous mail delivery by air.

5.7 Turn left to cross Ohio Drive and to continue along the tidal basin. As you cross Ohio, you'll want to take the path to the right that heads down to the basin. Ride around the entire tidal basin to the Jefferson Memorial in a clockwise direction. Along the way you'll pass the FDR and MLK Memorials.

5.9 The FDR Memorial is to the left. You can also see the Martin Luther King Memorial up ahead.

6.1 The MLK Memorial is to your left.

6.3 Turn right onto Independence Avenue and ride over the Kutz Bridge, the path will continue to the right along the water's edge. Look around for the first two Japanese cherry trees planted in the tidal basin; they are marked with a large bronze plaque and a Japanese lantern commemorating the occasion.

6.7 Continue following the trail to the right. You'll see the paddle boat station to the right and a refreshments stand to the left.

6.9 After circling around the Jefferson Memorial, we'll come back to this point to continue to the east side. Note: at the time of this writing there was considerable construction going on around this area. Several detours were in effect, and several bike paths were being improved and added.

7.1 Turn right to head into the Jefferson Memorial Grounds. Pick up the path to the right as the driveway curves left so that you can ride around the memorial in a counterclockwise direction. After riding around the memorial, return this point.

7.3 You are in front of the memorial; from here you have some great views of the basin and the Washington Monument to the north.

7.5 Turn right on the same driveway you came in to enter the memorial grounds. When you reach the barriers, turn left to head back in the same direction you came in.

7.7 Turn right onto the crosswalk to cross Ohio Drive and then left onto the path across the street.

7.8 Turn right onto Maine Avenue to go under I-395; you are now entering the Anacostia Riverwalk Trail and the Eastern Waterfront.

8.0 You reach Pruitt Seafood. Work your way down to Water Street to the right to ride along the waterfront and to continue south.

8.7 Water Street, ends but the Anacostia River Trail continues to the right. Continue riding south along the Riverwalk.

8.9 You've reached the Titanic Memorial. There are some great views of Haines Point to the west. Turn left and head toward 4th and P.

9.0 Turn left onto 4th Street.

9.3 Turn left onto M Street.

9.4 Continue to the right; you're now on Maine Avenue. Arena Stage will be to your right.

9.8 Reach 9th Street. Cross 9th and then pick up the trail that splits Benjamin Banneker Park to the right and follow it to the top of the hill. Make a left where the trail intersects the sidewalk.

9.9 Turn left onto the trail shortly before the bridge that spans I-395; do not go over the bridge. The left trail will take you over Maine Avenue and 12th Street along the Francis Case Memorial Bridge. Along the way you'll get to see some great views of the waterfront and markets below.

10.3 After crossing the bridge, make a sharp left (U turn) to head down to Haines Point. The Bubble will be on your left.

10.4 Turn right onto Ohio Drive SW. You'll now stay on Ohio Drive as it curves around the length of Haines Point.

10.8 Turn left and quickly right to continue on Ohio Drive in the same direction. Restrooms are available here to your right.

11.8 You reach the "tip" of Haines Point. Continue following Ohio Drive as it heads back to the northwest. Stay on Ohio Drive through the next two intersections.

12.0 Restrooms are available to the right.

13.4 As Ohio Drive ends with a left turn only, turn slightly right onto the path that runs along the right curb. The entrance to the George Mason Memorial will be to your right. Head east toward the Jefferson Memorial and the Capital Bikeshare racks ahead.

13.5 As you reach the Capital Bikeshare station, make a sharp right turn (U turn) to head up and over the 14th Street Bridge.

14.1 Turn left at the stop sign to continue north on the Mount Vernon Trail.

14.3 Turn right and immediately right again and ride around the Navy and Maritime Memorial to head back toward the Columbia Island Marina and the starting point of the ride.

14.5 Go under the tunnel and turn left to head into the marina. Turn right into the parking area. Restrooms are available to your right. Continue straight toward the Lyndon B. Johnson Grove.

14.6 Enter the grove and follow the path to the left toward the bridge to the Pentagon's north parking.

14.8 Turn left and over the bridge and then left again to exit the grove.

14.9 The loop is complete.

RIDE INFORMATION

Local Events and Attractions
Cherry blossoms, The National Mall, The Navy Yard, Nationals Stadium
The Southwest Waterfront, the nation's oldest continuously operated fish market

Restaurants
Pruitt's Seafood (Market): 11th Street & Maine Ave. SW, Washington, DC 20001; (202) 554-2669
Captain White's Seafood City (Market): 1100 Maine Ave. SW, Washington, DC 20024; (202) 484-CRAB; www.captainwhitesseafood.com
Phillips Flagship: 900 Water St. SW, Washington, DC 20024; (202) 488-8515; www.phillipsseafood.com

Restrooms
Restrooms are available in the Columbia Island Marina, the Jefferson Memorial, and in East Potomac Park (Haines Point).

The Alexandria Loop

This ride will take you through the third most densely populated city in the United States, Alexandria, Virginia. You'll spin down some of Alexandria's most interesting bike paths. Along the way we'll ride through upscale neighborhoods, ethnically diverse areas, and the north side of Old Town. You can also make a pit stop at the Masonic Memorial, or continue on through an industrial complex that will lead you to Alexandria's newest Brewery, Port City.

NOTE: At the time of this book's development there was considerable construction along Potomac Avenue, and the bike path was detoured from one side of the road to the other. By the time you read this you should be able to ride the length of Potomac Avenue without having to hop from side to side.

Start: Cameron Run Regional Park Area

Length: 17.2 miles

Approximate riding time: 2–3 hours

Best bike: Road bike

Terrain and trail surface: Mostly on bike paths and some sections of asphalt road

Traffic and hazards: Other trail users and vehicle traffic on the road sections

Things to see: Holmes Run, Old Town Alexandria historic sites, the Masonic Memorial, Port City Brewing Company

Getting there: From I-495, take exit 174 to the Eisenhower Connector. Follow the signs for Great Waves Waterpark. Park at the Cameron Run Regional Park parking area. GPS: 38.804417,-77.101868

Fees: None

THE RIDE

When I first moved to the area, back in the late '70s, Alexandria seemed like such a faraway place. We lived in Montgomery County, Maryland, and only made the trek down the Beltway to Old Town a couple of times a year. Back then all I really knew of Alexandria was the historic portion of the city. It wasn't until I returned to the area in the early '90s that I began to discover the rest of Alexandria, the third most densely populated city in the United States.

Back then we lived in an area that straddled Arlington and Alexandria called Arlandia. It was from there that I started to visit and discover the rest of the city. Our ride will take us through several of its neighborhoods, including Eisenhower Valley, the West End, North Gate, Arlandia, and Potomac West. Along the way we'll ride alongside rushing streams, secluded parkland, bustling neighborhoods, and national monuments before making our way back to the beginning.

Our ride starts in one of the most popular parks in Alexandria, Cameron Run Regional Park, and home of Great Waves Waterpark. Not long ago the area was nothing more than an unflattering industrial zone. Nothing much grew in the surroundings of the floodplain of Cameron Run and Holmes Run, and no one lived there. That all changed in the mid '80s with the creation of Cook Lake, a small lake that serves as the backdrop for the park and where locals can go for some "urban" fishing. With the lake came new trees, homes, and eventually a new trail that runs along Holmes Run toward Baileys Crossroads in Arlington. The beginning of the ride will run along this trail, which I think is one of the most interesting in the region.

As you enter Holmes Run from Eisenhower Avenue, the landscape will turn somewhat surreal. Because of the surroundings, this section of Holmes Run has retained the industrial feel of its past. The landscape of nearby bridges and the large concrete tunnels that channel Holmes Run's water give it a post-apocalyptic feel. That feeling carries on as you reach I-395 and ride under the Van Dorn overpasses and then through the I-395 tunnel, one of the most interesting sections of trail in the region. As

Bike Shops

Spokes Etc.: 545 N. Quaker Ln., Alexandria, VA; (703) 820-2200; www.spokesetc.com

Wheel Nuts Bike Shop: 302 Montgomery St., Alexandria, VA 22314; (703) 548-5116; http://wheelnutsbikeshop.com

you exit the tunnel, the concrete surroundings give way to a tree-covered trail and a totally different feel. Last time I rode here, I came out of the tunnel and encountered a family of deer. It was like being transported to a different world.

Pete makes his way past the George Washington Masonic Memorial.

Holmes Run continues, eventually turning into Dora Kelley Park, a small stretch of land that is a gem in the area.

It's quite remarkable how a park like this shields you from the surrounding neighborhoods. The park would not have been possible if not for one of its citizens, Mrs. Dora Kelley, a local Alexandria City resident who fought hard to maintain and preserve the woodlands near her home. Her dream became a reality in 1973 when the City of Alexandria acquired nearly 26 acres of land for the establishment of a nature park and wildlife sanctuary. The acquired land became part of a 50-acre parcel that now includes oak-hickory forests, a stream and floodplain, a freshwater marsh, and a variety of native plants and wildlife not found anywhere else in the city. For her efforts, the Alexandria City Council passed a resolution in 1976 to name the area after Mrs. Kelley, recognizing the outstanding contribution she made to preserve the character of the area.

As we continue, we'll head through the campus of Northern Virginia Community College before merging with the Four Mile Run Trail, an extremely popular trail in the area. Four Mile Run will take us through Shirlington, a small enclave of shops and restaurants that has evolved over the years. When we lived in Arlandria, on the other side of I-395, we often came here for dinner at one of the sidewalk cafes. Since then apartments and condos have sprouted along its perimeter, giving the area a city vibe within its 1-block length. We'll continue across I-395, this time over it, into the North Ridge neighborhood and the "hilly" portion of our ride. I purposely came in this direction to avoid some climbing

The Pineapple Means Business

Port City Brewing Company is one of Alexandria's newest landmarks, and likely to become one of its most visited. Port City Brewing hopes to continue a tradition started back in the late 1800s by the Portner Brewing Company, which operated in the city for nearly 50 years until prohibition forced it to close its doors. At the time, the Portner Brewery was the largest brewery in the southern United States and the biggest employer in Alexandria. Opened in January 2011, Port City hopes to revive that tradition by producing high-quality crafted beer. During a recent group ride, we stopped to visit and tour the facilities and felt right at home. A bike rack is available out front for riders following this route. If the pineapple is on the sign, it means they are open for business, so stop by for a tour. Tell them we sent you! The brewery is open for tours Wed through Sun; check their website for specific details.

Port City Brewing Company, 3950 Wheeler Avenue, Alexandria, VA 22304; (703) 797-2739; www.portcitybrewing.com

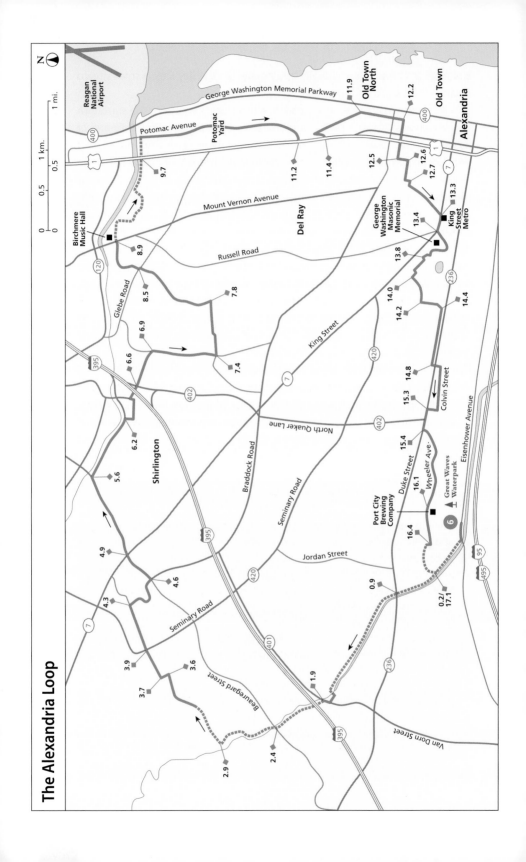

The Alexandria Loop

some of the bigger hills; still, we'll have to ascend a little before descending into Arlandria and the second half of our ride.

Arlandria was our neck of the woods. I often rode north toward Pentagon City on my way to work and down to the Four Mile Run to play soccer along some of the fields near Mount Vernon Avenue. On many occasions we spent late nights listening to quality music at the Birchmere and had several meals in one of the many Latin American restaurants that dotted the area. We often headed into the Del Ray Area from here as well, and I encourage you to do so since it has turned into quite a lovely destination for a meal or a drink during a warm summer evening.

The ride concludes through the west side of Old Town via the George Washington Masonic Memorial and the industrial streets of the Eisenhower Valley. Before closing out the loop you'll pass by one of the area's newest landmarks, Port City Brewing Company. By this point you're almost done, so treat yourself to a cold one, you've deserved it by now.

MILES & DIRECTIONS

0.0 Start at the Cameron Run Regional Park parking lot. We'll start measuring at the entrance to the lot in front of the park sign. Head west on the paved bike trail that runs parallel to Eisenhower Avenue.

0.2 Follow the trail to the right away from Eisenhower Avenue and alongside Holmes Run. Continue staying to the right at the next intersection.

0.7 Immediately before you reach the playground, make a left turn and then an immediate right to continue on the trail along Holmes Run.

0.9 Turn left to enter Holmes Run Park.

1.8 Turn left at this intersection to follow the scenic trail, NOT the urban trail. You'll go over Holmes Run and then turn right again. Note that after heavy rains this section of trail may be difficult to ride.

1.9 Go under Van Dorn Street and then through the tunnel that goes under Route 395. Yell through the tunnel, I do.

2.4 Cross Beauregard and then just hop on the sidewalk on the right on Morgan Street to pick up the trail to enter the Dora Kelley Nature Park. This is a surprising little oasis amidst the suburban sprawl.

2.5 Cross Holmes Run again and turn left to continue following the paved concrete path.

2.8   Continue straight through this intersection.

2.9   Turn right onto Chambliss Street.

3.0   Continue straight onto the bike path.

3.3   Exit the Dora Kelley Nature Park and continue straight on North Chambliss Road.

3.5   Stay to the right at this intersection to enter Fillmore Street.

3.6   Turn left onto Stevens Street.

3.7   Turn right onto Dawes Avenue.

3.9   Cross Seminary and continue on Dawes Avenue.

4.3   Turn right onto Campus Drive. You're now on the grounds of the Northern Virginia Community College Alexandria campus. I took several classes here when I was in the Army way back in the day.

4.6   Turn left onto Beauregard. At this point you have two options: ride on the sidewalk on the near side, or cross and turn left and hop on the sidewalk on the opposite side. You can also ride along the road if you choose. I recommend the latter since it will make crossing King Street a little farther ahead a bit easier. The original Five Guys is at the intersection of Beauregard and King.

4.9   Cross King Street (Beauregard becomes Walter Reed) and work your way to the left lane to cross to the other curb and hop on the designated bike path. You can also cross King Street and then use the designated crosswalk to cross South Walter Reed and then make a right onto the designated bike trail to continue in the same direction.

5.1   The trail will curve slightly to the left and then right to cross Dinwiddle Street.

5.6   Continue straight at this intersection, and at the light cross South Walter Reed to continue following the trail. You are basically making a right turn from South Walter Reed Drive onto South Arlington Mill Road. You are now on the Four Mile Run Trail.

6.2   Turn right onto Randolph Road and then immediately left onto Campbell Avenue to ride through the center of Shirlington. There are plenty of shops and restaurants here. My personal favorite is Capitol City Brewing Company.

6.3 Cross Quincy Street so that you end up on the sidewalk directly in front of the entrance of the WETA Building, then turn left to catch the ramp for the bridge that will take you over I-395.

6.6 Cross the bridge and ride over Martha Custis Drive to continue east on Gunston Road.

6.9 Turn right onto Valley Drive.

7.4 Turn left onto Allison Street.

7.5 Continue straight/slight left to stay on Allison Street.

7.8 Turn left onto Old Dominion Boulevard.

8.1 Stay to the right at Beverly Circle so that you remain on Old Dominion Boulevard.

8.5 Make a left onto West Glebe Road and then an immediate right to continue on Old Dominion Boulevard.

8.6 Turn left onto Notabane Drive. Use caution as you ride through this parking area. Notabane will turn into 4 Mile Road.

8.9 Cross Mount Vernon Avenue. The Four Mile Run Trail is straight ahead.

9.0 Turn right at this intersection.

9.4 After crossing the bridge, continue following the trail to the left and then right around the baseball field; continue straight through the next intersection.

9.7 Cross Route 1 and continue straight through the parking area to the back side of Pier 1 Imports and turn right onto the Potomac Avenue bike path. Alternatively you can cross Route 1, turn left onto the bike path, and then immediately after crossing over the bridge that spans the Four Mile Run turn diagonally right over the grass to the sidewalk alongside the first set of buildings, then turn right onto the Potomac Avenue bike path.

10.4 The bike path continues on the opposite side of Potomac Avenue.

11.2 Cross Main Line Road and then turn left to go over the Route 1 Bridge.

11.4 Immediately after crossing the bridge, turn left onto Slater Lane and then immediately right onto Powhatan Street. Vaso's Kitchen will be ahead to your left—great gyros and Greek beers, perfect place for a mid-ride break.

11.9 Turn right onto Columbus Street.

12.2 Turn right onto Pendelton Street.

12.5 Turn left onto North Payne Street.

12.6 Turn right onto Oronoco Street.

12.7 Turn left onto Earl Street and then immediately right onto Sutter Street. Sutter will dead-end; turn left onto the bike path.

13.1 Turn right onto Cameron Street and head toward the King Street Metro Station. This can be an alternate starting point if you took the train.

13.3 Turn right onto King Street and head up toward the George Washington National Masonic Memorial. You can ride on King Street or on the sidewalk on the opposite side.

13.4 Turn left onto Callahan and then immediately right and left onto the road that will climb up to the main entrance of the memorial.

13.6 Continue following the road as it curves around the left side of the memorial.

13.7 Look for the access path adjacent to the first small parking lot to the right. Turn right onto it and then left onto Park Road right after crossing the gate.

13.8 Turn left to follow Ridge Lane and the fence line for the memorial. This little alley offers an alternate view of the memorial seldom seen, except for the lucky residents who live along this lane.

13.9 Turn left onto Carlisle Road and then immediately right onto Hilltop Terrace.

14.0 Turn left onto Upland Place.

14.2 Turn left onto Hilton Street.

14.4 Hilton will curve to the right and turn into Duke Street.

14.8 Turn left onto Roth Street to cross the main Duke Street travel lanes.

14.9 Turn right onto Colvin Street.

15.2 Turn right onto South Quaker Lane. Before reaching Duke Street, work your way to the sidewalk on the opposite side of the road.

15.3 Turn left onto Duke Street, staying on the near sidewalk.

15.4 Turn left onto Wheeler Avenue.

16.1 Pass right in front of Port City Brewing Company. If the pineapple is on the sign, it means they are open for business. By the time you read this Port City will be hosting food trucks. What better way to almost end your ride than with a tasty Pale Ale?

16.4 Turn right onto South Gordon Street and then make an immediate left onto the bike path.

16.6 Veer to the left at this intersection.

16.7 Turn left onto Holmes Run to head back to the starting point of the ride. You will backtrack for approximately 0.5 mile.

17.0 Stay left.

17.1 Stay left.

17.2 The loop is complete.

RIDE INFORMATION

Local Events and Attractions

Visit the **Old Town Alexandria** website for information and links about upcoming events: www.visitalexandriava.com

One of my favorite Old Town Events is the annual **Saint Patrick's Day Celebration and Parade** and the September open air Arts Festival.

Restaurants

Vaso's Kitchen: 1225 Powhatan St., Alexandria, VA 22314; (703) 548-2747
Capitol City Brewing Company: 4001 Campbell Ave., Arlington, VA 22206; (703) 578-3888; www.capcitybrew.com

Restrooms

Various commercial establishments along the route.

Burke Lake Park

If there was ever a "family" ride, the Burke Lake loop is it. The loop takes riders on a mostly flat path along flower gardens. You'll enjoy the panoramic vistas of Burke Lake, a man-made body of water that also serves as one of the busiest fishing reservoirs in the metro Washington, DC area.

Start: All options start from the South Run Trails trailhead adjacent to the South Run Recreation Center Field House

Length:
   Burke Lake Loop: 6.5 miles
   Mercer Lake Loop: 4.1 miles
   Both Loops: 10.5 miles

Approximate riding time: Depends on route chosen, generally 45 minutes–2 hours

Best bike: Hybrid, mountain, or cross bike; kid bikes will do fine here

Terrain and trail surface: Mostly doubletrack hard-pack paved and unpaved trails in a wooded environment circumventing Burke and Mercer Lakes

Traffic and hazards: Other trail users

Things to see: Waterfowl, occasional bald eagles, panoramic lake views

Getting there: From the Capital Beltway (I-495), take exit 54 for Braddock Road W. Continue on Braddock Road for approximately 1.5 miles and turn left onto Burke Lake Road. In approximately 2.5 miles turn left onto Lee Chapel Road (VA 643) and continue for 2 miles to the Fairfax County Parkway. Turn left onto the parkway and then right onto Preservation Road. Follow the road into South Run Park until it ends in a small gravel lot behind the South Run Recreation Center Field House. GPS: 38.747708,-77.275922

Fees: None if you start your ride from the point detailed here. If you choose to do only the Burke Lake loop and decide to park in one of the Burke Lake parking areas, you will have to pay a fee unless you are a Fairfax County resident.

Charge for noncounty residents on weekends and holidays only (no charge on weekdays), Apr through late Oct.

The park grounds are open from sunrise to sunset. Please be aware that these times change throughout the year.

THE RIDE

It's hard to imagine what the mood was like in the 1950s in the vicinity of what is now Burke and Mercer Lakes. After World War II, the aviation industry around the country was thriving. One particular area of the country to benefit from this boom was the Washington, DC area. The federal government saw the need for a second airport to service the region. That second airport, it was decided, would be built in the town of Burke and the area where Burke Lake currently sits. The proposed location of the new international airport would occupy nearly 4,500 acres and would displace hundreds of families. According to a June 14, 1951, article in *The Evening Star*, the proposed airport would be completed by 1955 and would "dwarf both Washington National and Baltimore's Friendship terminals."

Understandably, Burke residents vehemently opposed the proposal, and thanks to some great leadership from the town, the federal government reconsidered and, in 1958, decided instead to build its planned modern-age facility farther out to the west in the town of Willard, what is now present-day Chantilly. That airport, as we all know it today, is Washington Dulles International Airport, perhaps one of the busiest international airports in the country.

With the airport battle behind them, Fairfax County acquired the land the federal government had set aside for the airport project at auction in 1959. Instead of an airport, the county opted to follow the suggestions of its citizens to create a recreational area, including a public fishing lake. In 1961, after identifying a suitable location and completing dam construction, the Fairfax County Park Authority began the process of filling in the 218 acres that would become Burke Lake. Nearly 2,000

Bike Shop
The Bike Lane: 8416 Old Keene Mill Rd., Springfield, VA 22152; (703) 440-8701; www.thebikelane.com

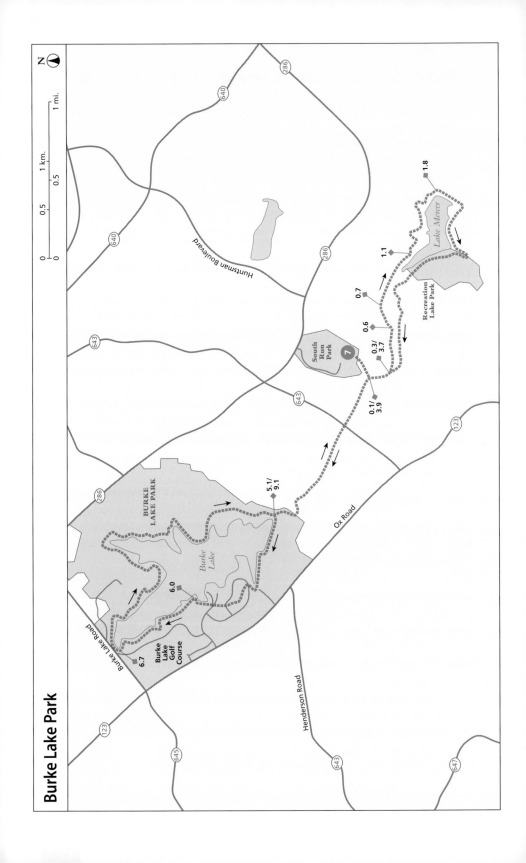

Burke Lake Park

N

0   0.5   1 km.

0   0.5   1 mi.

BURKE LAKE PARK

Burke Lake Road

6.7
Burke
Lake
Golf
Course

6.0

Burke
Lake

5.1/
9.1

Ox Road

Henderson Road

South
Run
Park

7

0.1/
3.9

0.3/
3.7

0.6

0.7

1.1

Lake Mercer

1.8

Recreation
Lake Park

Huntsman Boulevard

123

645

286

640

643

643

286

286

640

643

123

647

people attended the facility's opening ceremonies on May 25, 1963. Today, that lake is surrounded by nearly 900 additional acres of wooded parkland making it one of the county's largest lakes and also one of its most beautiful. It is a peaceful place to spend time, and lucky for us, it includes a bike trail around its perimeter. From the trail you can catch a glimpse of an elusive bald eagle or one of the many waterfowl that call the lake home and live on Vesper Island, a state refuge.

The lake is extremely popular during the spring and summer months, primarily because of its family-oriented attractions, including camping, several picnic areas, a playground, and a Frisbee golf course. The park also operates a miniature railroad that has been running in the park for over 40 years. It's not uncommon to see parents who as kids rode the train themselves enjoying it with their children. The second miniature replica of the Central Pacific Steam Engine chugs around the 1.75 miles of track in about 10 minutes. There is also an old-fashioned carousel for further enjoyment. And if you tire of everything the park has to offer, you can take a quick ride over OX Road (VA-123) to the adjacent driving ranges and golf courses, which include a school for aspiring golfers of all ages, or farther south to the Lorton Arts Center, where local artists have studios open to the public.

MILES & DIRECTIONS

0.0 Start from the gravel lot at the far end of the South Run Recreation Center by the field house. The South Run Trail entrance is clearly marked with a trail map kiosk.

0.1 Turn left toward Mercer Lake.

0.3 Turn left and away from the paved trail and onto the gravel trail.

0.6 Continue following the gravel path to the left.

0.7 Cross the cul-de-sac onto the gravel path directly opposite on the other side.

1.1 Turn left and head up the short hill and turn right onto the paved path at the top.

1.8 Go through the trail barrier and continue straight over the dam. (Note: The left fork takes you through the South Run Stream Valley Park and ends within close distance of the Cross County Trail). After crossing the dam, continue following the main trail to the right to stay along the perimeter of the lake. You'll pass several neighborhood "feeder" trails.

Generations: Old and young enjoy the loops at Mercer and Burke Lakes.

3.7. Turn right at this T intersection and head over the bridge. Continue following the trail to the left toward the starting point of our loop.

3.9. Turn left at this intersection and head toward Burke Lake. (A right turn will take you back to the parking area and your vehicle.) Stay straight on this path for 1.1 miles until you reach the Burke Lake Loop at mile marker 5.1.

5.1 You've reached the Burke Lake loop. At this point you can go either direction; the trail is easy and follows the perimeter of the lake. If you ride in a counterclockwise direction, just stay to the left at pretty much all intersections. If you ride clockwise, which is the direction we will be heading, stay to the right. As you reach the parking areas, there are clear signs that point you in the right direction to stay on the "Park Trail."

6.0 Signs of the miniature railroad tracks.

6.7 Continue following the trail to the right as it parallels the road and then immediately back into the woods to the right.

9.1 Turn left and backtrack to your vehicle.

10.2 Veer left at the intersection and continue up to the parking area.

10.5 Finish the loop.

Local Events and Attractions

Burke Lake Park offers fishing, boating, and a great Frisbee golf course. Farther north is the **Fairfax Station Railroad Museum.**

Restaurants

Glory Days Grill: 9526 Old Keene Mill Rd., Burke, VA 22015; (703) 866-1911; www.glorydaysgrill.com
BBQ World: 6050 Burke Commons Rd., Burke, VA 22015; (703) 503-7100; www.bbqworld-restaurant .com

Restrooms

After Oct 28, all facilities are closed until Apr. Park grounds remain open sunrise to sunset.

You can easily combine the Mercer/Burke Lake Loop with the Laurel Hill Loop for a nice long day in the saddle by connecting both trails with the bike path that runs parallel to Route 123. Or you can also follow the left fork at mile marker 1.8 across the South Run Stream Valley Park to Pohick Road and the Cross County Trail for even more options.

The Arlington Beltway

This ride will take you around the city of Arlington along three of the area's "back-bone" trails. You'll ride along a busy highway—though at times you may not know it—get a glimpse of some of DC's most notable landmarks, and ride through what was once George Washington's land and a prosperous railroad corridor.

Start: Intersection of Washington Boulevard and Quincy Drive (Quincy Park) in Arlington, Virginia

Length: 16.8 miles

Approximate riding time: 2 hours

Best bike: Any bike will do

Terrain and trail surface: Designated paved bike trails

Traffic and hazards: Other riders, pedestrians, and several busy intersections

Things to see: Views of the Lincoln Memorial and the Washington Monument, planes landing/taking off from Reagan National Airport at Gravely Point (Rugby matches in the Fall).

Getting there: From the Capital Beltway, take the exit for I-66 east toward Washington, DC. Take exit 71 for Fairfax Drive toward Glebe Road and drive for approximately 0.5 mile. Turn left onto Quincy Street. Quincy Park will be to your right at the intersection of Quincy Street and Washington Boulevard. GPS: 38.885822,-77.108059

Fees: None

THE RIDE

I like to refer to this ride as "Arlington's Beltway," simply because the nearly 17-mile loop we'll take will circumnavigate one of DC's nearest and most "urban" suburbs. Arlington is highly influential to the nation's capital. Because of its close proximity to the capital, is where you'll find the Pentagon and a multitude of other federal government agencies and facilities. Arlington's economic activity is highly tied to the government; it is also home to many regional iconic landmarks, including the Iwo Jima Memorial, Ronald Reagan National Airport, and the home of valor: Arlington National Cemetery.

Originally, Arlington was part of a parcel of land that belonged to Fairfax County and was donated to the federal government by the State of Virginia so that it could be used as part of the new federal capital district. By the mid-1840s, however, the federal government saw no need for the land and returned the nearly 26 square miles back to Virginia.

For nearly a century thereafter the land was known as Alexandria County, but to avoid confusion with the neighboring Alexandria City, the General Assembly of Virginia renamed the area Arlington County in 1920. The name Arlington was originally taken from the plantation that existed along the banks of the Potomac River in early colonial times. That land traded many hands and was ultimately inherited by Mary Anna Custis, wife of Confederate General Robert E Lee. The couple's home, Arlington House, was located high atop a hill overlooking the river and the young nation's capital. During the Civil War their land and mansion was confiscated by the federal government and chosen as the site of Arlington National Cemetery.

Bike Shops

Fresh Bikes Arlington: 3924 Wilson Blvd., Arlington, VA 22203; (703) 248-9600; www.freshbikescycling.com
REI: 3509 Carlin Springs Rd., Bailey's Crossroads, VA 22041; (703) 379-9400; www.rei.com
Bikenetic: 922 W. Broad St., Falls Church, VA 22046; (703) 534-7433; www.bikenetic.com

Our ride will start in one of Arlington's several "self-contained" communities, Ballston, and then circle around in a clockwise direction using three of its most traveled and busiest cycling trails. We'll ride the Custis Trail along the east side of the county, the Mount Vernon Trail along the south, and finally the Washington & Old Dominion (W&OD) trail to the west.

The first portion of our ride will take us along the Custis Trail, a 4-mile paved path that was built alongside Route 66 in the mid-'70s and early '80s and extends from the W&OD in the west to Rosslyn in the east. The trail borrows its name from the highway that it parallels. The highway that was named for the First Lady of the United States, Martha Washington Custis, was a controversial project when it was first proposed by congress in the mid part of the 20th century. Residents of Arlington County vehemently opposed the project because of air quality and noise concerns and took legal action in order to stop its construction.

This spot at Gravely Point is an area favorite for watching jet planes come in and land at Reagan National Airport.

It took nearly 20 years for the involved parties to reach a compromise and for work on the east/west highway to get started. The compromise was a reduced-width highway in the urban corridor that offered additional mass transit alternatives. For that reason, Route 66 inside the Capital Beltway is a high-occupancy road during peak hours. In addition, the construction of the highway also included a path running along its side, and for our benefit, it is the one we will be riding.

As you travel along the Custis Trail, it is clearly evident that the engineers took great care in shielding you from the highway. Yes, it is obvious that you are riding alongside a heavily used transportation corridor, but for the most part the ride is highly enjoyable. This portion of the ride will be the most challenging for many riders since the Custis, unlike the later portions of our ride, does experience some elevation changes. You will be forced to use those leg muscles in several spots to climb over several of the hills that will come your way. But don't fret, they are nothing out of the ordinary and will only last for a short portion of our trip.

Upon arriving in Rosslyn, the narrow asphalt path will give way to a wide sidewalk that will parallel Lee Highway. The ride will lead you across several busy streets, so be cognizant of your surroundings and the traffic that lies ahead. Rosslyn is a travel hub for many, and it may be very busy during peak hours; it is where drivers hop on Route 50 and where commuters often make their way to and from Route 66. It is also a converging point for several cycling commuting sites and the home of one of several Metro hub stations.

As you cross Lynn Street at the far end of Rosslyn, you'll hop on the genesis of the Mount Vernon Trail and continue south along the banks of the Potomac.

You'll find that this portion of the ride is also included in another ride in this book (see Ride 4, The Four Bridges), so you can easily combine them to create a lengthier loop.

The portion of the Mount Vernon Trail you will be riding this time offers great vistas of the monuments and Washington, DC along the other bank of the Potomac River. You'll get to see what I consider to be one of the best vantage points of the Lincoln Memorial and the Washington Monument. You'll also ride under the Memorial Bridge and onto Gravely Point, a favorite spot for many area residents to watch planes take off and land into Reagan National Airport. Gravely Point is also a local hotspot to catch a rugby match. During cool autumn weekends, several men's and women's Virginia Rugby leagues play on the vast fields adjacent to the river. I highly recommend hanging out and watching a game if you get the chance.

After passing the airport you'll turn right and head west on the Four Mile Run Trail toward Shirlington and the W&OD. Both of these trails were once the foundations of a busy railroad line that connected Alexandria with the western Virginia suburbs. The W&OD at one point extended all the way from Alexandria to Purcerville, Virginia, nearly 50 miles to the west, and offered a vital regional link. Tough times after the Great Depression and an improved regional road system ultimately forced the closure of the railroad in the late 1960s and the 100-foot right-of-way was purchased by the Virginia Department of Highways with the intent of using the land for Route 66.

The land was later purchased by Virginia Power, and then between 1978 and 1982, it was sold to the Northern Virginia Regional Park Authority (NVRPA). By 1988 the NVRPA had completed the construction of the 45-mile W&OD Asphalt Trail. Our ride will only include a short portion of the extensive trail.

Once we enter the W&OD in Shirlington, we'll pick up the Custis Trail again to complete our loop. While on the W&OD, pay close attention to several important landmarks, including a corner marker for George Washington's property where Long Branch meets Four Mile Run (Glencarlyn Park) and an old caboose along Bluemont Bypass that serves as Alexandria and Arlington's only railway museum.

MILES & DIRECTIONS

0.0   Head north on Quincy toward Route 66.

0.3   Immediately after crossing over Route 66, turn right into the entrance for the Custis Trail, then left at the immediate stop sign to head east on the Custis Trail. You want to remain on the Custis Trail until you reach Key Bridge in Rosslyn.

1.0   Stay to the left and go over 66 to continue on the Custis Trail. After crossing over 66, remain to the right.

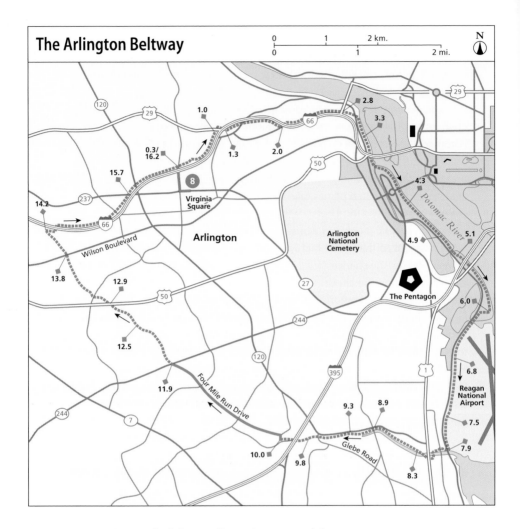

1.3 Stay to the left; 66 will now be on your left.

2.0 Continue following the trail to the left and over 66. Courthouse is to the right. 66 will now be on your right.

2.1 Continue following the trail to the right (east) toward Rosslyn and the Key Bridge. You will now be riding parallel to Lee Highway and will have to cross several intersections. Stay alert in and around this area.

2.8 You've reached the end of the Custis Trail immediately after crossing Lynn Street. You now want to continue straight on the Mount Vernon Trail. Follow the signs for Roosevelt Island, Crystal City, and Alexandria. The trail will take you over the George Washington Memorial Parkway and follow the banks of the Potomac. Remain on the Mount Vernon Trail for a little over 5 miles.

3.3 Continue to the left to follow the boardwalk. The right fork will take you over to the Roosevelt Bridge and the Kennedy Center.

4.3 Continue straight.

4.9 Stay to the right at this intersection. The left fork takes you to the Navy, Maritime Memorial, and the Lyndon B. Johnson Grove on the other side of the parkway.

5.1 Continue straight (slight left) through this intersection. The right fork will head up and above the 14th Street Bridge.

6.0 Gravely Point. Hang out and watch the planes take off and land at Reagan National Airport.

6.8 Continue straight at this intersection. The fork to the right will take you to Crystal City in the vicinity of Crystal Drive and 18th Street, where you can find all kinds of shops and restaurants, including Revolution Cycles on 20th Street.

7.5 Continue straight through both of these intersections.

7.9 Stay to the left and follow the signs for the Four Mile Run Trail.

8.3 Turn left and follow Four Mile Run toward Shirlington.

8.8 Stay to the left and remain on Four Mile Run.

8.9 Remain to the left and follow the trail under Mount Vernon Avenue.

9.3 Turn left and continue heading west on Four Mile Run.

9.6 Turn left and follow the signs to the W&OD Trail.

9.8 Continue straight and follow the trail under Route 395.

10.0 Turn right on Shirlington Drive and follow the signs to the W&OD and Custis Trails. Immediately after turning right, you will reach a light and have to turn left to access the W&OD Trail, which is clearly visible on the opposite side of the street. The Four Mile Run Trail is to the left and basically runs parallel to the W&OD Trail you will be riding. We've saved that route for a different ride. Remain on the W&OD for a little over 4 miles until you reach the Custis Trail.

11.9 Cross Columbia Pike. The W&OD Trail is clearly visible on the opposite side.

12.5 Continue straight over the small bridge. Restrooms are available to the left.

12.9 Continue straight and follow the trail under Route 50. Continue straight past the next two intersections to remain on the W&OD.

13.6 Continue straight through this intersection; we'll ride the trail to the right on another ride. This is the vicinity of Blue Moon Junction.

13.8 Stay to the right and go under Wilson Boulevard. Continue on the W&OD after you cross Wilson.

14.2 Turn right onto the Custis Trail and remain on it for the next 2 miles.

14.4 Turn left and ride under 66 and follow the trail to the right as it parallels 66.

15.7 Go over the bridge that spans 66 and then continue to the right, heading east on the Custis Trail.

16.2 Turn left to head back up toward Quincy Street and then immediately left again on Quincy to head back to the starting point of our ride.

16.6 The loop is complete.

RIDE INFORMATION

Local Events and Attractions

This ride covers a considerable footprint that includes the cities of Ballston, Rossyln, Clarendon, and Ballston, all of which offer a multitude of events and attractions. Check **www.arlingtonvirginia.com** for a comprehensive list of local events and attractions.

Restaurants

Rockland's BBQ: 3471 Washington Blvd., Arlington, VA 22201; (703) 528-9663; www.rocklands.com

Potbelly Sandwiches: 4250 Fairfax Dr., Arlington, VA 22203; (703) 807-4100; www.potbelly.com

> Arlington County is the geographically smallest self-governing county in the United States.

Restrooms

Restrooms are available along the W&OD and Four Mile Run Trails in Arlington. Porta-potties are also available at Gravely Point.

Laurel Hill

The ride through the hills and meadows of Laurel Hill will take you through a parcel of land that was once home to a Revolutionary War hero, thousands of reformatory inmates, and a magazine of inter ballistic missiles.

Start: Giles Run Meadow Trailhead parking lot by the playground; alternate start points: Barret House, Lorton Workhouse Arts Center Parking Area

Length: 10.9 miles; optional 2-mile Reformatory loop (good for kids)

Approximate riding time: 1–2 hours depending on ability

Best bike: Mountain bike

Terrain and trail surface: Mostly doubletrack and singletrack trails with a short section of hard surface on the CCT Trail

Traffic and hazards: Roots, rocks, and a couple of stream crossings. Watch out for hikers. In the spring and summertime, check yourself for ticks during and after the ride; Laurel Hill is notorious for them.

Things to see: Remnants of the old prison and reformatory facility, the 18th-century Lindsay house and William Lindsay's grave, and the renovated arts center

Getting there: Laurel Hill is in Lorton, Virginia, approximately 20 miles south of Washington, DC. From I-95, take Lorton Road exit, head west at bottom of ramp (a right turn whether coming north- or southbound on I-95). The Giles Run entrance is on the right about 0.25 mile down Lorton Road. Follow the driveway up until you see the prison complex. The parking lot is on the left, next to the playground. GPS: 38.709006,-77.238715

Fees: None

Laurel Hill, located in Lorton, Virginia, is a relatively new addition to a growing list of off-road cycling trails in Fairfax County. Named after the original hometown of one of the area's first settlers, Joseph Plaskett, Lorton has a very colorful history. And Laurel Hill, the geographic area where this ride takes place, is no different. The ride will take you through what was once the home of a Revolutionary War hero, thousands of the most hardened criminals, and a magazine of six Nike inter ballistic missiles aimed toward the Soviet Union.

Lorton's history starts well before the arrival of Joseph Plaskett in the mid-1800s. The area had been home to the Powhatan people, a confederation of tribes that farmed and hunted the lands of the coastal plains and tidewater region. Like so many regions in the east, it didn't take long for the Native Americans to be displaced by the arriving settlers. Yet it really wasn't until Joseph Plaskett added a post office to his popular country store that Lorton was finally placed on the map.

Roughly around the same time that Lorton gained postal recognition, another prominent American and contemporary to both George Mason and George Washington settled in the area, giving it prominence. William Lindsay, a major in one of Virginia's militias during the Revolutionary War and a presumed aide to George Washington himself, built a home for his family on a hilltop overlooking his 1,000-acre plantation and named it Laurel Hill after what is believed to have been the original Lindsay family estate in Ireland. In 1871 Lindsay suffered severe wounds in the battle of Guilford Courthouse and returned home, where he spent his last decade alongside his wife and 16 children. Upon his death, the major was buried in the estate, where his grave remains visible to this day. Over the years

"Please Break for Snakes," really. You'll also see lots of bunnies, a snake's favorite treat—no need to brake for those.

his home was renovated and expanded, and was even once occupied by the superintendent of the Lorton prison. Today, unfortunately, it stands in disrepair.

The area remained in the shadows until the early 20th century, when then-President Theodore Roosevelt commissioned the building of a progressive penitentiary and reformatory for the District of Columbia in the meadows of Laurel Hill. Roosevelt firmly believed that the natural surroundings of the area and exposure to nature and hard work provided an ideal environment suitable for the rehabilitation of prisoners. With that in mind, the Lorton Reformatory and Penitentiary was built, and at its peak grew to accommodate over 7,000 inmates within nearly 3,000 acres of land. The prison's dwindling popularity, changing attitudes, and the sprawl of the late 20th century toward the Virginia suburbs forced its closure and transference from the federal government to Fairfax County by the beginning of the 21st century.

Lorton's proximity to Washington, DC also made Lorton the perfect location for a Nike missile site. During the peak of the Cold War, when the arms race between the United States and the Soviet Union was at its height, the Army acquired 30 acres from the federal government on the grounds of the penitentiary and built a double pad with six Nike missile magazines. The site maintained operations until the early 1970s, when Secretary of Defense James R. Schlesinger ordered its closure. As a result, most of the missile structures were razed, and today very little evidence of their existence remains.

Prior to acquiring the land from the federal government, Fairfax County was mandated to develop a "Reuse Plan that would maximize use of land for open space, parkland, or recreation." In 1999 a citizen task force was appointed to develop the plan, which was later adopted by the county's board of supervisors and presented to Congress. Then, by November 2001, with the transfer of the last of the prisoners from the penitentiary complete, the Lorton prison was officially closed. By July 2002, after an extensive survey, over 2,000 acres of land in the facility were transferred to Fairfax County at a cost of $4.2 million, and thus began the renovation of the Lorton facilities.

Today the area is most commonly referred to as Laurel Hill to honor the legacy of William Lindsay and to preserve its historical significance. The phased approach toward development outlined in the Reuse Plan is well under way, and over the past decade the facilities have seen a dramatic change. Several of the

Bike Shops

The Bike Lane: 8416 Old Keene Mill Rd., Springfield, VA 22152; (703) 440-8701; www.thebikelane.com
Olde Town Bicycles: 14477 Potomac Mills Rd., Woodbridge, VA 22192; (703) 491-5700; www.oldetownebicycles.com
Village Skis & Bikes: 12383 Dillingham Sq., Woodbridge, VA 22192; (703) 730-0303; www.vsbsports.com

You May Run into Anne Mader (@thebikelane)

I first met Anne several years ago through MORE and often see her at Laurel Hill, Wakefield, and Fountainhead. Anne has been cycling the trails of Fairfax County for nearly 15 years, and in that time she has become an influential cycling advocate in our community. Her efforts over the years have directly influenced the development of two of the most popular area trails, Laurel Hill and the new trails at Fountainhead.

She was bitten by the biking bug when a work friend took her mountain biking one afternoon; the rest, as they say, is history. Since then, she and her husband have opened The Bike Lane, a local bike shop that has become an integral part of the community.

"I love everything about cycling," says Anne, "especially mountain biking. Rocks are fun! A bike is something special, it brings so many things to people's lives, freedom, excitement, fitness, transportation . . . "

PHOTO COURTESY ANNE MADER

But for Anne it's not just about the riding; she's made cycling an integral part of her life and has chosen to share what she loves with others, especially kids, through her Junior Mountain Bike Program. "Having 20 to 30 kids show up for a ride on the trails has just been very exciting," said Anne. "Some kids have been riding with us for five years and it has been so cool to see them still riding, racing, and even working in one of our shops."

So, next time you're riding Laurel Hill or Wakefield and see a cool woman leading a pack of kids, stop her and say hi, and thank her for making cycling in our region that much better, and for being a positive healthy influence on local children.

old penitentiary buildings have been restored and now house a thriving community of artists and craftsmen that host cultural and community events. An environmentally oriented 18-hole golf course is up and running, and, luckily for cyclists, an extensive system of trails has been built and is now open for the enjoyment of the community. Future plans include the restoration of the original 18th-century Lindsay home and additional work to the penitentiary

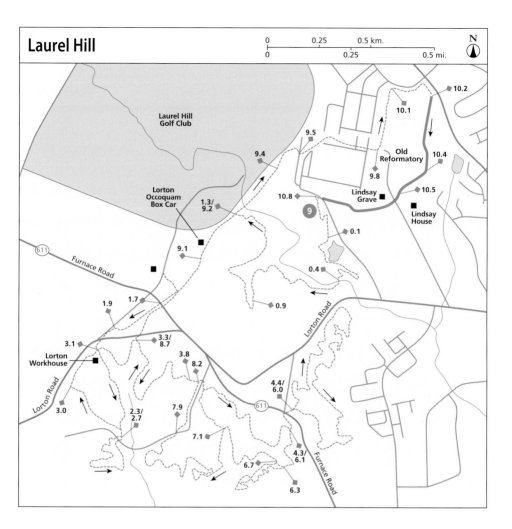

Laurel Hill

and reformatory buildings to include residential units, restaurants, retail shops, and educational facilities.

MILES & DIRECTIONS

Main loop:

0.0   Start the ride from the far end of the parking area where the paved path begins by the small playground with the climbing apparatus. Head down the path and turn left to enter the single track. The trail will then turn right and head toward the meadow pond.

0.1   Pass the meadow pond. The trail is easy to follow and well marked from here on.

0.4   Cross the creek and continue on the other side to the right. The trail will curve left and then right as it climbs to the wood line.

0.9   Stay right at this intersection to continue on the Giles Run Meadow Trail.

1.3   Turn left on the doubletrack. You are now on the Cross County Trail (CCT).

1.5   Stay left to continue on the CCT.

1.7   Right before the Barrel Arch Bridge there is a trail to the right. This is a short connector that will take you to the Barret House and an alternate starting point for this ride. Continue straight under the barrel bridge and past the trail intersection to the left.

1.9   Turn left on the pavement and cross Lorton Road. Use caution. The trail is clearly visible on the other side of the road. Follow it and turn left at the first intersection then follow the trail to the right.

2.2   Turn left at this intersection and then immediately right at the bottom and left again to enter the Slaughterhouse loop.

2.3   Pass the Slaughterhouse and turn right to follow the trail as it climbs to the top of the hill via a series of switchbacks.

2.7   You're back where you started the Slaughterhouse Loop. Exit and head back up the way you came in. Upon exiting, turn right and then immediately left to climb back up to the Workhouse loop.

2.8   Turn left, following the arrow labeled "to CCT."

3.0   Turn right on the CCT and continue back to the point where we started this first loop. If you turn left on the CCT, it will take you to the Lorton Workhouse, an alternate starting point for the ride.

3.1   Turn right and then immediately left to head down into the other side of the Workhouse loop.

3.3   Continue straight. We will take the trail to the left on our way out.

3.8   Stay to the left at this intersection to head toward the yellow (Pasture Loop). Cross the road, pick up the trail, and then turn left to follow the yellow loop.

4.3   Turn left at this intersection to head up toward Furnace Road and the Apple Orchard Loop. After the Apple Orchard Loop we'll return to this spot.

4.4 After crossing the road, you'll be on the Apple Orchard Loop. You can go either direction; we'll go left and follow the loop in the clockwise direction. There are a couple of well-marked intersections on the loop; just make sure to stay to the right on both (left if you're heading counterclockwise).

6.0 Back at the entry point of the Apple Orchard Loop. Turn left to head back to the Pasture Loop.

6.1 Turn left onto the Pasture Loop (yellow trail) and head south toward the incinerator.

6.3 Veer left at this intersection to enter the Power Station Loop.

6.7 Turn left to continue on the Pasture Loop.

7.1 Continue following the trail to the left to enter the Dairy Barn Loop. If you were to turn left and head back up, you would reach the Workhouse Loop.

7.9 Cross the dirt road and pick up the Workhouse Loop directly across the road to the left. If you head down the road to the left, you would reach the Slaughterhouse Loop. To the right is the entrance to the Pasture Loop (mile marker 3.8 above).

8.2 Stay left at this intersection. We'll double back on the Workhouse Loop for a short distance before making our way back to the Giles Run Area.

8.7 Turn right at this intersection to cross Lorton Road and head back toward the CCT.

8.8 Turn right on the CCT and head back the way you initially came in. The Barrel Bridge will be to your immediate right.

9.1 Stay to the right to continue on the CCT. The old Lorton Occoquan box car will come up on your left.

9.2 To the right is the intersection of the Giles Run Meadow Trail. You can head back up and ride it in the opposite direction to your vehicle if you wish. We'll continue straight over the bridge.

9.3 Immediately after crossing the bridge, stay to the left. The short hill to the right will take you back to the parking area. We're going to go on a quick sightseeing loop around the perimeter of the penitentiary.

9.4 Continue to the left and circle the pond in a clockwise direction. You are heading up to the path you see along the side of the reformatory.

9.5 Turn right and then immediately left to go around the reformatory. If you continue straight after turning right, you'll end up in the parking area.

9.8 Continue following the path to the left; the main prison wall will be to your right.

10.1 The blacktop ends. Turn left on the sidewalk and follow it to the stop sign. At the stop sign turn right and follow the dirt path around the next watch tower.

10.2 Turn left on the road when the dirt path ends. The prison wall will now be immediately to your right.

10.4 The wall ends; continue following the fence line along the perimeter of the road.

10.5 You'll get a good glimpse of the Lindsay house to the left and his grave immediately to the right by the prison gates. Continue straight on the road.

10.8 Turn left into the parking lot and head back toward the playground and the starting point of the ride.

10.9 The loop is complete.

Optional maximum security prison loop:

This loop is excellent for kids or if you're looking to do a quick run after or before your ride.

0.0 Start at the Giles Run parking area by the playground. We start measuring from the first access point to the parking lot, by the yellow pylons. Exit the lot by turning right and then follow the left fork along the perimeter of the reformatory. You'll now be on the Cross County Trail (CCT).

0.3 After a short down and up, you'll reach the first watch tower. To the right is the Lindsay house, to the left his grave.

0.5 Reach the second watch tower. There is a gap in the fence that allows you access to the athletic fields. You can get a closer look at the facilities around here. Continue following the road that runs along the reformatory wall.

0.6 At the time of this writing, there was a chain-link fence blocking the road. Turn right as you reach the fence and then follow the dirt path to the left to continue riding along the perimeter of the reformatory.

0.7 Turn left onto White Spruce Road. Stay on the near sidewalk; this will put you on the paved blacktop trail. Turn left onto the path to follow the perimeter of the reformatory. If you're lucky, you'll get a glimpse of the new prison residents. Virtually every time I ride through here I have seen gophers, groundhogs, and red foxes running around.

1.0 Turn right onto the brick path.

1.3 You have three options here: turn left to head back to the parking lot. Follow the middle path to head down to the CCT, or turn right and quickly left to take a slightly longer route to the CCT. We'll turn right and then immediately left and follow the path around the pond.

1.4 Turn right.

1.5 Don't cross the bridge; make a sharp left and head back up toward the parking lot.

1.6 Follow the path toward the right between the watch tower and the guard house to complete the loop, or turn left and do the loop in the opposite direction. I'd opt for the latter.

1.7 Complete the loop.

RIDE INFORMATION

Local Events and Attractions
Workhouse Arts Center: www.lortonarts.org/calendar.php
Historic Occoquan: www.occoquan.org

Restaurants
Antonelli's: 8212 Gunston Corner Ln., Lorton, VA 22079; (703) 690-4500; www.antonellis-pizza.com
Glory Days Grill: 9459 Lorton Market St., Lorton, VA 22079; (703) 372-1770; www.glorydaysgrill.com

Restrooms
Go before you go.

At its peak, the Lorton penitentiary and reformatory held over 7,000 prisoners. On November 19, 2001, amidst little fanfare, the last handful of prisoners left the correctional facility for transfer to other federal facilities across the country.

Prince William Forest Park

These rides will take you through the paved and dirt roads, and trails of Prince William Forest Park offering unique views of one of the National Park Service's few remaining and best examples of a piedmont forest ecosystem. Within the park's 15,000-forested acres, the largest green space in the Washington, DC Metropolitan Area, you'll also find over 35 miles of hiking trails, hundreds of acres open to primitive camping, and a plethora of wildlife and plant life to enjoy.

Start: Both the Scenic Road Loop and the off-road loop start from the far end of the parking area adjacent to the Pine Grove Picnic Area. The Bike Lane Loop starts from Parking Area D.

Length: Varies, depending on route chosen

Approximate riding time: Varies, depending on route chosen

Best bike: For the Scenic Road Loop, I recommend a road bike. For the off-road loop I recommend a mountain or hybrid bike. Any bike will do for the out-and-back Bike Lane Loop.

Terrain and trail surface: Varies, depending on route chosen

Traffic and hazards: Occasional vehicles on the scenic ride; roots, rocks, and some natural obstacles on the off-road ride

Things to see: Prince William Forest Park represents the largest example of an eastern Piedmont forest ecosystem in the National Park System.

Getting there: The park is in northern Virginia, 32 miles south of Washington, DC along I-95. From I-95 south take exit 150 west, Route 619 (Joplin Road), and follow the signs to the park entrance on the right. Proceed to the visitor center, where you'll find road and trail maps and additional information. Restrooms are available both next to the visitor center, in the main Pine Grove Picnic Area, and in the Oak Ridge Campground. To reach the Travel Trailer Village, take exit 152 west toward Manassass (Route 234, Dumfries Road) for 2.5 miles to the Trailer

Village entrance on the left. The off-road loop can be easily accessed from the Route 234 bike path via the trailer village and Burma Road.

Fees: $5.00 per vehicle, 7 consecutive days. $3.00 per person walk-in, bike in or per motorcycle (also 7 days). $20.00 Annual Pass (best value), provides entry for pass holder and occupants of a single personal vehicle (capacity of 14 passengers or less). GPS: N/W 38.561187,-77.349887

THE RIDE

The story of Prince William Forest Park goes beyond the first Scottish settlers who arrived on the shores of Quantico Creek in the late 1600s. Through his travels in the early 1600s, Captain John Smith reported the existence of a Doeg Indian community along the banks of the creek. The tribe predated the area's early settlers by thousands of years. The tribal community unfortunately dissipated with the arrival of Scottish settlers around 1690. Around that time a gristmill was erected in what is now the town of Dumfries and soon after, with the lifting of

> ### Bike Shop
> **Olde Towne Bicycles:** 14477 Potomac Mills Rd., Woodbridge, VA 22192; (703) 491-7000; www.oldetownebicycles.com.

the Navigation Laws of the late 1600s and early 1700s, and the building of a port along the creek, a thriving tobacco industry flourished west of the then-navigable creek. The growth of this bountiful cash crop had an adverse effect on the creek, and by the late 1700s that growth caused the lands to erode and eventually fill the creek with silt, making it no longer navigable.

The demise of tobacco farming saw the emergence of another harmful industry along the banks of the creek. Gold and pyrite mines flourished in Independent Hill and in Dumfries, and turned out to be a significant source of pollution for the lands around the creek and the creek itself. Sulfuric acid, a by-product of pyrite mining operations, and mercury, used extensively in the gold extraction process, were present in the waters of Quantico Creek in great quantities. Reports from that time tell us that at one point the waters of Quantico Creek were as acidic as vinegar and void of life. Mine operations prospered and operated continuously until the 1920s, but falling prices and labor troubles forced its closures, and thus the ending of a destructive chapter in the creek and area's history.

A decade later, as the nation fought the ravages of the Great Depression, only a few small working farms remained in the area. As part of Franklin Delano Roosevelt's "New Deal," the Chopowamsic Recreation Demonstration Area

You May Run into Scott Scudamore

I've known Scott for nearly 20 years, and in that time he's become one of my best friends. We met shortly after he started biking again during an organized Mid-Atlantic Off-Road Enthusiasts (MORE) ride. Back then I lived in Maryland and he in Virginia in Prince William County along the perimeter of Prince William Forest Park.  I clearly remember his incredible enthusiasm toward mountain biking and the new sport he had discovered. Not long after joining MORE, Scott became actively involved and has continued to be since he straddled two wheels. A recent article in *Spokes Magazine* featured Scott and everything he's accomplished for mountain biking in the region, including clearing a big hurdle at Prince William Forest Park.

"Some of my early mountain biking was on the forest roads of Prince William Forest Park," Scott told me, "but after discovering singletrack I ventured to other places, including Fountainhead and Schaeffer Farms in Maryland, and stopped riding very much at the park. In 1998 I accompanied the International Mountain Biking Association (IMBA) trail crew to a visit and we were basically told that the trails in the park would likely never be opened to bikes because of the environmental impact bikes would have on the trails."

After establishing a close rapport with the Friends of Prince William Forest Park, and years of keeping communication channels with the park's staff open, Scott helped convince the park to allow IMBA and MORE to build a short connector trail from the Pine Grove Picnic Area (where the MTB ride starts) to South Orenda Road so that riders could ride an actual off-road loop. It took a little over five years of planning and studies, but in 2010 the trail was built by volunteers with the help of IMBA and opened to bikes. The goal of the trail is to show the National Park Service that bikes can use the parks' resources without the feared impact. "After a heavy rain the new trail is ready for use due to the environmentally sound design practices used to design it," Scott said. "There is still a lot of work to do for more mileage to open in the park, but this special project is proving it can be done."

Scott is right. When I presented this ride to the park managers, they agreed that the trail was a step in the right direction and were optimistic about the future. For now, if you chance upon Scott on the trail, chances are he'll say hi first, thank him for his efforts and for working hard to make Prince William Forest Park an even better riding destination.

(RDA) was created in 1933, and reforestation and reclamation of the "ravaged" lands around Quantico Creek were authorized. In an effort to reduce unemployment and teach job skills, the task of building what would later become Prince William Forest Park fell on the hands of the Civilian Conservation Corps (CCC). In 1936 the Chopowamsic RDA became a unit of the National Park Service and was mandated to "conserve the scenery and the natural and historic objects and the wildlife therein and to provide for the enjoyment of the same in such a manner and by such means as will leave them unimpaired for the enjoyment of future generations." Over 2,000 CCC enrollees would work on what became a model for the entire nation: a new type of camp where low-income children and their families could get away to experience the great outdoors. By 1941, the CCC had built roads, bridges, dams, and five rustic camps for inner city children.

For a brief period during World War II, the park served the nation in a different capacity: as a top-secret military installation. Members of the Office of Strategic Services used the lands as a training ground for covert operations, and by 1946, the park was returned to the National Park Service for use by the public. Today the park offers visitors a myriad of activities, including cycling. Biking on the park's hiking trails, unfortunately, is prohibited. However, there are a couple of exceptions: a short but highly enjoyable singletrack section built by the International Mountain Biking Association (IMBA) adjacent to the Pine Grove Picnic Area that is perfect for introducing young children to the joys of singletrack. There is also a section of Taylor Farm road that was once closed to bikes that allows us to actually create a highly enjoyable off-road loop. These sections, along with many of the dirt roads in the park, are featured in the off-road ride detailed here. I also highlight the well-maintained Scenic Drive Loop and the dedicated bike lane, both perfect for experienced cyclists and for a quick spin with your kids, respectively.

Witnessing one of the finest piedmont forest ecosystems in the National Park Service, and how the land has repaired itself from the ravages of tobacco farming and the destructive effects of mining, is a wonderful experience. As you ride through the scenic loop or the off-road loop, you can take an up-close look at the forest reclamation process in action. I urge you to not just bike this wildlife oasis but also hike some of the more than 35 miles of trails in the park. The trails will take you along ridges, into valleys, and beside the banks of the two main creeks that are within the park. Along the way, in addition to the bountiful wildlife, you may even see hints of the early settlers who once lived here. Small family plots are scattered throughout the park and offer a glimpse to a not-so-distant past. Parking areas along the scenic drive make all of these trails and features easily accessible. Also take a moment to visit the park visitor center to have a look at some of the exhibits and videos that highlight the rich history of this wonderful resource.

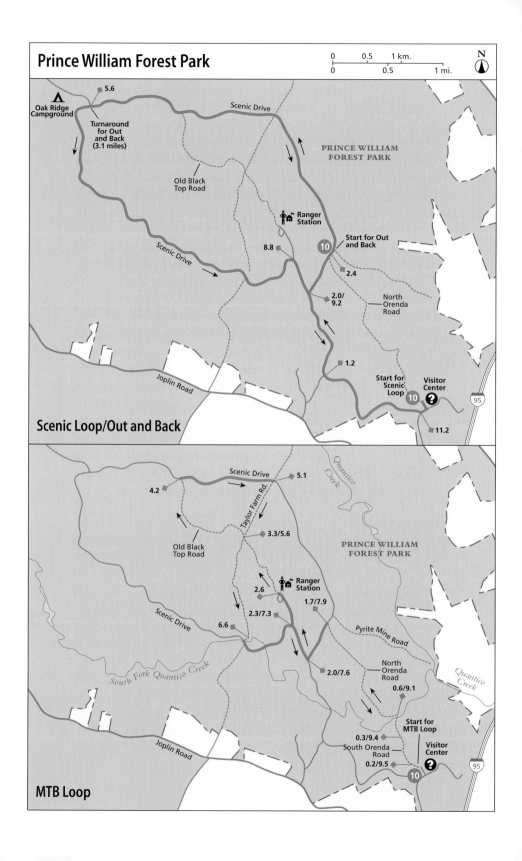

Prince William Forest Park

0   0.5   1 km.
0   0.5   1 mi.

N

Scenic Loop/Out and Back

Oak Ridge
Campground

5.6

Turnaround
for Out
and Back
(3.1 miles)

Scenic Drive

Old Black
Top Road

PRINCE WILLIAM
FOREST PARK

Scenic Drive

Ranger
Station

8.8

Start for Out
and Back

10

2.4

2.0/
9.2

North
Orenda
Road

Joplin Road

1.2

Start for
Scenic
Loop

10

Visitor
Center

?

95

11.2

MTB Loop

Scenic Drive

4.2

5.1

Quantico Creek

Taylor Farm Rd.

3.3/5.6

Old Black
Top Road

PRINCE WILLIAM
FOREST PARK

2.6

Ranger
Station

1.7/7.9

2.3/7.3

Scenic Drive

6.6

Pyrite Mine Road

South Fork Quantico Creek

2.0/7.6

North
Orenda
Road

0.6/9.1

Quantico Creek

Joplin Road

Start for
MTB Loop

0.3/9.4

South Orenda
Road

0.2/9.5

10

Visitor
Center

?

95

MILES & DIRECTIONS

Scenic road loop:

0.0 Start at the far end of the parking area of the Pine Grove Picnic Area and head back toward the park entrance. When you reach the stop sign, turn right. The stop sign marks the beginning of this ride. Make an immediate right into the park's scenic drive.

1.2 Stay to the right and follow the signs for the Scenic Loop.

2.0 Stay right at this intersection to ride the Scenic Loop in a counter-clockwise direction. You can if you want turn left. At this point we'll be staying on the main park's Scenic Loop for a little over 7 miles.

2.4 You've reached parking Area D and the start of the one-way traffic section of the Scenic Loop. The left lane is reserved for cycling and running.

5.6 Stay to the left at this intersection. Oak Ridge Road will take you to the campground. This is a great little side detour. The road that circles the campground is nice and narrow and in a secluded, tree-covered area of the park. It will add a couple of extra miles to your ride.

8.8 Stay to the right at this intersection to remain on the Scenic Loop. The road to the left will take you to the Turkey Run Campground Area. This road is part of our off-road loop.

9.2 Turn right to head back toward the Park Entrance. Turn left to do the Scenic Loop again.

11.2 Turn left to head back to the starting point of the ride. The loop is complete.

Prince William Forest Park MTB loop:

0.0 Start at the far end of the parking area for Pine Grove Picnic Area and head toward the wood fence along the picnic tables and open field. A hard gravel trail shoots off to the left from the fence line; the IMBA biking trail starts to the right off the gravel trail. This is where our ride starts (singletrack).

0.2 Turn right on South Orenda Road (double track gravel path).

0.3 Stay right at this intersection. The left fork is clearly marked with a "permit use only" sign.

0.6 Cross the short hanging bridge (walk your bike as suggested) and then immediately turn left onto North Orenda Road and continue on the dirt road for a little over a mile.

1.7 Turn left on the park's Scenic Drive (paved).

2.0 Turn right to continue onto Scenic Drive and get ready for a short climb (paved).

2.3 Turn right and follow the signs for the Turkey Run Ridge Campground (paved).

2.6 Shortly after the parking area for the campground you'll see the gate for Old Black Top Road and the point where the pavement ends. Continue onto Old Black Top Road (dirt).

3.3 Continue straight through this intersection and remain on Old Black Top Road.

4.2 Old Black Top Road ends, turn right onto the Scenic Drive (paved). Parking Area "F" will be to your left.

5.1 Turn right onto Taylor Farm Road. Burma Road will be to your left. Although Taylor Farm is called a "Road" it is no more than a wide path. The entrance to Taylor Farm Road has a distinctive boardwalk.

5.6 Continue straight through this intersection (Old Black Top Road). We crossed this spot at mile marker 3.3.

6.6 Follow the short boardwalk to the right. Taylor Farm Road ends, turn left onto Scenic Drive (paved).

7.3 Say right at this intersection and get ready for a fast road descent. At this point you begin to back track to the ride's starting point.

7.6 Turn left at this intersection and continue on Scenic Drive.

7.9 Turn right onto North Orenda Road (dirt).

9.1 Turn right and go over the short hanging bridge and continue up on South Orenda Road.

9.4 Continue on South Orenda Road. This is the same intersection from marker 0.3.

9.5 Turn left onto the singletrack trail.

9.7 Come out of the singletrack and make a left onto the gravel path and then an immediate right to head back to the wood fence along the picnic area and the parking area. The loop is complete.

The new section of IMBA-built singletrack at Prince William Forest Park is one of Ari's favorite trails.

Bike lane:

The bike lane is a little over 3 miles in length and runs from parking Area D to the entrance to the Oak Ridge Campground. In between there are two additional parking areas, E and F. Our ride takes us out and back from parking Area D to the entrance of Oak Ridge Campground and back to parking area D.

3 .1   Make a U turn and head back the way you came. You can turn right on Oak Ridge Road to head toward the Oak Ridge Campground area. This will add a couple of extra miles to your ride.

6.2   The loop is complete.

RIDE INFORMATION

Local Events and Attractions

Potomac Mills Shopping Mall features over 200 retail outlets, over 25 eateries, and 18 state-of-the-art theatres. 2700 Potomac Mills Circle, Woodbridge, VA 22192; (703) 496-9330; www.simon.com/mall/Potomac-mills .

Regular mall hours: Mon to Sat 10 a.m. to 9 p.m., and Sun 11 a.m. to 6 p.m. Restaurant, cinema, and store hours may differ from mall hours.

Restaurants

Tio Julio's: 14900 Potomac Town Place, Ste. 150, Woodbridge, VA 22191; (703) 763-7322

Wegman's (yes, it's a grocery store, but trust me, their seafood and sushi bars are phenomenal): 14801 Dining Way, Woodbridge, VA 22191; (703) 763-5500

Restrooms

Adjacent to the visitor center and in the Pine Grove Picnic area.

Fall Line: Prince William Forest Park lies along the border between two physiographic zones: the Piedmont and the Coastal Plain. Many of the faulted rocks represent the fall line, a unique geological feature. Streams form falls or rapids as they leave the harder rocks of the Piedmont and enter the softer rocks of the Coastal Plain.

Arlington and the Pentagon

This ride, which requires you to carry your identification, will take you by one of our national capital's most iconic memorials, as well as right by some of its newest. By the time you close out this loop, you will have ridden past the Iwo Jima Memorial, through one of the nation's oldest forts, through hallowed ground, and by the 9/11 Memorial at the Pentagon. This moving and tranquil memorial is the scene of one of the most pivotal moments in our nation's recent history.

Start: Lyndon B. Johnson Memorial Grove Parking Area along Boundary Channel Drive, Pentagon North Parking

Length: 9.8 miles

Approximate riding time: 1–2 hours, more if you spend time getting to really know the memorials

Best bike: Any bike will do for this particular ride. You can grab one of the Capital Bikeshare bikes available in Crystal City.

Terrain and trail surface: Mostly road and designated bike lanes, as well as hard-pack trails. One short portion is an unpaved trail along Route 110.

Traffic and hazards: Vehicle traffic in and around the memorials and in the Pentagon and Crystal City.

Things to see: The Iwo Jima Memorial, Arlington Cemetery, the Pentagon 9/11 Memorial, the Air Force Memorial, and panoramic views of Washington, DC

Getting there: From Springfield: Take I-395 north toward Washington and take exit 8B. Then merge onto Washington Boulevard toward the Pentagon/Arlington Cemetery/Rosslyn. Take the first exit toward VA 110/Pentagon North Parking. Turn left at the stop sign at Boundary Channel Drive. The Lyndon B. Johnson parking area will be on your left as the road curves right.

From the National Mall: Take 14th Street south to I-395 south. Take exit 10A for Boundary Channel Drive toward the Pentagon North Parking. Drive for approximately 0.5 mile on Boundary Channel Drive. The parking area will be on your right as the road curves to the left. GPS: 38.877453,-77.052848

Fees: None. You will be biking through a military installation. Helmets and IDs are mandatory.

THE RIDE

This route holds a very special place in my life. When I first moved to Arlington in early 1991, I was a brand-new private in the US Army. I lived in the barracks at Fort Myer, a stone's throw away from the entrance to Arlington Cemetery, the Old Post Chapel, and the Army's Old Guard Caisson. During those times I made lasting friendships and began my relationship with Arlington County and our national capital on board my trusted bike.

My love affair with cycling preceded my arrival to Arlington, but it is here where it really blossomed. I recall exploratory dawn patrol rides from the Army barracks down Meigs and Sherman Drives through the Cemetery and over Memorial Bridge into the city. I can't even begin to tell you how I felt while riding in and around the monuments while the vast majority of the city still slept. Seeing the mist rise from the Potomac from the grounds of the Netherlands Carillion and the Iwo Jima Memorial rivaled any 4th of July fireworks display. Riding toward Memorial Bridge as the sun rose in the eastern horizon above the Capitol Dome is a sight that has been forever embedded in my memory. I also recall late-night urban rides through Arlington led by my good friend Andy Carruthers and the Mid-Atlantic Off-Road Enthusiasts Band of Brothers. Those late-night and early-morning bike ride sessions solidified my love for the sport, my appreciation for the beauty of the Washington, DC landscape, and deepened my respect for all the veterans who came before me. It's simply impossible to do this loop and not feel the honor, valor, and sacrifice that permeate through every location you pass through.

Unlike my Army days, when I generally started this ride from within Fort Myer, we'll start our adventure from what is likely one

Bike Shops

Revolution Bikes: 220 20th St. S, Ste. A, Arlington, VA 22202; (703) 415-4560; www.revolutioncycles.com
Hudson Trail Outfitters: 1101 S. Joyce St., Ste. B29, Arlington VA 22202; (703) 415-4861; www.hudsontrail.com

The section of road open to bikes in Arlington Cemetery is becoming a favorite for commuters.

of the most iconic locations in the DC metro area, the Pentagon. Then we'll quickly make our way to one of the area's most recognizable monuments, the Iwo Jima Memorial. The concept for the Marine War Memorial was born from the Pulitzer-winning photograph that Joe Rosenthal crafted in 1945 of five Marines and one Navy corpsman raising the US flag during the Battle of Iwo Jima during World War II. Within 72 hours of seeing the image, sculptor Felix Weldon had created a clay replica that was presented to President Truman. By 1946, work on the massive sculpture that replicated the moment, and the likeness of the five Marines (Ira Hayes, Franklin Sousley, Harlon Block, Michael Strank, and Rene Gagnon) and the Navy corpsman (John Bradley) had begun, and eight years later, thanks to the efforts of hundreds of artisans, it was completed and dedicated by President Dwight D. Eisenhower on November 10, 1954.

As you ride past the massive statue, you can't help but think about the sacrifices that Marines have made over the years in defense of our country and freedom. Those sacrifices are clearly visible as we continue our ride through Fort Myer and Arlington National Cemetery. I urge you to pace yourself as you ride through here. Truly, our ability to enjoy ourselves the way we do is largely in part to the sacrifices the people buried here made. As you exit the cemetery, you'll also pass by an inconspicuous memorial that is often overlooked. At the intersections of Shelby and Memorial Drives, you'll find the Women in Military Service for America Memorial. The memorial pays tribute to every woman who has served in the military and is a vehement reminder that women have played— and continue to play—a critical role in our nation's history.

As you continue on Memorial Drive, you'll get to enjoy and savor one of the city's grandest views, Memorial Bridge and the Lincoln Memorial. Although we will not cross this span over the Potomac on this ride, you'll have an opportunity to do so in Ride 4 and enjoy its grandeur. We will then pass along the west side of the Pentagon, one that has been considerably transformed since I walked its halls between 1991 and 1994. As you ride past the new massive wall that separates Washington Boulevard from the Department of Defense (DoD) facility, try to imagine the chaos that followed the crash of American Flight 77 into its façade. It's hard to believe, but prior to the attacks of September 11, 2001, you could literally walk from the point you are riding onto the Pentagon's heliport or to the walls that collapsed with the crash of the plane. Today, a solemn memorial to the heroes of 9/11 sits along the path of our ride. If you have not visited this location before, I highly recommend it. The designers of the memorial have been able to create a place both somber and peaceful. The location and serenity of the memorial allows you to reflect not only on all of the innocent lives that were lost but also on all of the things we hold dear. It really does put things into perspective and provides us with a reality check—to not take the things we have for granted—not even the simple joy of a bike ride through the streets of Arlington.

We then climb to within view of the newly dedicated Air Force Memorial. It's hard to believe that the addition of a memorial to honor our nation's airmen would become such a polarizing issue, but the Air Force memorial did just that. The memorial to honor our nation's aviators was originally intended to be built near the grounds of the Iwo Jima Memorial, opposite the Netherlands Carillion and down the hill from where the Marine Memorial now stands—at the intersections of Route 100 and Marshall Drive, roughly where our ride started. But opposition from prominent Marine veterans in Congress and the Friends of Iwo Jima forced the Air Force Memorial Foundation to reconsider its location. In order to avoid lengthy legal battles and litigation, the current site was selected. President George W. Bush—himself an aviator—dedicated the memorial on October 14, 2006. Over 30,000 people attended the ceremony.

The three spires reaching for the skies are meant to represent the image of "contrails" from the soaring jets of the Air Force Thunderbirds as they peel back in a precision "bomb burst" maneuver. Although the maneuver is performed with four jets, the memorial only includes three, evoking the image of the "missing man formation" performed by airmen during traditional funeral fly-overs. The memorial itself is made of concrete and steel. Its three spires range from 200 to 270 feet in height.

We then head toward Pentagon Row and Crystal City, where you can break for a smoothie or lunch, visit a shop, or rest in one of the neighborhood parks along the way. You can use this location as an alternate starting point for the ride. There are several Capital Bikeshare stations where you can pick up a bike and follow this loop. Finally, we'll make our way back through the north side of the Pentagon to close out the loop.

Arlington and the Pentagon

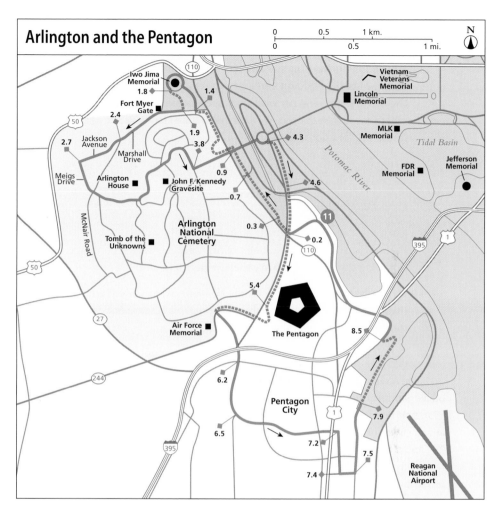

This ride passes through an active military installation and access may be revoked at any time without notice. Please respect and obey all traffic laws while riding in Fort Myer and do not stray from the bike path. ID and helmet required!

MILES & DIRECTIONS

0.0   From the Lyndon B. Johnson Memorial Grove parking area, follow Boundary Channel Drive north along the perimeter of the Pentagon's North Parking toward the ramp for Route 110.

0.2   Go straight through the stop sign toward the underpass for Route 27, Washington Boulevard, ride under Route 27 as if you were going to Route 110.

0.3 Immediately after going through the underpass, get on the grassy area to the right and pass a brick control building. Turn right immediately after the building and then left on the driveway that parallels the metro tracks. The narrow dirt/gravel path will be straight ahead where the driveway ends. You will ride parallel to the Metro and Route 110 for approximately 0.75 mile.

0.7 Carefully cross the ramp. Although vehicles are warned there could be pedestrians crossing, few reduce their speed.

0.9 Cross Memorial Drive and turn left.

1.0 Cross the exit ramp and make an immediate right onto the bike path that will run along the perimeter of Arlington Cemetery. Continue following the bike path to Marshall Drive.

1.4 Turn right into the entrance for the US Marine Corps War Memorial (Iwo Jima) and circle around the memorial in a counterclockwise direction to get a nice view of the statue.

1.8 Enter the bike path and follow it to the Netherlands Carillion. The path is adjacent to a line of porta-potties—great chance to take a "P" break.

1.9 Follow the trail to the right along Marshall Drive and toward Fort Myer's Wright Gate. Get your ID ready to go through the gate and into Fort Myer.

2.4 Continue straight at this intersection. (Note: You can turn left onto McNair as well to head toward the Cemetery entrance, but you would miss one of the nicest portions of Ft. Myer.) Marshall Drive becomes Jackson Drive at this point.

2.7 Turn left onto Lee Avenue. These are the general officer quarters at Ft. Myer. The officer's club is to your right.

2.9 Cross over McNair Road. The Old Post Chapel will be on your left. Continue straight through the Arlington Cemetery entrance. The bike route is clearly marked. Please do not deviate from it.*

3.8 Turn left onto Memorial Drive. The Memorial Bridge and Lincoln Memorial can be seen ahead. Soak in the view. Continue straight along the path that parallels the road on the right to Memorial Circle.

4.3 Cross over the ramp from the George Washington Memorial Parkway and then turn right onto the designated bike path. A left turn would take you over to cross Memorial Bridge. (We'll do just that on Ride 4,

Four Bridges Ride.) Continue and cross over a second road ramp. Use caution in these crossings.

4.4 Stay to the right at this fork and to another ramp crossing. The bike path will now follow the edge of Route 27, Washington Boulevard, toward the Pentagon.

4.6 Cross this ramp and continue following the trail toward the Pentagon ahead. This is a bail-out point; if you choose, turn left and head down toward the Pentagon's north parking and your vehicle.

5.4 Make a quick left and then right to stay on the trail. You can also bear to the right on a short section of "beaten path" along the edge of the ramp. The Heroes of 9/11 Memorial will be to your left (9/11 Memorial). Restrooms are also available here. Bike racks are available to lock your bike and visit the memorial.

5.5 Turn right and follow the designated bike path along Columbia Pike toward the Air Force Memorial.

5.8 Turn left onto Joyce Street.

6.2 Cross over Army Navy Drive and continue straight on Joyce Street. Pentagon Row will be on your left. There are ample dining and shopping opportunities here. Hudson Trail Outfitters is up ahead to your left.

6.5 Continue straight at this intersection. You will now be on 15th Street. Joyce continues to the right.

6.7 Cross over Hayes Street toward Crystal City. Once you cross Hayes, you will lose the designated bike lane for approximately 200 yards. You are free to use the entire lane during that time. This is an alternate starting point for our ride. There is ample parking along 15th Street and a Capital Bikeshare bike station.

7.2 Immediately after going under Route 1, take a right on Bell Street and continue toward the Metro.

7.4 Turn left onto 20th Street. Revolution Cycles will be on your right along 20th. Stop by and say hi, tell them who sent you! Revolution Cycles has organized rides into downtown and the monuments, they'll be happy if you join them.

7.5 Turn left onto Crystal Drive and follow the designated bike trail along the right. Alternate starting point.

7.9 Crystal Drive veers to the left and becomes 12th Street. At this point you have the option of continuing on 12th Street and then right onto Long Bridge Road, or veering off into Long Bridge Park to the right. If you veer off into Long Bridge Park, simply follow the sidewalk along the train track until it ends and then turn left to head down toward Long Bridge Drive. Turn right onto Long Bridge Drive. There is a great view of the Washington Monument along Long Bridge Park. Note: At the time of this writing there was considerable construction taking place on Long Bridge Park and Long Bridge Drive, so things may have changed a little by the time you read this.

8.5 Turn right onto Long Bridge Road.

8.6 Turn left onto Boundary Channel Drive and head under I-395. Follow Boundary Channel Drive back to your vehicle.

9.5 Complete the loop.

*Arlington Cemetery allows limited access to bicycles in an east-bound (downhill) direction only. Identification and helmets are required.

Alternate route to Arlington Cemetery:

If you prefer not to ride the "off-road" portion of this ride along Route 110, you can use these alternate directions.

0.0 From the ramp to enter the grove, turn right and head over the pedestrian bridge. Immediately after crossing the bridge, turn right and follow the stone path toward the marina parking area.

0.1 Bear right away from the stone path and ride on the asphalt path. Continue to the right and enter the parking lot. There is a narrow path that travels along each side of the parking area if you choose to ride that.

0.4 Turn left at the stop sign and then immediately right to enter the path that will take you toward the Mount Vernon Trail. Ride under the parkway and soak in the great views of the Jefferson Memorial and the Washington Monument across the river.

0.6 Continue straight to head north on the Mount Vernon Trail toward the Memorial Bridge; the Navy and Maritime Memorial will be on your left.

1.4 Turn left at this intersection to leave the Mount Vernon Trail and to cross over the George Washington Memorial Parkway. Use caution.

1.5 Continue following the trail to the right to cross over the Washington Boulevard ramp.

1.6 Turn left to cross over Washington Boulevard and to head toward Arlington Cemetery.

1.8 Turn right to cross Memorial Drive and then quickly left to continue in the same direction. (Now follow the same directions as above from mile 1.0; you'll have to adjust your markers accordingly.)

RIDE INFORMATION

Local Events and Attractions

Tuesday evenings during the summer, the Marines host **Sunset Parades** on the Parade Deck of the Marine Memorial. During the 1-hour performance, the US Marine Drum and Bugle Corps presents music from "the Commandant's Own," and the Marine Corps Silent Drill Platoon showcases precision drills. The Sunset Parade is open to the public at no charge. Cycling around the Iwo Jima Memorial is not allowed during this time.

Arlington National Cemetery: Lock up the bike after entering from Fort Myer and visit Kennedy's and Pierre L'Enfant's gravesites.

Restaurants

Pentagon Row offers a multitude of restaurants. You can choose from a variety of cuisines. Dining opportunities are also available in Crystal City along Crystal Drive. My personal favorites include:

Noodles and Company: 1201 S. Joyce St., Arlington, VA 22202; (703) 418-0001

Chipotle: 2231 Crystal Dr., Arlington, VA 22202; (703) 920-8779

> The Netherlands Carillon adjacent to Arlington National Cemetery and the Iwo Jima Memorial was a gift from the Netherlands to the United States in 1954 and stands as a symbol of friendship between the two countries. The Carillon plays automated music each day at noon and 6 p.m.

Restrooms

Porta-potties are available on the Iwo Jima Memorial grounds as well as by the entrance to the 9/11 Memorial. The 9/11 Memorial restrooms are cleaner and nicer.

Wakefield Park

Wakefield Park is quite possibly the most popular mountain bike destination in the Metro Washington, DC area. Its close proximity to the Capital Beltway makes it a popular location for all the northern Virginia suburbanites who live and/or work inside the Beltway. On any given afternoon, the parking lots of Wakefield Park are brimming with activity from people using the soccer fields, Audrey Moore RECenter, skate park, tennis courts, and the extensive network of bike trails that run parallel to Accotink Creek and the nearby power lines.

Start: Start in the Aubrey Moore Recreation Center parking area. The loop outlined here starts immediately adjacent to the recycling bins.

Length: 5.6 miles

Approximate riding time: 1 hour

Best bike: Mountain bike

Terrain and trail surface: Mostly singletrack trails with a short section of hard-surface CCT trail

Traffic and hazards: Roots, rocks, and a couple of stream crossings; watch out for hikers

Things to see: Creeks, forests

Getting there: The park is less than 0.5 mile from the Capital Beltway off Braddock Road in northern Virginia. Exit west on exit 54a, Braddock Road, and turn right less than 2 miles into Wakefield Park. Drive straight for approximately 0.5 mile and then turn left where the tarmac ends into the main Audrey Moore Recreation Center parking area. Park adjacent to the recycling bins to the right. GPS: 38.821755,-77.222857

Fees: None

THE RIDE

Sometimes it's interesting to see where you will find challenging trails. More often than not, Washingtonians and nearby DC suburbanites have to venture far out to the west or north of the city to find natural-surface trails that criss-cross the forested spaces of Frederick County in Maryland and the George Washington National Forest in Virginia. But, as it turns out, there are surprising opportunities closer to home for dirt lovers to enjoy. One such location is the network of trails that exists only minutes from the Capital Beltway in Wakefield Park. For those nature enthusiasts who can't afford to venture out and drive over an hour to distant trail networks, Fairfax County's Wakefield Park has become an oasis for indoor and outdoor recreational activities.

Wakefield Park is the home of the Audrey Moore Recreational Center, a facility that includes a multitude of activities for Fairfax County residents and visitors alike. The RECenter, dedicated to longtime Fairfax County politician Audrey Moore, measures in at nearly 76,000 square feet, houses a 50 x 25m pool with various diving boards and spectator seating, a spacious sundeck, locker rooms, saunas, and showers. There is also a large gym with multiple basketball hoops and volleyball nets. The RECenter also includes a cycle studio, should you feel compelled to cycle indoors. If you want to mix in a strength workout before or after your ride, there is also a spacious fitness center with a multitude of cardio equipment, free weights, and a stretching area.

On the outside you'll find seven well-maintained athletic fields, including five softball fields, a football field, and a soccer field. You'll also see a basketball court, a skate park, and eleven lighted tennis courts to go along with the more than 6 miles of natural surface singletrack mountain biking trails.

The trails at Wakefield have been through a drastic transformation over the past decade. The early popularity of mountain biking in the mid 1990s and subsequent 2000s brought a tremendous number of riders into the park. Unfortunately, the original power line and wooded trails that existed within its boundaries were not originally designed for off-road cycling, thus they suffered considerably with the amount of riders that used them on a daily basis. Park managers and the Mid-Atlantic Off-Road Enthusiasts (MORE)—a local mountain bike advocacy group—recognized the problem and took action to improve and preserve the network of trails.

> **Bike Shop**
>
> **The Bike Lane:** 8416 Old Keene Mill Rd., Springfield, VA 22152; (703) 440-8701; www.thebikelane.com

With the help of the International Mountain Biking Association's trail crew, the muscle of area volunteers, and the support of the Fairfax County government, regional riders set out to improve the trails of this Beltway destination.

12

You May Run into Tom Jackson (@fuel95)

I've known Tom for several years through my involvement with the Mid-Atlantic Off-Road Enthusiasts (MORE). I first met him at Wakefield when he was a ride leader. During organized MORE rides, you could always find him in the parking area by the recycling bins rounding up all the new riders who had somehow found the club and getting them ready for a spin in the park's trails on one of his extremely popular beginner rides. Tom's lived in Virginia for over 20 years and got started mountain biking when his brother took him out to Seneca Creek State Park. "I love singletrack trails," he told me, "the ability to just get out into the woods, even in an

PHOTO COURTESY TOM JACKSON

urban setting, and get away from the world for a while is what I love the most. It's the ability to see the world in a way most people don't," he added. His love for the sport and desire to get involved led him to become active within MORE. At first he filled in by leading rides. Then he served as ride coordinator and helped out as trail boss, and later provided significant impact to the club as its vice president for handling sponsorships. Thanks to his efforts, MORE has reached new heights and continues to succeed through the relationships he fostered with area businesses that support the club. When you see him, say hi and thanks for all he's done. He deserves it.

Thanks to the efforts and dedication of those biking advocates, today the park in Wakefield houses over 6 miles of sustainable, enjoyable, and challenging trails, all within 0.5 mile from the Capital Beltway.

Our loop will take you through those renovated trails and partially through part of the loop of the popular Wednesdays at Wakefield (W@W) summer series of mountain bike races. While challenging, it is a ride that can be easily conquered by beginner riders and enjoyed by accomplished dirt lovers alike. I highly recommend you change directions on this loop or change it around to make it your own. To add a little distance to your ride, also venture out and include sections of "The Bowl," a small area of the park that lies between the Beltway and the park entrance road that offers a couple of extra miles of singletrack. You may also want to give the trails a shot at night. Thanks to a well-crafted partnership between Fairfax County and MORE, night riding is allowed in the park on Mon, Tues, and Thurs nights from dusk to 10:30 p.m. Bear in mind that night riding is not allowed in any other Fairfax County parks, and to ensure this privilege remains, please don't ride the trails during any non-designated nights.

MILES & DIRECTIONS

This is a suggested route, my best piece of advice is to just go out and explore all of the trails around the power lines to find the loop that you like best. I have not included "The Bowl" or the adjacent Accotink trails in this write-up, but you can easily double your ride by adding these.

0.0 Start immediately adjacent to the recycling bins and turn left on the gravel road toward the pedestrian bridge that spans over the Capital Beltway.

0.1 As you reach the pedestrian bridge, take the narrow singletrack trail that shoots up to the left. Follow this trail as it zigzags through this small section of woods.

0.3 Cross the dirt road and ride on the singletrack that runs parallel to I-495. When the trail splits, take the fork to the left along the perimeter of the power station.

0.4 Continue on the singletrack trail toward the left after crossing the small creek. The trail will then veer to the right slightly before reaching the CCT. Continue on it over the short boardwalk and rock section, and immediately after this short section, head into the woods to continue on the trail that runs parallel to the power lines.

0.6 Cross over a small wood bridge and continue straight across this intersection. Get ready for a short "burst."

0.7 Continue straight past this intersection and continue the short climb.

0.8 After a short downhill and "whoop," turn left and then immediately left again into the main trail (basically a big U turn).

0.9 Turn immediately right onto the creek trail.

1.2 Continue bearing to the right (follow the yellow arrows) to return to the main trail.

1.3 Turn left at the first intersection; there is a yellow arrow marker clearly visible here. Follow the trail to the right for a short climb until it ends at the next intersection.

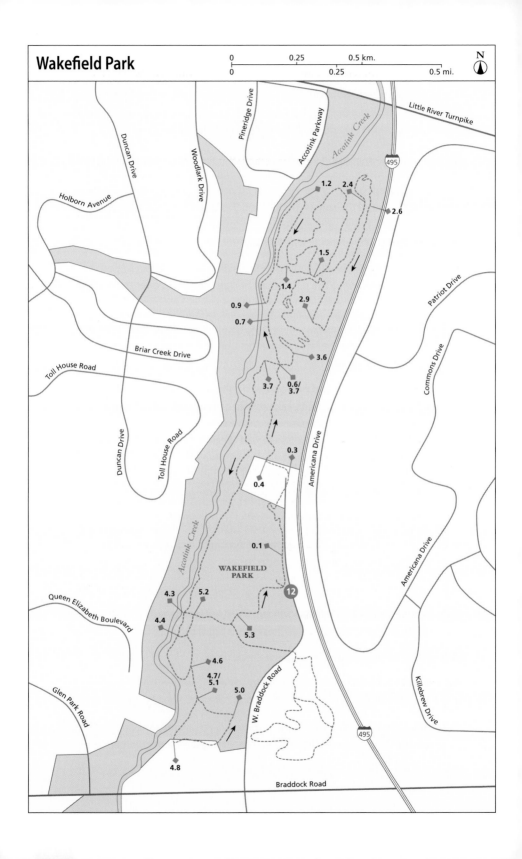

Wakefield Park

0   0.25   0.5 km.

0   0.25   0.5 mi.

N

Pineridge Drive

Accotink Parkway

Accotink Creek

Little River Turnpike

495

Duncan Drive

Woodlark Drive

Holborn Avenue

1.2
2.4
2.6

1.5

1.4

0.9
2.9

0.7

Briar Creek Drive

3.6

Toll House Road

3.7
0.6/
3.7

Patriot Drive

Commons Drive

Duncan Drive

Toll House Road

0.3

Americana Drive

0.4

0.1

WAKEFIELD
PARK

12

Queen Elizabeth Boulevard

4.3
5.2

4.4

5.3

Accotink Creek

4.6

4.7/
5.1

Glen Park Road

5.0

W. Braddock Road

Americana Drive

Killebrew Drive

495

4.8

Braddock Road

1.4 Turn left and pass one intersection, the exit of phase 4. We'll be back at this point shortly.

1.5 Turn left. This is the second intersection and the entrance to phase 4. Remain on phase 4 and go over 8 small wood bridges.

2.1 Turn left onto the trail we were just on; this time continue straight past the entrance to phase 4 and out into the power lines. The trail will veer to the left under the power lines. At this point you'll ride toward and around the back of the second set of towers visible from where you are.

2.4 The trail will veer to the left as you reach the second tower and then back to the right and behind the tower. After a short switchback climb, you'll emerge on the top adjacent to the two towers.

2.6 You are now at the base of the two towers. Follow the trail as it runs parallel to the Beltway. You will again ride to the base of the next second base of towers.

2.9 Turn right to ride the trail on the inside of the two towers. Immediately after passing the second tower (single pylon), turn right to head back down a series of whoops that end with a sweeping left-hand berm turn into the woods at mile 3.0.

3.1 Continue following the trail to the left for approximately 0.5 mile. The right fork takes you back to the entrance of phase 4. This trail will gradually climb and then descend via a series of switchback berm turns along the power lines.

3.6 Turn right before the trail shoots out into the open and then immediately right again. You'll see the wooden bridge spanning the creek, which we crossed at mile marker 0.6. Continue straight until you reach the CCT and turn left at mile 3.7.

3.7 After turning left onto the CCT, go over a small bridge and immediately turn right onto the creek trail. You will now remain on the creek trail for nearly a mile.

4.3 Stay to the right to remain on the creek trail.

4.4 Stay to the right to remain on the creek trail.

4.6 The creek trail will come out of the power lines and veer to the left and back and intersect the CCT. Make a sharp right. Our return trip will bring us back to this intersection shortly.

4.7 Continue to the right and cross the creek.

4.8 Turn left onto the CCT. A right turn will take you to Lake Accotink.

5.0 Immediately before reaching the parking area, turn left to follow the trail along the outfield fence line.

5.1 Turn right to return to the trail we were just on a few minutes ago and then right again when the trail comes out into the power lines.

5.2 Go over the bridge and turn right to remain under the power lines. As soon as you reach the two large towers, turn right to head up to the soccer fields and the Audrey Moore Recreation Center.

5.3 Turn right onto the paved trail that runs around the perimeter of the soccer field and then right again to head up between the skate park and the RECenter to reach the parking area.

5.5 You're back at the lot and the starting point of the ride.

RIDE INFORMATION

Local Events and Attractions

Wakefield Farmers Market: Wed, May 2 through Oct 31 from 2 to 6 p.m. Mountain bike races are conducted throughout the summer, including Wednesdays at **Wakefield (W@W) Mountain Bike Race** series. Trail running races are conducted within Wakefield Park as a part of the **Backyard Burn** race series coordinated by Ex2Adventures in the spring and fall.

Restaurants

Kilroys: Ravensworth Shopping Center, 5250-A Port Royal Rd., Springfield, VA 22151; (703) 321-7733; www.kilroys.com; www.facebook.com/restaurantandbar. Tell them we sent you!

Restrooms

Restrooms are available in the Audrey Moore RECenter and also adjacent to the softball fields in the satellite parking areas.

The Cross County Trail (CCT) runs through Wakefield Park, and area riders often combine this ride with other CCT-accessible trails to create "epic" loops easily exceeding the century mark.

Arlandia

This ride will take you south down the Mount Vernon Trail, through Historic Old Town Alexandria, and return north along Potomac Avenue and Crystal Drive. This is a ride of contrasts. You will see some of the newest and oldest sections of Arlington and Alexandria. Not quite the real "Arlandia," but close enough.

Start: Lyndon B. Johnson Memorial Grove Parking Area along Boundary Channel Drive Pentagon North Parking

Length: 14.5 miles

Approximate riding time: 1.5–2 hours

Best bike: Road bike

Terrain and trail surface: Paved bike paths and road; one section in Old Town is over cobblestones

Traffic and hazards: Other trail users and vehicle traffic on the roads

Things to see: Gravely Point offers great views of aircraft landing and taking off from Reagan National Airport. As you ride through Old Town Alexandria, you'll pass many historical sites including the Athenaeum, the Apothecary Museum, and Gatsby's Tavern. Views of the monuments from the Mount Vernon Trail and from Long Bridge Park.

Getting there: From Springfield: Take I-395 north toward Washington and take exit 8B. Then merge onto Washington Boulevard toward Pentagon/Arlington Cemetery/Rosslyn. Take the first exit toward VA 110/Pentagon North Parking. Turn left at the stop sign at Boundary Channel Drive. The Lyndon B. Johnson parking area will be on your left as the road curves right.

    From the National Mall: Take 14th Street south to I-395 south. Take exit 10A for Boundary Channel Drive toward the Pentagon North Parking. Drive for approximately 0.5 mile on Boundary Channel Drive.

The parking area will be on your right as the road curves to the left. GPS: 38.876067,-77.052183

Fees: None

THE RIDE

Alexandria, along with Arlington, have been two of my favorite places in the region ever since I moved to the Washington, DC area. Having lived in both, and experienced their subtleties, I have an appreciation for each. When my wife and I were married, our first apartment was located in "Arlandia," an area that serves as an overlap of the two cities. We lived just blocks away from Mount Vernon Avenue and a stone's throw from Crystal City and Potomac Yards, two of the three areas our ride will navigate and two places that have been experiencing considerable change in recent years. The third area included in this ride is Old Town. Unlike Crystal City and Potomac Yards, Old Town has somehow managed to retain its charm over the years, perhaps because of its historic designation.

Alexandria, the third oldest historic district in the nation, has served an important role in our history and was the home to several of our nation's most important figures. It was George Washington's hometown, and his memorial service was held at the Old Presbyterian Meeting House. Its bell tolled in mourning for 4 days between his death and burial. Robert E. Lee, one of the country's most famous Civil War figures, also called it home. He moved with his family to within the city's borders at age 4. Thomas Jefferson frequented Gatsby's Tavern (we ride past it), still in operation today, and President Gerald Ford called the city home, living in its Clover neighborhood until shortly after being appointed president.

Founded in 1749 by Scottish merchants, Old Town continues to bustle with activity. Old Town Alexandria, and portions of the ride in Arlington, were originally part of the District of Columbia and hold the unique distinction that the lands were returned to Virginia. George Washington was the city's original surveyor, and

Bike Shops

Revolution Cycles: 220 20th St. S, Ste. A, Arlington, VA 22202; (703) 415-4560; www.revolutioncycles.com
Wheel Nuts Bike Shop: 302 Montgomery St., Alexandria, VA 22314; (703) 548-5116; www.wheelnutsbikeshop.com
Big Wheel Bikes: 2 Prince St., Alexandria, VA 22314; (703) 739-2300; www.bigwheelbikes.com
Bike and Roll: 1 Wales Alley, Alexandria, VA 22314; (703) 548-7655; www.bikethesites.com

A Bike and Roll employee preps a rental bike for a family of tourists.
PHOTO COURTESY BIKE AND ROLL

later, when the capital of the new nation was to be established in 1791, he included the port city, along with Arlington, within the confines of the capital. In 1846, however, when the capital city was reduced in size, Arlington and the portion of the city south of the Potomac were retro ceded to Virginia.

Alexandria has played a part during many of our nation's most tumultuous times. It was taken by the British in the War of 1812, and it served as an important strategic location during the American Civil War. As a gateway to the south, and a major slavery trading port, the Union occupied it early on during the hostilities and used it as a major supply depot, transport, and hospital center. The occupation of Alexandria by Union troops also provided freed slaves with unprecedented opportunities. Not only did they find their freedom behind the protection of the Union Army, but also employment.

Along the Old Town portion of the ride, you'll pass by several sites of historic significance, actually too many to list here, so I encourage you to stop and read the plaques and markers along the way. Also, the town's residents have always been extremely cautious of "urban renewal" and have fought hard to preserve the town's architectural integrity, so look at the buildings and appreciate the structures you are riding past. We do cycle by Gatsby's Tavern (on the corner of Cameron and Royal), past the Waterfront Park, the Torpedo Factory, and over a cobblestone street that's been preserved to illustrate Alexandria's past to Old Town's hordes of visiting tourists.

As we exit Old Town, we'll make our way toward Arlington and one of the newest (as far as development goes) sections of the area, known as Potomac Yards (The Pot). So new in fact that it is still under construction. The Pot straddles the southeast portion of Arlington County and the northern portion of Alexandria. Although it's not quite the "real" geographic location of Arlandia (that's just a tad farther to the west), it is close enough for me to borrow its name for this ride.

Over years, Potomac Yards served primarily as a transportation hub. At first, C&O Canal barges that crossed the Potomac over the Aqueduct Bridge (see Ride 2, The Capital Crescent Trail and Rock Creek Park) brought their cargo for trains to transport to The Pot. Later, in the early 20th century, The Pot boomed as a direct result of the McMillan Plan (see Ride 3, The National Mall – L'Enfant's Grand Avenue) and the construction of the Long Bridge (see Ride 4, The Four Bridges). Ultimately, railroad usage diminished and The Pot was decommissioned. Years of industrial use left it in disrepair and contaminated. A large-scale cleanup effort was completed in 1998, even though, at the time, its future remained uncertain.

Mr. Jack Kent Cooke, who at the time was the owner of the Washington Redskins, had failed to convince Alexandria's residents to allow him to build a new stadium for his team in the early '90s. The Washington Nationals also tried and failed, and so did DC United. Ultimately residents did agree to transform The Pot's reclaimed land into a residential and retail hub, and plans are under way to add more condominiums, townhomes, and a 25-acre park.

Farther beyond The Pot we'll enter Crystal City, an area that is also in a period of developmental flux, much like The Pot was at the end of its cleanup in 1998. Until recently, Crystal City had been a federal business hub. Its high-rises were densely populated by a myriad of government agencies and offices, primarily that of the Department of Defense and its contractors. The recent Defense Base Closure and Realignment (BRAC) Commission virtually emptied out several buildings, forcing the city of Arlington to take a close look at the future of the city and surrounding area. Arlington has taken the stance that BRAC is an opportunity to redevelop and reinvent the area. As I write this, studies are being conducted on the feasibility of remodeling or rebuilding some of the structures. A new 50-year plan will go into effect soon, and that plan will undoubtedly change the look of Crystal City and the open spaces within it. Plans would add a street car line that will connect Pentagon City to The Pot, and to reconfigure the open spaces around Crystal Drive to make them easier to walk and navigate. There is no doubt that cycling is included in the long-term initiative.

As you ride through Old Town Alexandria and make your way across The Pot and into Crystal City, you'll navigate through an area of contrasts. At first through a community that has succeeded in preserving the past, then through another that's on the path to rebuilding itself, and finally through one that is just beginning to reinvent itself.

MILES & DIRECTIONS

At the time I documented this ride, there was considerable construction taking place along Potomac Avenue in Potomac Yards and along Long Bridge Park in Crystal City. The directions will remain the same, but some of the trails may have been finished and you may be able to alter the route slightly.

0.0   Head down the ramp to enter the grove and turn right and ride over the bridge. Immediately after the bridge turn right and follow the stone path toward the marina parking area.

0.1   Bear right away from the stone path and ride on the asphalt path. Continue to the right and enter the parking lot. There is a narrow path that travels along the parking area if you choose to ride that.

0.4   Turn left at the stop sign and then immediately right to enter the path that will take you toward the Mount Vernon Trail. Ride under the parkway and enjoy the great views of the Jefferson Memorial and the Washington Monument.

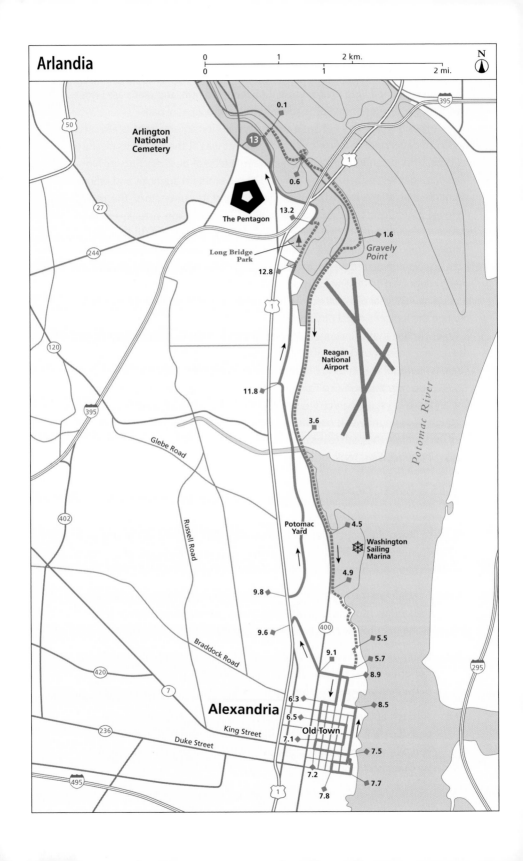

Arlandia

0   1   2 km.
0   1   2 mi.

N

Arlington
National
Cemetery

13

0.1

0.6

13.2

The Pentagon

Long Bridge
Park

1.6

Gravely
Point

12.8

Reagan
National
Airport

11.8

3.6

Glebe Road

Potomac
Yard

4.5

Washington
Sailing
Marina

4.9

Potomac River

9.8

9.6

Russell Road

400

9.1

5.5

5.7

8.9

Braddock Road

6.3

8.5

Alexandria

6.5

Old Town

7.1

King Street

Duke Street

7.5

7.2

7.7

7.8

0.6 Turn left at this intersection slightly past the Navy and Marine Memorial, and then turn left at the T intersection to join the Mount Vernon Trail.

0.8 Continue past both intersections to remain on the Mount Vernon Trail until we reach Alexandria.

1.6 Continue through Gravely Point.

2.5 Continue straight on the Mount Vernon Trail. The right turn will take you toward Crystal City and Crystal Drive around 18th Street.

3.6 Stay right at this intersection to continue toward Alexandria.

4.5 The marina is to your left. This can be an alternate start point to your ride.

4.9 Veer to the left to follow the more "scenic" river ride.

5.5 Continue to the right and then left to follow the trail along the railroad tracks. The left fork is a nice walking trail.

5.7 Turn right onto Canal Center Plaza/First Street and continue until it dead-ends; turn left onto Royal.

6.2 Turn right onto Pendelton Street.

6.3 Turn left onto St. Asaph Street.

6.5 Turn left onto Princess Street. To the right you can see the historic section of Princess, still paved with its original stones. We'll ride some of these a little later.

6.7 Turn right onto Lee Street.

6.8 Turn right onto Cameron Street. The Carlyle House will be on your left, and slightly farther up on the corner of Cameron and Royal will be Gatsby's Tavern.

7.1 Turn left onto St. Asaph and then immediately (7.2) left again on King Street to ride through the historic "main" street. You can see the Friendship Firehouse across the street as you make the turn. Farther down King Street are several other historic locations, including the Apothecary Museum and Market Square. The Ramsey House visitor center will be at the intersection of King and Fairfax to the left as you head down King Street. The visitor center is worth a stop to get info and additional maps with historic markers.

7.5 Turn right onto Union and then make an immediate left onto Wales Alley. Bike the Sites will be to your left. Make an immediate right onto Strand and continue toward Big Wheel Bikes.

7.6 Turn left onto Prince and then immediately right to continue on Strand. Big Wheel Bikes and Chadwick's will be on your right.

7.7 Turn right onto Duke Street.

7.8 Turn right onto South Fairfax. The Old Presbyterian Meeting House is at this intersection.

7.9 Turn right onto Prince Street. You'll ride over a section of pavers and then a section of old stones that have been preserved to show what the streets of Old Town used to look like.

8.0 Turn left onto Union Street and continue on Union until it ends just past Oronoco Park. You'll pass the Torpedo Factory after crossing King Street. Great place to lock up the bike and explore Old Town a little by foot. You can also walk through the Torpedo Factory to access the Alexandria waterfront. This is one of my favorite places in the DC area.

8.5 Turn left onto Pendelton Street.

8.6 Turn right onto Fairfax Street.

8.9 Turn left onto Montgomery Street and continue until you reach Washington Street. The block before Montgomery on Fairfax has a couple of nice little shops, including a wine store, Au Domaine, with a great selection of European wines and a wonderful coffee shop, Extra Perks, that shows European soccer on weekend mornings when the English Premiere League (EPL) is in session.

9.1 Cross Washington Street and continue right on Powhatan Street.

9.4 At the intersection of Bashford and Powhatan is Vaso's Cafe, a great place to have a Greek lunch on their outdoor patio.

9.6 Shortly before the light for Slaters Lane, turn left on the crosswalk to ride on the sidewalk toward Route 1 and the bridge that crosses over the railroad tracks. At the light (9.7) turn right and go over the Rt. 1 Bridge toward Potomac Yards.

9.8 Turn right onto Potomac Avenue and pick up the bike path immediately after crossing Main Line Avenue. Note: At the time of this writing, there was considerable construction taking place along the sides of Potomac Avenue—the trail or designated bike lane will be on both curbs of Potomac Avenue. By the time you read this, Potomac Park will likely be in place and offer many amenities.

11.8 Turn right onto Crystal Drive.

12.8 Crystal Drive veers to the left and turns into 12th Street. You'll want to continue straight into Long Bridge Park and the path that parallels the railroad tracks. You'll get a phenomenal view of the Washington Monument. Note: At the time of this writing, there was considerable construction taking place along Long Bridge Park so the path layout may have changed slightly.

13.2 Take a left and then another immediate left to head down toward Long Bridge Road. When you reach Long Bridge, turn right to continue north. Restrooms are available by the athletic fields.

13.5 Turn left onto Boundary Channel Drive and continue for 1 more mile until you reach the starting point.

14.5 Complete the loop.

Although our ride starts at the Lyndon B. Johnson Memorial Grove, the route is easily modifiable so you can start in Old Town and do a historic cycling tour. Old Town is an incredibly friendly cycling location, and getting lost in its neighborhoods is not as stressful as you may imagine. Still, if you don't want to venture out on your own and would rather have someone show you the way, visit the folks at Bike and Roll. Their shop is midway through this ride on the corner of The Strand and Wales Alley (1 Wales Alley). Bike and Roll offers guided tours through Mount Vernon and other destinations. If you don't have a bike and you want to ride, they should be your first stop. They are active members of the Alexandria Visitor's Association, so if you want to take this ride a little further, they can offer you some pretty cool guided tours. On Bike to Work Day and Car Free DC Day, they offer free rentals and participate in the Washington Area Bicycle Association's learn-to-ride programs. If you pay them a visit, tell them I sent you.

13

RIDE INFORMATION

Local Events and Attractions
www.visitalexandriava.com
Old Town Farmers Market, year-round, Saturday
Art Night at the Torpedo Factory, every second Thursday browse open studios and interact with the artists
Alexandria's Food and Wine Festival, mid-June

Restaurants
Extra Perks: 822 N. Fairfax St., Alexandria, VA 22314; (703) 706-5886; www .extraperkscoffeeshopandcafe.com. Great little coffee shop and restaurant— not exactly in Old Town but the route goes right by it. Tell them we sent you.
Thai Royal: 835 N. Royal St., Alexandria, VA 22314; (703) 535-6622; www.thai landroyalst.com
Paisano's: 3650 S. Glebe Rd., Ste. 185, Arlington, VA 22202; (703) 416-7000; www.pizzapaisanos.com

Restrooms
Restrooms are available at various locations through the ride. In Old Town Alexandria you can find them at the visitor center (corner of King and Fairfax), and at the Torpedo Factory on Union Street. In Crystal City you can find restrooms by the athletic fields at Long Bridge Park.

14

Elizabeth Furnace

This is by far the most difficult ride in the book, but one of the most rewarding. I won't sugar-coat it: this ride is demanding, technical, steep, fast, and dangerous. If the ride itself doesn't do you in, a bear might. When you finish you'll ask yourself "why?" And then, out of nowhere, you'll start planning your return, or researching other rides in the Forest—there are plenty, over 400 miles of singletrack to choose from. This demanding and technical ride has become a rite of passage for mountain bikers in the Washington, DC region and serves as the perfect introduction to the type of trail you'll find elsewhere in the George Washington National Forest and the Catoctin Mountains to the north.

Start: Massanuten Mountain/Signal Knob parking area

Length: 11.7 miles

Approximate riding time: 2–3 hours

Best bike: Mountain bike

Terrain and trail surface: Mostly singletrack, one section of gravel road

Traffic and hazards: Trail obstacles, extremely technical trail

Things to see: Strasburg Reservoir, Historic Front Royal, Skyline Drive, Skyline Caverns

Getting there: From Washington take Route 66 west toward Front Royal. Take exit 6 for US 340/US 522 South toward Front Royal. Turn right onto US 55W, Strasburg Road, and then left onto Fort Valley Road. The parking area will be to your right and clearly marked as you enter the George Washington National Forest. GPS: 38.924428,-78.332176

Fees: None

I remember the first time I ventured out into the George Washington National Forest (GWNF)... I thought it would be the last. I headed out west of Washington on Route 66 to Front Royal with a group of friends from the Mid-Atlantic Off-Road Enthusiasts (MORE) group to ride Elizabeth Furnace for the first time. I had already been riding my mountain bike in the region for several months and had ridden Wakefield, Patapsco, and Loch Raven Reservoir to the north in Baltimore, and all the other usual spots. But none of those rides would prepare me for what I was about to experience in the foothills of the GWNF and the Appalachian Mountains.

The first part of our ride will use a gravel road that was once used to transport the pig iron that was created in the furnace below to the other side of Massanutten Mountain. Iron ore was mined in the area and then brought to the Elizabeth Furnace, where it was purified. Unfortunately not much is left of the furnace that produced nearly three tons of the pig iron daily until the Federals burned it during the Civil War. The furnace was rebuilt shortly after the war, but it only stayed in operation for a short time and never operated again. Today some of the structure remains, but it is in disrepair and often covered by overgrown vegetation during the spring and summer months.

Bike Shops

Element Sports: 2184 S. Pleasant Valley Rd., Winchester, VA 22601; (540) 662-5744; www.elementsport.com
Hawksbill Bicycles: 20 W. Main St., Luray, VA 22835; (540) 743-1037; www.hawksbillbicycles.com

Once past the dirt road, which really is a pleasant climb, we will enter the canopy and begin a journey toward the Strasburg Reservoir and Signal Knob. The singletrack trails continue in an upward direction and offer a series of highly enjoyable technical sections with several creek crossings. They are technical enough to keep you focused on the ride and what lies ahead. The beauty of this ride is that at its midpoint you can veer right and visit Strasburg Reservoir, and during a hot summer day, take a dip in its cool waters before confronting the hike a bike to Signal Knob, the high point of the ride.

To get to Signal Knob, however, you must endure one of the toughest 0.5-mile sections of trails in the region. Once up high you'll be treated to fantastic panoramic views of the valley below. It's no surprise that Confederate soldiers climbed the very same trail you will use to observe Union troop movements and relay signals from its peak to their counterparts. After enjoying the view and recovering your strength, you'll descend on what is perhaps one of the best downhill runs in the region. "Boulder gardens" that will tame the most seasoned

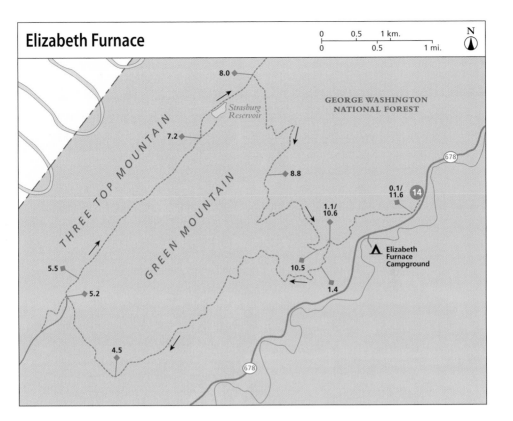

0   0.5   1 km.

0   0.5   1 mi.

N

mountain biker will open up and treat you to one of the most technical and rewarding downhills you'll ever experience, and, before you know it, deliver you to the starting point of the ride. You'll likely spend a quarter of the time in this last section, and although exhausted you will undoubtedly be asking for more.

If more is what you want, don't fret; there are hundreds of miles of trails in the Forest and lots of them have been documented in another guide: *Mountain Biking Virginia*, by my good friend Scott Adams, with whom I coauthored *Mountain Biking the Washington, DC/Baltimore Area*.

MILES & DIRECTIONS

0.0   Start from the Massanuten Trail, Signal Knob parking area. The trailhead is on the west side of the parking area. Enter the trail and stay to the left.

0.1   Stay to the right as you reach the group camping sign. The trail will be blazed orange.

0.4   Stay to the right and follow the blue blazes.

A rider negotiates the rocks and boulders of the Elizabeth Furnace Trail.

1.1 Turn left at this trail intersection. Massanuten Mountain West is on the right fork; this is the direction we will be returning in.

1.4 Turn right onto the fire road and get ready for a nice grinder up the mountain.

4.5 The fire road ends. Enter the singletrack and then stay to the right at the trail fork.

5.2 Cross Mudhole Gap and then turn right on the gravel road. Continue following the orange blazes.

5.5 Continue straight through the gate on the gravel road.

7.2 Turn left and follow the signs for Signal Knob. If you continue straight, less than 0.25 mile ahead is the Strasburg Reservoir. On a blistering hot day you can take a dip in the reservoir.

8.0 Turn right onto the blue trail. This is the beginning of the last, and most brutal, climb of the ride.

8.8 You've reached the top. I highly suggest you take a break and prep yourself for the downhill ride. The trail is to the left and blazed blue.

10.5 Stay left at this intersection and continue on the blue trail.

10.6 Stay to the left at this intersection. You can turn right and ride the entire loop again if you want. At this point we'll be backtracking on the trail we initially started on.

11.6 Stay to the left.

11.7 Turn right to return to the parking area and close out the loop.

RIDE INFORMATION

Local Events and Attractions

Front Royal is only a stone's throw from the nation's capitol and offers a gateway to the Shenandoah Valley: www.discoverfrontroyal.com

Restaurants

Jalisco Mexican Restaurant: 1303 N. Royal Ave., Front Royal, VA 22630; (540) 635-7348

Restrooms

Restrooms are available in the Elizabeth Furnace day-use area a little farther down the road.

> The Appalachian Mountains are over 450 million years old and were once as tall as the Alps and the Rocky Mountains.

Loudoun County Roads

This ride will take you through some of Loudoun County's nicest back roads, including portions of the Washington & Old Dominion (W&OD) Trail. Along the way you'll ride past local vineyards and the historic town of Waterford.

Start: Loudoun High School parking lot, intersection of Dry Mill Run and Catoctin Circle

Length: 41.2 miles

Approximate riding time: 2.5–4 hours

Best bike: Road bike

Terrain and trail surface: Paved bike paths and roads

Traffic and hazards: Other trail users in the W&OD and vehicle traffic in the road sections

Things to see: Historic Waterford, Northgate and Doukénie Vineyards

Getting there: Toll free: Take the Capital Beltway I-495 and take exit 47 to VA 7 West, Leesburg Pike toward Tysons Corner. Follow VA 7 for 23 miles and exit onto US 15 South. Merge onto US 15 Business North/South and turn left onto Fairfax Street. Turn right onto Catoctin Circle; the high school will be ahead to your left.

  Toll road: Take the Capital Beltway I-495 and take exit 45 and merge onto Route 267 West (toll) toward Dulles Airport. Continue on Route 267 for approximately 25 miles and exit onto US 15 toward Leesburg. Follow the signs for US 15 Business toward Leesburg and turn right onto US 15 Business North/South, King Street. Make a U turn at Fairfax Street and then a right turn onto Catoctin Circle. The high school will be up ahead to the left. GPS: 39.111515,-77.578776

Fees: None

THE RIDE

This is a variation of an extremely popular road ride through the back roads of northern Virginia's Loudoun County. Chances are that when you head out to do this ride, you'll likely see other folks headed out to do a variation of their own. Since parts of the ride use the popular W&OD Trail, it is very feasible for you to head out from Arlington or Alexandria and do an epic version of this loop. For our purposes, however, we'll stick with the modest 40-miler that I detail here, which will take you through some of the county's most beautiful roads and one of its most historic towns, Waterford.

Waterford, originally known as Janney's Mill, after its founder Amos Janney, was established in 1732. The town grew quickly in an unlikely place around a mill that produced flour and quickly became a center for commerce. Over the years the town grew to include a second mill, and at its peak had a little over 500 residents, all Quakers. The town was the site of a fierce battle between Confederate troops and Union soldiers. At one point several of its residents migrated to Ohio because of Virginia's failure to abolish slavery, and because the effect that the war was having on the town. Since the Quakers were Unionist and pacifists they were often taken advantage of and raided by confederate troops.

Waterford never quite recovered from the ravages of the Civil War and lost much of its economic strength. The completion of the C&O Canal along with the construction of the B&O Railroad at Point of Rocks replaced Waterford as a major commercial route. Slowly, residents began to leave the area, and the town fell into disrepair.

Because it offered no commercial value, the town was left virtually undisturbed for many years. There simply was no reason to invest in demolishing an area that had little value. This pretty much ensured that the historic integrity of the buildings remained untouched for years. In the mid-1930s, a historical survey found that most of the buildings in the town were dilapidated, but by that time residents from neighboring Washington and other Virginia towns began expressing an interest in the town's historic

Bike Shops

Bicycle Outfitters: 34-D Catoctin Cir. SE, Leesburg, VA 20175; (703) 777-6126; www.bikeoutfitters.com

Plum Grove Cyclery: 16286 Rockland Ln., Leesburg, VA 20176; (703) 777-2252; http://plumgrovecyclery.com

significance. Many buyers came to the area to purchase the historic homes and then renovate them. Others came to build new homes, but were careful to match the character of those around it. By the early 1940s several families took it a step further and established the Waterford Foundation to ensure that the integrity of the town was preserved in the hopes of re-creating the rural

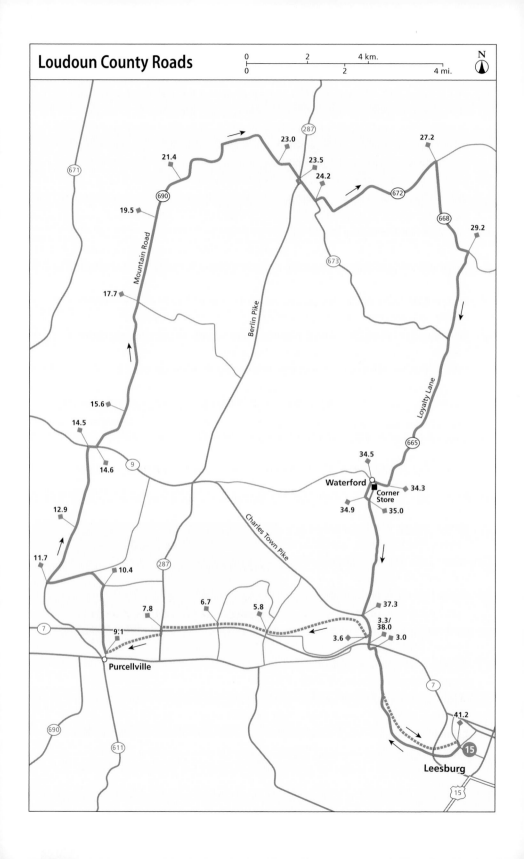

Loudoun County Roads

0   2   4 km.

0   2   4 mi.

N

287

672

671

690

668

27.2

23.0

23.5

24.2

29.2

21.4

19.5

17.7

673

Mountain Road

Berlin Pike

15.6

14.5

14.6

9

Loyalty Lane

665

34.5

Waterford

34.3

Corner
Store

34.9

35.0

12.9

11.7

10.4

287

Charles Town Pike

7.8

6.7

5.8

37.3

3.3/
38.0

9.1

3.6

3.0

7

Purcellville

690

611

41.2

7

15

Leesburg

15

ambience of the town, just like it was when it was first founded. Ultimately that effort paid off, and Waterford was listed as a Virginia Historic Landmark in 1969. One year later, in 1970, Waterford and the surrounding countryside were declared a National Historic Landmark.

As you ride through 2nd Street, you'll understand why. Entering the town past the old corner store, and then riding in front of its historic houses is like taking a trip into the past. The residents of Waterford are proud of the heritage they have preserved and hope to carry it into the future. Annual historic tours of homes and buildings are highlights in this proud community, and I urge you take the time to explore it.

MILES & DIRECTIONS

0.0   Start from the Loudon High School parking lot on the entrance by Dry Mill Road. Turn right and head west on Dry Mill Road.

2.5   You get a glimpse of the W&OD on the right side; we'll join it shortly and also return on it shortly.

2.6   Turn right and then immediately left to get on the W&OD trail.

3.0   Turn right onto Dry Mill Road.

3.3   Turn right onto Charles Town Pike.

3.6   Turn left onto Simpson Circle and then hop on the W&OD again to the right.

4.1   Cross Simpson Circle.

5.8   Cross Hamilton Station Road.

6.7   Cross Ivandale Road.

7.8   Cross Berlin Turnpike and then turn left to continue on the W&OD. After riding under the route, turn right to continue following the W&OD.

9.1   Turn right onto North Hatcher Avenue.

10.4   Turn left onto Alder School Road.

11.7   At the traffic circle turn right onto Hillsboro Road.

12.9   To the left is Northgate Vineyard (www.northgatevineyard.com).

14.5   Turn right onto Charlestown Turnpike.

This is what "they" mean by "rolling country roads."

14.6 Turn left on Mountain Road. (This should be named "Joy" as in fun Road.)

15.6 Doukénie Winery is to the left (www.doukeniewinery.com).

17.7 Turn left and then quick right to continue on Mountain Road.

19.5 Take a look at the bison to the right at Destiny's View farm.

21.4 Turn left onto Irish Corner Road. (This is the poster road for rolling country roads.)

23.0 Continue to the left to remain on Irish Corner Road.

23.5 Circle around the small park in a counterclockwise direction and then turn right on East Broad Way. There is a 7-Eleven here, perfect time for a break.

24.2 Turn left onto Lovettsville Road.

27.2 Turn right onto Taylorstown Road.

29.2 Turn right onto Loyalty Road. The trail is directly across from the Taylorstown General Store and Anna Road.

34.0 Welcome to Historic Waterford.

34.3 Stay right on Water Street.

34.5 Turn left onto 2nd Street. Lock up your bike here and visit the Corner Store and do a short walking tour of Waterford.

34.9 Continue to the left; 2nd becomes Factory Street.

35.0 Turn right onto High Street.

37.3 Turn left onto Charlestown Pike (VA-9).

38.0 Turn left onto Dry Mill Road on the near crosswalk and hop on the W&OD Trail.

38.3 Continue straight on the W&OD Trail. We are now double backing on the initial portion of the ride and will finish it off on the W&OD.

41.2 Turn right onto Catoctin Circle and then immediately right into the Loudoun High School parking lot to complete the ride.

RIDE INFORMATION

Local Events and Attractions
Historic Waterford: www.waterfordvillage.org or www.waterfordhistory.org
Northgate Vineyard: 16031 Hillsboro Rd., Purcellville, VA 20132; (540) 668-6248; www.northgatevineyard.com
Doukénie Winery: 14727 Mountain Rd., Hillsboro VA 20132; (540) 668-6464

Restaurants
Waterford Market: 15487 2nd St., Waterford, VA 20197; (540) 882-3631

Restrooms
Available at a couple of commercial establishments along the route (gas stations, etc.).

Meadowood Recreation Area

This ride will take you through mature hardwood forests in the Mason Neck Peninsula. The trails we'll be riding are relatively new, and chances are that by the time you are reading this, the 3.1-mile loop will be transformed into a larger and longer network of mountain bike trails. Plans are in motion to nearly double the length of the existing mountain bike loop with a directional trail that will take advantage of the terrain's natural features and offer cyclists a challenging and enjoyable ride.

Start: Old Colchester Road parking area

Length: 3.1 miles

Approximate riding time: 0.5–1 hour, longer if you do multiple loops

Best bike: Mountain bike

Terrain and trail surface: Mostly singletrack, one long elevated boardwalk

Traffic and hazards: Other trail users, trail obstacles

Things to see: Mason Neck, Gunston Hall

Getting there: Take the Capital Beltway, I-495 toward northern Virginia and follow the signs for I-95 South. Take exit 163 for VA 642 toward Lorton and turn left onto Lorton Road. Follow Lorton Road for approximately 1 mile and turn right onto US 1 south. In 2.1 miles turn left onto Hassett Street and then left onto Old Colchester Road. The parking area will be clearly marked to your right. GPS: 38.680545,-77.219717

Fees: None

THE RIDE

The Meadowood trails and recreation area are a relatively new leisure destination operated by the Bureau of Land Management (BLM). The nearly 800 acres of meadows, ponds, and hardwood forests where the trails currently lie were transferred in a land swap between Pulte Home Builders, Fairfax County, and the federal government in 2001. In late October of the same year, the land was assigned to BLM, which currently manages it to ensure an open space for recreation and environmental education.

Before the land was acquired and transferred to the BLM, it had been a working farm with horse stables. It also included a series of wooded trails that were in varying states of disrepair. Many of the trails were along steep lines, causing erosion and posing safety and water issues. Once BLM took over the day-to-day management of the location, they fixed some immediate problems and developed an integrated activity plan in which they outlined their vision for the area and identified the potential use scenarios. These included hiking, fishing, horseback riding, and cycling (mountain biking). The plan also identified and recognized that the legacy ATB and old farm equestrian trails should be abandoned and replaced with new sustainable routes.

Meadowood is physically divided into two distinct areas by Belmont Boulevard. The east side of the system, and closest to the Meadowood Field Station (management offices) and adjacent to the existing horse boarding stables, is primarily an equestrian destination; bikes are not allowed there. The west side had remained undeveloped, and since mountain biking would be one of the allowed activities in the system, BLM worked with International Mountain Biking Association (IMBA) representative and trail specialist Dan Hudson to lay out a potential biking and hiking loop. The area surveyed included some of the old farm trails, and it was recommended that many of these be rerouted or rebuilt.

Bike Shops

Olde Towne Bicycles Inc.: 14477 Potomac Mills Rd., Woodbridge, VA 22192; (703) 491-5700; www.oldetownebicycles.com

Village Skis & Bikes: 12383 Dillingham Sq., Woodbridge, VA 22192; (703) 730-0303; www.vsbsports.com

In 2009 the BLM, using American Recovery and Reinvestment Act (ARRA) funds, hired two term staff members, Doug Vinson and David Lyster, with trail building experience to oversee the recommendations made by Dan Hudson and IMBA. After a period of additional planning, Vinson and Lyster begin building the recommended loop in early 2011. By January 2012 they had completed the South Branch Trail, the loop I detail here. Not satisfied with their effort, Doug and David set out to begin phase 2 of the Meadowood project. Enlisting the

You May Run into Doug Vinson

Doug Vinson is one of the trail-building experts whom BLM staffed to complete and build the trails at Meadowood. His vision is what's shaping the development of the area and influencing the future of several other trails in the region. Doug has been in the area for approximately five years and is already making a mark for himself. His love for cycling and the outdoors led him to form Vinson Trailworks, a full-service trail contractor specializing in design, layout, and construction. "I just love that moment of clarity when trail, bike, and rider all come

PHOTO COURTESY DOUG VINSON

together," he said. The "trail" part is what is most important to him. For us, it translates to well-built, sustainable routes that are built by cycling-loving folks. "I'm proudest of the trails at Meadowood. These trails are my babies," he added. "I'm inspired by the recent work on area trail systems like Fountainhead and Rockburn, and wish to build upon their success and take my efforts to the next level. David Lyster and I have been building trails at Meadowood for the last four years, from surfaced equestrian paths to super-fun mountain bike trails. The South Branch Loop Trail packs more fun in 5 miles than any other trail around!" You'll definitely run into Doug at Meadowood, so make sure you give him a high five for a job well done.

help of volunteers and the Mid-Atlantic Off-Road Enthusiasts (MORE), they began to solicit and raise funds for an extension to the loop. Again, with the help of IMBA, they crafted a design that will add an additional directional loop, accessible from the South Branch Trail to the system. The new loop will have more advanced trail features, including banked turns, rock outcroppings, narrow log crossings, and steep climbing turns. The second phase is expected to be completed in 2013, and hopefully by the time you have this book in your hands, the trails at Meadowood will have nearly doubled in length.

MILES & DIRECTIONS

0.0 Start at the parking area of Old Colchester Road. We will start at the gate. Immediately after crossing the gate, turn left to enter the South

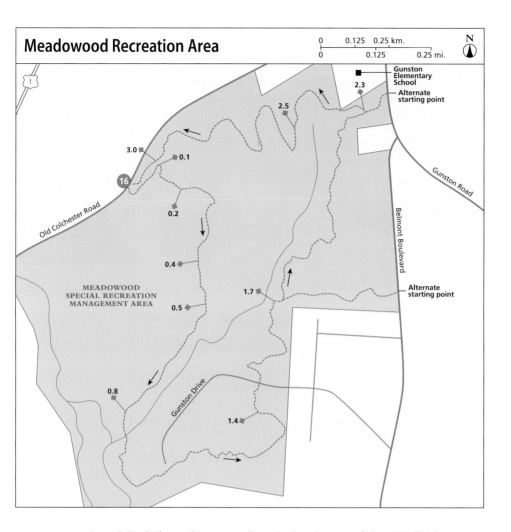

Meadowood Recreation Area

0 0.125 0.25 km.

0 0.125 0.25 mi.

N

Gunston Elementary School

2.3

Alternate starting point

2.5

3.0

0.1

16

0.2

Old Colchester Road

Gunston Road

Belmont Boulevard

0.4

MEADOWOOD SPECIAL RECREATION MANAGEMENT AREA

1.7

0.5

Alternate starting point

0.8

Gunston Drive

1.4

Branch Trail. The trail is very well marked and easy to follow. We'll ride it in a counterclockwise direction.

0.1 Turn right to begin the loop.

0.2 Continue straight through this intersection. Pause to take a look at the provided map.

0.4 Continue straight through this intersection.

0.5 Continue to the left. You'll come up through a series of three additional trail junction points; remain left at all of them and follow the clearly marked South Branch Trail.

0.8 You've reached the boardwalk. Cross it and continue straight and up on the trail.

Yours truly riding the long deck at Meadowood.

1.4 Continue straight into the singletrack at this intersection.

1.7 Continue straight through the next two intersections. The trail to the right will take you to Belmont Boulevard, an alternate starting point.

2.3 Make a sharp left. Straight will take you to Gunston Road and an alternate starting point.

2.5 Bench; the trail continues to the right.

3.0 Continue to the right. The left will start the loop again (mile marker 0.1).

3.1 The loop is complete.

RIDE INFORMATION

Local Events and Attractions
Workhouse Arts Center: www.lortonarts.org/calendar.php
Historic Occoquan: www.occoquan.org

Restaurants
Glory Days Grill: 9459 Lorton Market St., Mason Neck, VA 22079; (703) 372-1770; www.glorydaysgrill.com
Vinny's Italian Grill: 7730 Gunston Plaza, Lorton, VA 22079; (703) 339-7447; www.vinnysitaliangrill.net

Restrooms
None on or near the trail; go before you go.

Mount Vernon Loop

Everyone rides the Mount Vernon Trail out to Washington's home and then back along the same route; that's easy. Instead, for this ride we will head out to Washington's home along the Mount Vernon Trail, but for the return we will ride through neighborhood streets and not-often-used bike paths to make it a far more enjoyable (I think) loop.

Start: Bell Haven Marina

Length: 18.8 miles

Approximate riding time: 2–3 hours

Best bike: Cross bike or road bike

Terrain and trail surface: Paved bike paths and roads. One section along the Fort Hunt Road bike path is unpaved; however, you can ride on Fort Hunt and avoid this section.

Traffic and hazards: Other trail users and vehicle traffic on the road sections

Things to see: Panoramic views of the Potomac, Mount Vernon, and Mount Vernon's neighborhoods

Getting there: From VA: Take the Capital Beltway (I-495) to exit 1 headed south on Richmond Highway, Route 1. Once on Route 1, stay in the right lane to take the exit for Fort Hunt Road. Follow Fort Hunt Road for 1.1 miles and turn left onto Belle View Boulevard. At the end of Belle View Boulevard, turn left onto the George Washington Parkway. Turn right into the Belle Haven Marina and then immediately left toward the parking areas.

   From MD: Take the local lanes of the Capital Beltway (I-495) over the Woodrow Wilson and take the first exit toward Mt. Vernon. Merge onto Church Street and then make an immediate right onto Washington Street. Cross the Washington Street Deck (bridge over I-495) and you'll be on the George Washington (GW) Parkway. Drive 1.25 miles and turn left into Bell Haven Marina. Immediately turn left again toward the parking areas. GPS: 38.779146,-77.051883

Fees: None

THE RIDE

I've used the Mount Vernon Trail (MVT) on several rides in the book. Built in 1973, the trail serves as a backbone for many bike rides in the Washington, DC area. From its beginning at Roosevelt Island, you can connect with the Custis Trail or cross the Key Bridge and connect with the C&O Canal and Capital Crescent Trail—from which you can then hook up with the Rock Creek Trail to travel into Maryland. As you travel south from Roosevelt Island, you can cross any of the main Potomac bridges and access other routes around the city and into southern Maryland. If you turn west on the Four Mile Run, you can venture far into Loudoun County, Virginia, along the W&OD. With all of these options, it is often puzzling why people always just head down and back on the MVT when, with a little effort, they can craft a much more interesting loop.

Granted, the route from Theodore Roosevelt Island to Washington's home is scenic, and no matter which way you travel it is serene. And heading out and back is quite easy; you can get 37 miles with only a U turn involved. But for the sake of variety, I often look for alternative routes to make my outings more interesting. This is how this loop was conceived (and practically all the others in the book). I, like many, often pick a spot along the parkway ("America's Most Modern Roadway") to start on the MVT. One of my favorites has always been Belle Haven Park. It's at a midway point and has amenities that other parking spots don't. It has a rest-room, water fountains, and a great view across the river of Maryland, National Harbor, and the Wilson Bridge. From here you are minutes away from Old Town Alexandria, National Harbor, and Mount Vernon. I offer this as the starting point, but if you want to rack up the miles, you can always start at Roosevelt Island and work your way south to this spot; you won't regret the views—your legs, however, may question the decision.

Bike Shops

Spokes Etc.: 1506 Belle View Blvd., Alexandria, VA 22307; (703) 765-8005; www.spokesetc.com
Big Wheel Bikes: 2 Prince St., Alexandria, VA 22314; (703) 739-2300; www.bigwheelbikes.com

You May Run into Jim Strang

I've known Jim for a little over 20 years. We first met when I moved into the Arlandia area in 1991. From circumstances beyond my control (aka being in the Army), I arrived to my new home sans bicycle, so I headed to the closest shop, Spokes Etc. on Quaker Lane. Jim was the one who greeted me, and little did I know that the guy who spent several hours with me over the course of several days was the owner of the place. He was extremely patient and helped me select the right bike for the type of riding I was going to do. Ultimately I left the shop with a bike I still own to this day, a FAT Chance Yo Eddy.

PHOTO COURTESY JIM STRANG

Jim's been a Fairfax resident for over 40 years, a roadie by nature who's ridden across the country on two occasions and has done his share of racing. He's the guy who will tell you, "I remember when the Mount Vernon Trail didn't exist . . . " and share stories of the area's cycling past with you. He got his first "real" bike in 1972, a Gitane Interclub, which undoubtedly he rode on the brand-new Mount Vernon Trail. Now, he just rides for fitness and the pleasure of rolling on two wheels. Cycling is Jim's fountain of youth. "For me, cycling is a great mental break," he said. "It forces me to just focus on what I'm doing on the bike, and nothing else."

Through his shop's Saturday morning rides I discovered my first trails in the DC area, and indirectly because of him, I developed an appreciation and love for the sport that has led me to this day. Jim taught me early the importance of your Local Bike Shop (LBS) and how critical they are to helping you enjoy your sport. We are fortunate to have several great LBSs in the area, his included. The time he spent helping me walk out with the right bike always left an impression on me and set the standard by which I measure all other bike shops. The success of his business is a direct result of how much emphasis (he) they put on their customers. That original 1986 Quaker Lane location has grown into five area stores, one of which you'll ride in front of at the tail end of our loop (Belle View). "There is no better feeling than getting in a quick 40 miles before work," Jim told me the other day. "It's good for the body and the head." Perhaps he'll be riding the area when you spin by. If not, stop by his shop. Chances are pretty good that he'll be the one to greet you.

Fort Hunt Park is often overlooked by Mount Vernon Trail riders and offers a nice little extension to your ride and can serve as a destination in and of itself. The one-way section, similar to the one at Prince William Forest Park, offers parents a relatively safe area to take kids for a ride.

It's easy to understand why Washington chose the location of his home along the Potomac in Virginia and why several of our nation's leaders used the area for recreation. Before there was a parkway, or a Mount Vernon Trail, Eleanor Roosevelt rode her horse along the river's bank. The Washingtons themselves often ventured on excursions along the Potomac's banks as well, and Washington personally surveyed much of the land around here.

Relatively speaking, the trail is not that old. A short portion of the trail existed between the Arlington Memorial Bridge and the 14th Street Bridge in the very early '70s. Back then cyclists would ride on the parkway lanes, and on Sunday the northbound thoroughfare was closed off so locals could have it for recreational use. But as traffic increased, the presence of cyclists on the parkway became a safety issue and the practice was discontinued. In 1972, local Alexandria Waterfront activist Ellen Pickering began her push to have the National Park Service build what is now the MVT. Her efforts yielded a new section from the 14th Street Bridge to Alexandria, and later, the trail was extended systematically to the south and later to the north to Roosevelt Island. By 1975 the majority of the southern portion of the trail was completed. Most of it was loose gravel, but the steepest sections were paved to minimize erosion. By 1977 a reroute was made to take cyclist traffic away from West Drive, and finally in 1988, the northern terminus of the trail was built to Roosevelt Island.

Our ride will take us mostly along the southern portion of the trail and through Fort Hunt to Mount Vernon. We'll then back up via the Mount Vernon Highway before riding through various neighborhoods in the Mount Vernon

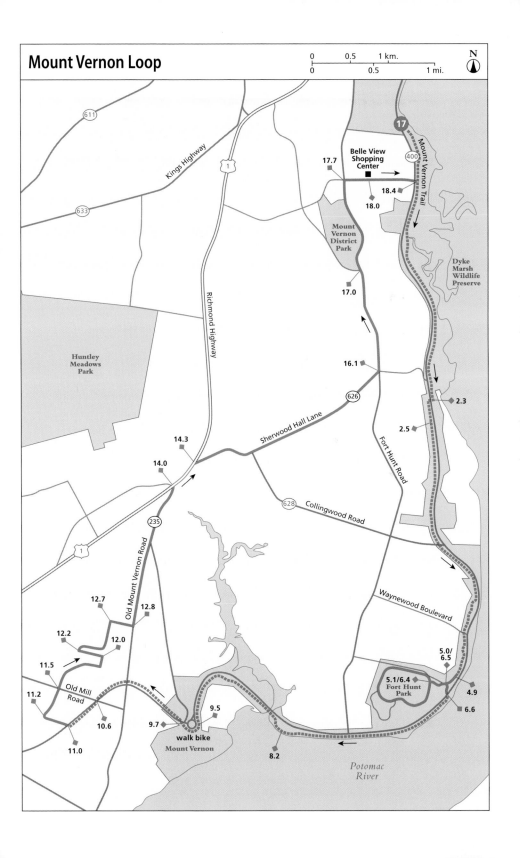

Mount Vernon Loop

0   0.5   1 km.

0   0.5   1 mi.

N

611

Kings Highway

1

633

Richmond Highway

Huntley
Meadows
Park

14.3

14.0

235

Old Mount Vernon Road

1

12.7

12.8

12.2

12.0

11.5

Old Mill
Road

11.2

11.0

10.6

9.7

9.5

walk bike
Mount Vernon

8.2

628 Collingwood Road

626

Sherwood Hall Lane

16.1

17.0

Mount
Vernon
District
Park

18.0

18.4

17.7

Belle View
Shopping
Center

400

17

Mount Vernon Trail

Dyke
Marsh
Wildlife
Preserve

2.3

2.5

Fort Hunt Road

Waynewood Boulevard

5.0/
6.5

5.1/6.4
Fort Hunt
Park

4.9

6.6

Potomac
River

Area, getting to know local residential areas. Finally we'll head up Fort Hunt Road before returning to Bell Haven via Belle View Boulevard.

MILES & DIRECTIONS

0.0 Start on the Mount Vernon Trail in the Bell Haven Marina in front of the restrooms and the Jones Point Historic Marker. Head south on the Mount Vernon Trail.

2.3 The Mount Vernon Trail continues on the road; follow Northbound Road.

2.5 Turn right onto Alexandria Avenue to go over the bridge that spans the George Washington Memorial Parkway and then immediately left to get on the Mount Vernon Trail.

4.9 Turn right onto Fort Hunt Road to head toward Fort Hunt.

5.0 Turn left and into Fort Hunt.

5.1 Turn right at the stop sign and follow the road around all of Fort Hunt in a counterclockwise direction. The fort Hunt loop is perfect for kids. It is designated a one-way shortly after the first parking lot. The left lane is reserved for walkers and bikes, and the right lane is designated for vehicle traffic, which is minimal.

6.4 Turn right to exit Fort Hunt and to head back to the Mount Vernon Trail.

6.5 Shortly after exiting the park, you'll see the entrance to the Mount Vernon Trail. Continue south on the trail.

6.6 The trail will put you back on the road for a short distance as you ride under the parkway. Use caution as you pick up the trail to the left immediately after riding under the short tunnel since there may be oncoming traffic.

8.2 Riverside Park; restrooms are available here. Continue straight.

9.5 You've reached the sidewalk for the Mount Vernon Historical Area. Walk your bike to the crosswalk immediately past the Mount Vernon Inn.

9.7 Turn right to cross the street and immediately left to pick up the trail that runs along VA-235 South (Mount Vernon Memorial Highway).

10.6 Old Mill Road intersection. The path continues on the opposite side of the street. Continue in the same direction.

11.0 The path veers right to cross 235 South. Cross and continue straight to enter Southwood Drive. The next couple of miles we'll ride through the Mount Vernon neighborhoods.

11.2 Turn right onto Adrienne Drive.

11.5 Cross Old Mill Road.

11.9 Turn left onto Beauchamp Drive.

12.0 Turn left onto Colonial Avenue.

12.2 Turn right onto Gibbs Street.

12.7 Turn right onto Woodley Drive.

12.8 Turn left onto Old Mount Vernon Road. There are sidewalks and paths available until you reach Route 1 on either side of Mount Vernon Road.

14.0 Turn right onto Route 1. I suggest riding on the sidewalks since traffic is pretty heavy here.

14.3 Turn right and continue east onto Sherwood Hall Lane. There is a nice wide shoulder on this road.

16.1 Turn left onto Fort Hunt Road. The bike trail is on the near curb so when you make the left make it into the off ramp area from Fort Hunt to Sherwood Hill. The trail entrance is easy to see. You can also ride on Fort Hunt Road if you prefer.

17.0 The paved path turns to a natural surface trail (unless you're on the road).

17.7 The trail will end in the parking area of the Martha Washington Public Library. Continue straight to the light and turn right onto Belle View Boulevard.

18.0 Continue straight on Belle View Boulevard, but first make a pit stop at Spokes Etc. to the left and say hello.

18.4 Cross the George Washington Memorial Parkway and turn left onto the Mount Vernon Trail. Use caution.

18.8 Complete the loop.

A rider rolls along one of the long bridges of the Mount Vernon Trail.

RIDE INFORMATION

Local Events and Attractions
Old Town Alexandria Events: www.visitalexandriava.com
Mount Vernon Trail: www.nps.gov/gwmp/mtvernontrail.htm
Historic Mount Vernon: www.mountvernon.org

Restaurants
Lots to choose from if you head north toward Old Town Alexandria; these are two of my favorites.
Union Street Public House: 121 S. Union St., Alexandria, VA 22314; (703) 548-1785; www.unionstreetpublichouse.com
Hard Times Cafe: 1404 King St., Alexandria, VA 22314; (703) 837-0050; www.hardtimes.com

Restrooms
Restrooms are available in Bell Haven Marina at the starting point of the ride and along the Mount Vernon Trail at Riverside Park.

Prince William Road Ride, Brentsville and Manassas Loops

After years of living in Maryland, we made the move down to the fringes of Northern Virginia, where I discovered the rolling backcountry roads of Western Prince William County. These loops are two I frequently ride. One starts in Historic Brentsville and will take you through some of the county's most scenic—and some of my favorite—country roads. The other virtually starts out my front door. I share the latter with you in the hopes that you share your "front door" ride with me as well.

Start:
> **Brentsville ride:** Parking area of the Old Brentsville Courthouse
> **Manassas loop:** Intersection of Route 234 and Waterway Drive in Prince William County, Virginia

Length:
> **Brentsville ride:** 25.1 miles
> **Manassas loop:** 31 miles

Approximate riding time (both rides): 1.5–3 hours

Best bike (both rides): Road bike

Terrain and trail surface:
> **Brentsville loop:** Paved country roads
> **Manassas loop:** Paved bike paths and one section of road

Traffic and hazards:
> **Brentsville loop:** Vehicle traffic
> **Manassas loop:** Other trail users and vehicle traffic

Things to see: Brentsville Courthouse, Prince William County farms, Prince William Forest Park, Quantico Marine Museum, Quantico National Cemetery, Manassas Battlefield

Getting there:
> **Brentsville loop:** From the Capital Beltway (I-495) take I-95 toward Richmond. Continue for approximately 17 miles and take exit 152B onto Route 234 north toward Manassas. After 7.5 miles turn left onto

Independent Hill Drive and then turn right onto VA 619 West/Bristow Road. The Brentsville Courthouse will be approximately 5 miles on your right.

Manassas loop: From the Capital Beltway (I-495) take I-95 south to exit 152B for Route 234 North/Dumfries Road toward Manassas. Continue for approximately 3 miles and turn right onto Waterway Drive and then turn right into the shopping center. Park close to the intersection of Route 234 and Waterway; the bike path parallels Route 234 along the southeast-bound lanes.

GPS:
  Brentsville loop: 38.688592,-77.498417
  Manassas loop: 38.608303,-77.359886

Fees: None for the ride, nominal fee if you want to visit the historic buildings

THE RIDE

The modest town of Brentsville is one of great historical significance in our nation's history since it played a key role during the Civil War. Situated virtually in the center of Prince William County and the junction of the Alexandria and Manassas Gap Railroads, it provided a key link to the South. During that time it also served as the seat for Prince William County. Confederate generals recognized its geographic significance, so they made it a primary mission to protect and maintain possession of the railroad junction. Allowing the Union to control it would mean they would have a key access point to the South's capital, Richmond, Virginia.

Bike Shops

Bull Run Bicycles: 9824 Liberia Ave., Manassas, VA 20110; (703) 335-6131; www.bullrunbicycles.com. Leads road rides out of their shop on Tuesday evenings and off-road rides Sunday. **Olde Towne Bicycles Inc.:** 14477 Potomac Mills Rd., Woodbridge, VA 22192; (703) 491-5700; www.olde townebicycles.com. Leads Friday mountain bike rides and Sunday road rides to the Prince William Forest Park.

The spot from where we begin our ride was virtually the same place where young men volunteered or were recruited into the Confederate Army. And it marks the spot from where they marched to meet the Union Army in the first major engagement of the Civil War, the First Battle of Manassas.

Only a few months had passed since the start of the Civil War when Northern citizens began clamoring for an advance on Richmond, the Confederate capital in Virginia. They thought that by taking the South's capital city, the rebellion would be quelled and hostilities would come to a quick end. Yielding to pressure from the public and from political leadership, Brig. Gen. Irvin McDowell led his inexperienced Army across Bull Run (where the Fountainhead ride is located) toward Manassas. Their aim was to capture Manassas Junction, the pivotal railroad town next to Brentsville that would give the North an overland route to the South's capital.

The Southern Army met the "surprise" attack planned by the North with determination and conviction on July 21, 1861. Led by a relatively unknown officer from the Virginia Military Institute (VMI), Thomas Jackson, the Southern forces held their ground and helped lead the Northern forces back toward Washington, DC. It was in that first battle that Jackson earned his nickname, "Stonewall." Jackson's brigade suffered considerable casualties that day, but they stopped the Union's assault and helped drive it back. It was another officer in the Southern forces, Brig. Gen. Barnard Elliott Bee Jr., who uttered the words, "Look at Jackson standing there like a stone wall," that earned him and his brigade the nickname. It was also the first time that Union soldiers heard the "Rebel Yell." It was Jackson who instructed his troops to "yell like furies" when they advanced and charged the enemy.

Both the South and North suffered great casualties in the First Battle of Manassas, and both armies came to the realization that the war would be longer, more arduous, and brutal than they had ever anticipated. Nearly 5,000 men died in the battle, proving how difficult the war would be. Years later, more than half a million Union and Confederate soldiers would lose their lives in Civil War battles. The Second Battle of Manassas in late August 1862 was of greater scale. Over 100,000 men fought in the fields of Prince William County, and over 12,000 died, most from the Union. Ultimately the North prevailed, and today Manassas is simply a historic reminder of some of our nation's most tumultuous times. Brentsville suffered tremendously during the war. Battles raged at its footsteps and the small town never quite recovered from it. The few buildings that remain in the Brentsville historic site are a reminder of a painful past that has long been gone, but one that shaped the county, the state, and our nation as a whole.

MILES & DIRECTIONS

Brentsville loop:

0.0   The ride starts from the parking area behind the old Brentsville Courthouse. We'll start measuring from the spot where the courthouse driveway intersects Bristow Road. Turn right onto Bristow Road as you head out of the parking area. Use caution since there is traffic here.

Prince William Road Ride–Brentsville Loop

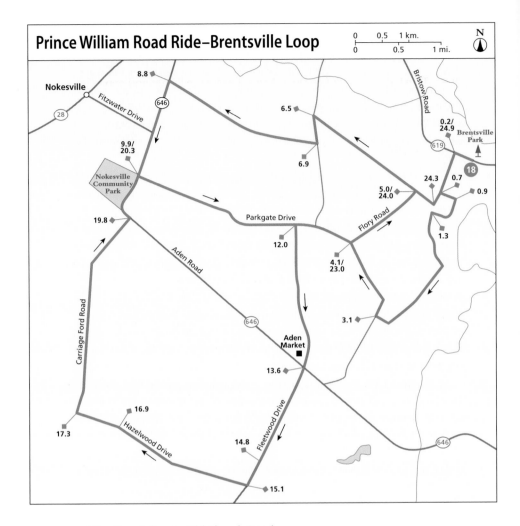

0.2 Turn left onto Old Church Road.

0.7 Turn left onto Oxford Court.

0.9 Turn right onto Oxfordshire Drive.

1.3 Turn left onto Old Church Road.

3.1 At the T intersection turn right onto Parkgate Road.

4.1 Turn right onto Flory Road.

5.0 Turn left onto Crockett Road.

6.5 Turn left onto Valley View Drive.

6.9 Turn right onto Colvin Lane.

8.8   Turn left onto Aden Road. Use caution and stay alert on Aden.

9.9   Turn left onto Parkgate Drive. Keep alert for the llamas and ponies on the left.

12.0   Turn right onto Fleetwood Drive.

13.6   Cross Aden Road. The Aden Grocery is at this intersection. Halfway mark of the ride.

14.8   Access to the Merrimac Wildlife Management area to the left, a property managed to provide opportunities for hunting, fishing, wildlife viewing, and outdoor education. Continue straight.

15.1   Turn right onto Hazelwood Drive.

15.7   "Snyder Farm," to your left offers an eclectic collection of garden sculptures to feast your eyes.

16.9   Evergreen Acres. If you're local, stop by around Christmastime to cut down your own tree.

17.3   Turn right onto Carriage Farm Road. The Prince William County Safety Training Complex will be up ahead to the left.

19.8   Turn left onto Aden Road. Nokesville Community Park is to the left. You can extend your ride by a mile or so if you ride into the park. Restrooms are available.

20.3   Turn right onto Parkgate Drive.

23.0   Turn left onto Flory Drive.

24.0   Turn right onto Crockett Road.

24.3   Turn left onto Old Church Road.

24.9   Turn right onto Bristow Road.

25.1   Turn left into the old Courthouse Drive to complete the loop.

Manassas loop:

Lots of people prefer doing this in a counterclockwise direction. Not me—I prefer the clockwise loop because you finish via some calm neighborhood paths and roads and some nice Lake Montclair views. I was not going to include this ride in the book originally, but I added it because it is one of the ones I do most often. It is literally out my front door. There's one of these in your neck of the woods, trust me; please find it and share it with me at www.bestridesdc.com.

18

0.0 Start at the Montclair Crossing Shopping center at the intersection of Waterway Drive and Route 234. Park close to the actual intersection; there is a sidewalk path by the bank. Ride or walk over to the crosswalk that will take you to the Route 234 Bike Path; begin calculating from there. Cross Route 234 and make a right onto the bike path.

6.9 Turn left onto Whitting Drive and make an immediate right onto Canova Drive to continue in the same direction as you were traveling on the path.

7.8 Canova ends. Pick up the path again and continue northwest.

9.4 Continue to the left on Olympic Drive.

9.7 Olympic ends. Pick up the path again and go over the bridge that spans the waterway. The dam is to your left.

10.0 Cross Coles Drive and continue following the path.

10.5 Cross Coles Drive again and continue riding on Plant Drive.

10.8 Continue right in front of Meadow Farms; the trail will pick up to the right. Continue following the path to the next light.

11.0 Reach the intersection of Route 234, Brentsville Road, and the Prince William Parkway. Turn right, cross Route 234, and continue on the Prince William Parkway.

13.2 Cross the Prince William Parkway to pick up the bike path on the opposite side and turn right.

20.5 Turn right to continue on Hoadly. There is a "sporadic" bike lane on Hoadly, but there is a wide shoulder to ride on as well.

23.0 Turn left onto Spriggs Road. There is a bike path you can use until you reach Lake Terrapin Drive.

26.6 Turn left onto Lake Terrapin and continue to the T intersection.

27.3 Turn right onto Leatherback Road and then make an immediate left onto the short connector path. This will put you on Tallowood Drive. Continue straight on Tallowood.

27.7 Turn left onto Spring Branch Boulevard.

28.1 Turn right onto Holleyside Drive.

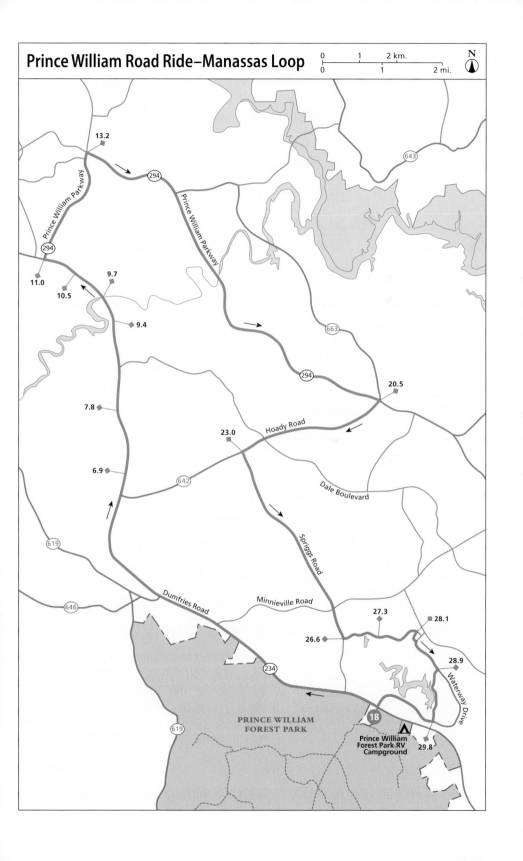

Prince William Road Ride–Manassas Loop

0   1   2 km.
0   1   2 mi.

N

13.2

643

294

Prince William Parkway

294

Prince William Parkway

11.0

9.7

10.5

9.4

663

294

20.5

7.8

Hoady Road

23.0

Dale Boulevard

6.9

642

619

Spriggs Road

646

Dumfries Road

Minnieville Road

27.3

28.1

26.6

28.9

Waterway Drive

234

619

PRINCE WILLIAM
FOREST PARK

18

Prince William
Forest Park RV
Campground

29.8

Those bikes belonged to a trespasser. Stay on this side of the fence.

28.2 Turn right onto Waterway. (Use caution when turning onto Waterway Drive since there is considerably more traffic than other portions of the ride.)

28.9 Turn right onto Golf Club Drive and follow it until it ends.

29.2 At the end of Golf Club, you'll see the entrance to the bike path. Follow the path over the dam and onto the Dolphin Beach parking area.

29.5 Continue straight through the parking area and through the entrance gate to get on Dolphin Drive.

29.8 Turn right onto Ashgrove and then make an immediate right onto Waterway Drive. Continue straight on Waterway.

31.0 As you reach the shopping center, make your way to the opposite side to pick up the sidewalk that will lead you to your car and to complete the loop.

RIDE INFORMATION

Local Events and Attractions
Prince William County: www.princewilliamcounty.com

Restaurants
Okra's Louisiana Bistro: 9110 Center St., Manassas, VA 20110; (703) 330-2729; www.okras.com
City Square Cafe (outdoor dining in season): 9428 Battle St., Manassas, VA 20110; (703) 369-6022; www.citysquarecafe.com
Lagniappe "on the bayou": 12635 Galveston Ct., Manassas, VA 20112; (703) 730-7774; lagniappeonthebayou.com. Tell them I sent you!
Brother's Encore and Pub: 5135 Waterway Dr., Dumfries, VA 22025; (703) 680-0032; www.brothersencore.com
Armetta's Italian Grill & Pizzeria: Staples Mill Plaza, Dale City, VA 22193; (703) 878-9977; www.armettasrestaurant.com

Restrooms
For the Brentsville loop there are restrooms in the Brentsville Courthouse Historic Center in the Site Offices Building and in Nokesville Community Park. For the Manassas loop there are several pit stops along the way, including a BP gas station at the corner of Route 234 and Hoadly Road, and an Exxon station at the corner of the Prince William Parkway and Liberia Avenue.

The CCT, North to South

This ride will take you on the Cross County Trail (CCT) from its northern terminus in Great Falls, Virginia, to its southern end at Occoquan Regional Park. Along the 40 miles we will travel past three other rides included in this book, making it possible to create a "mega" epic ride, should you have the legs for it.

The CCT includes a combination of singletrack, dirt, bike paths, gravel roads, and on-road surfaces and is best completed on a mountain bike or reliable cross bike. I generally ride it on a rigid mountain bike with "slicks." The trail is well marked with brown plastic pylons throughout its entirety, but there are certain intersections and points where it is not very obvious. Just follow the directions here and you should be fine. While on the trail, look for the distinguishable brown pylon CCT markers. If you don't see one, chances are you've veered off course. For the most part, all branches out of the CCT are feeder trails into the CCT.

Start: Difficult Run Parking Area, Great Falls

Length: 39 miles

Approximate riding time: 3–4 hours

Best bike: Mountain bike

Terrain and trail surface: Off-road trails, gravel and paved bike paths, and one section on street roads

Traffic and hazards: Trail obstacles, several creek crossings, and vehicular traffic in the road section

Things to see: The natural splendors of Fairfax County, the Lorton Prison and Penitentiary, the Occoquan

Getting there: From Maryland take I-495 south over the American Legion Bridge and take exit 44 onto Georgetown Pike, Route 193 toward Langley/Great Falls. The Difficult Run parking area will be to your left in approximately 3.7 miles. From Virginia take I-495 north to exit 44 and follow the same directions as above. GPS: 38.978311,-77.249293

Fees: None

THE RIDE

The Cross County Trail (CCT) is a unique achievement for Fairfax County. It is a trail nearly 40 miles in length that connects the county from one end to another. Along its path it links hills and valleys, streams and meadows and intersects urbanized landscapes and neighborhoods. Its very creation was a catalyst that united government agencies with citizen activists, environmental groups, trail enthusiasts, and private sector organizations, and has been serving as an example of what can be achieved regionally when everyone puts differences aside and works together toward a common goal.

The trail was conceived in the mid-1990s when Fairfax resident and hiking enthusiast Bill Niedringhaus approached the county with an idea to connect existing trails in an effort to create one long corridor from Great Falls to Occoquan Regional Park. Park staff was extremely busy back then, but they entertained Niedringhaus's idea. With support from the county, Niedringhaus and a few friends created the Fairfax Streams and Trails group and did considerable research on his proposal before presenting it to the County Board of Supervisors in 1998. Then-Chairman Gerry Connolly realized that Niedringhaus was

Bike Shops

The Bike Lane: 11943 Democracy Dr., Reston Town Center, Reston, VA 20190; www.thebikelane.com
Spokes Etc.: 10937 Lee Highway, Fairfax, VA 22030; (703) 591-2200; www.spokesetc.com

onto something great, so he presented a resolution to create the Cross County Trail, which the board unanimously approved. The county then sought and later received additional resources and federal support for the project.

Shortly thereafter, other groups became involved. The Mid-Atlantic Off-Road Enthusiasts (MORE) and the group Fairfax For Horses jumped in, and by early 2000 construction to connect several portions of the trail began. By December 2005 the entire route was mapped and completed, and today the CCT is a jewel in Fairfax County.

Much of the trail follows the stream valleys of Difficult Run and Accotink Creek. The northern portion of the system begins near Great Falls and follows the Difficult Run into the heart of Fairfax. Because the county has banned construction in floodplains, the trail offers a linear park that stretches for nearly 15 miles. Most of the traffic here is via off-road singletrack trails. As you reach the southern portion of the system, you'll have to ride on a short section of road before rejoining the trail. At this point the trail splits between natural surface and paved paths, yet it does not lose its character as it continues to follow streams en route to Occoquan.

You May Run into Pete Beers (@I_am_Dirt)

The day I met Pete my life changed, as I'm sure it has for everyone who has had the pleasure of meeting him. The guy is a human powered vehicle and is one of the very few people I know who practices what we all preach. "I live to show people that they can leave their car home," he told me. "I'm not a talker. I never have been. I never will be. I'd much rather let my legs do the talking." And he does. Pete rides his bike everywhere, to and from work, for errands, for fun, and even to haul things he used to tuck in the trunk of his car. He rides to our rides. When we all plan a 20-mile loop around a given park, Pete rides the 25 miles to get there, and then the 25 miles to get home. Last year alone he logged over 13,000 miles. Yes, you read that right, over 13,000 miles! In the process he spared us nearly 13,000 pounds of CO2. He's also active with Bike Arlington and has helped others find safe routes to and from work.

PHOTO COURTESY OF PETE BEERS

Pete's been riding nearly all of his life. "I started out when I was very young, and it was all downhill from there," he kidded with me the other day. "Seriously, I made a conscious choice. Cycling became a way for me to go places. When I was young and on my bike, I was free to go where I wanted. Even when I learned to drive, the bicycle was still a huge part of my life. I simply love to ride."

When it came time for me to write this book, Pete was the first person I reached out to because he knows this city and its suburbs like the back of his hand. He'd prefer the French Riviera he says, "but DC is a gold mine of great places to ride." And he's right. Pete really served as a consultant on this book for me, and for that I am extremely grateful. He was also a trusted and patient companion on many of the rides I detailed here, including this one.

I'm certain that you'll spot him on the trail one day. He's easy to find. He'll either be riding a bike with an enormously large front tire, or one that is entirely pink. Or he'll be riding for the glory of the motherland (Mexico) and while doing it, practicing his "danger panda" maneuver: taking self-portraits as he spins. When you do run into him, say hello, and ask him to tell you all about his Mexican National Team experience.

Along the way you can access several other parks and trail systems in the region. From the CCT you can access Wakefield Park (see Ride 12, Wakefield Park), Laurel Hill (see Ride 9, Laurel Hill), the W&OD, Lake Accotink, and with a little extra effort places like Fountainhead Regional Park, Burke Lake, Holmes Run (see Ride 6, The Alexandria Loop), and the Custis Trail (see Ride 8, The Arlington Beltway). This makes the CCT yet another valuable natural resource and a backbone trail from which to launch your very own cycling adventures.

MILES & DIRECTIONS

0.0 Start from the Difficult Run Parking Area in Great Falls, Virginia. Look for the CCT sign to the right of the lot as you drive in. Head southwest on the CCT.

0.6 Reach the first of many stream crossings along the CCT.

1.0 Stay to the right at this intersection to continue on the CCT.

1.3 Come out onto Leigh Mill Road. The CCT continues to your right shortly before the bridge that crosses over Difficult Run.

1.7 You have a couple of options here. Stay on the bridle path as it circles to the right or climb up on the singletrack. We will climb up over a series of short and steep switchbacks to the left. When you come up on the road, turn left and as you reach the small cul-de-sac, look for the trailhead to the right.

1.9 Turn left onto the doubletrack. If we had stayed to the right at the previous marker, this is where we would have ended up.

2.0 Stream crossing number 2.

2.5 The trail comes out into a small parking area and continues on a paved road. Continue on the paved road until you reach Colvin Run Road. Turn left and cross Leesburg Pike (Route 7) at mile marker 2.7 and then turn left onto the clearly marked CCT shortly after you cross Route 7.

3.0 Stay to the right to continue on the CCT.

3.8 Reach Browns Mill Road. You can cross Browns Mill and then turn immediately left to cross the Difficult Run River or turn left and then pick up the CCT to the right. I will skip the river crossing and turn left and then right onto the CCT. The CCT is now paved.

3.9 Turn right at this intersection to continue on the CCT.

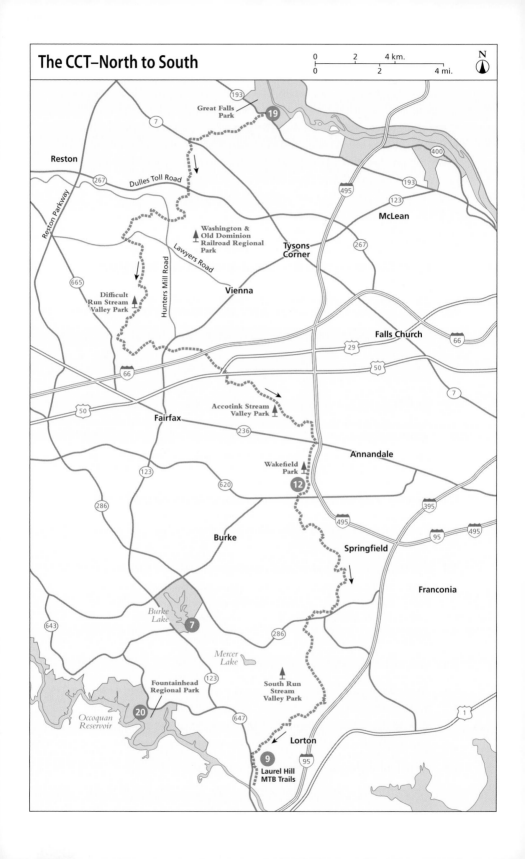

The CCT–North to South

0	2	4 km.
0	2	4 mi.

N

19 Great Falls Park

7

Reston

267 Dulles Toll Road

Reston Parkway

665

665

Hunters Mill Road

Lawyers Road

▲ Washington & Old Dominion Railroad Regional Park

▲ Difficult Run Stream Valley Park

Vienna

193

400

495

193

123

McLean

267

Tysons Corner

29 **Falls Church**

66

66

50

7

50

Fairfax

236

▲ Accotink Stream Valley Park

Annandale

123

620

▲ Wakefield Park **12**

395

286

Burke

495

95 495

Springfield

Franconia

643

Burke Lake **7**

286

Mercer Lake

Fountainhead Regional Park

123

▲ South Run Stream Valley Park

647

Occoquan Reservoir **20**

Lorton

1

9 Laurel Hill MTB Trails

95

4.3 Turn right onto the gravel path to continue on the CCT. The left fork is a feeder trail.

4.4 Ride under the Dulles Toll Road.

4.7 Stay to the right to go over the bridge and continue on the CCT.

4.9 Turn left to go over another bridge; then turn right. Continue to follow the "worn" trail.

5.9 Continue to the left as you come out on the field.

6.0 After leaving the field and crossing a small bridge, turn left onto the gravel path and then onto the singletrack.

6.1 Stay right at this T intersection. You are now on the W&OD, affectionately known as the "WOD" trail.

6.3 Use caution when crossing Hunter Mill Road.

6.9 Turn left onto the CCT. This intersection is easy to miss since you will be heading down fast on the W&OD. Don't hang out on the WOD at this intersection since riders from the opposite side of the WOD will be barreling down in your direction and could easily crash into you.

7.1 Turn right and head over the small wood bridge. (At the time of this writing this entire section was under significant construction and this area may be considerably different than what you are reading. It is safe to say, however, that the trail will be clearly marked and in better shape since the construction is a trail improvement project.)

7.5 Stay left and then right to continue on the CCT.

7.9 Reach Twin Branches Road. Cross the road and turn left to pick up the CCT on the other side. This section of the trail is called "The Turquoise Trail." As you enter the trail stay to the right.

8.5 After crossing the bridge, turn left at the T intersection.

8.6 Stay right at this intersection to continue on the CCT.

8.7 Cross Lawyers Road and continue on the CCT to the right. Then after a short steep gully continue to the left.

9.2 The trail continues to the right on the other side of the creek (Little Difficult Run).

9.5 The trail will descend to the right and then switchback to the left. At the bottom turn right to follow the CCT marker.

10.0 Cross this intersection and continue following the wood fence line to the right.

10.6 Cross Vale Road and turn left onto the CCT as it parallels Vale Road.

10.9 Turn right to continue on the CCT.

11.0 Cross the Rocky Branch and continue straight.

11.1 Cross a small bridge and stay to the right.

12.2 Turn right at this T intersection to continue on the CCT.

12.9 Turn right at this intersection to continue on the CCT.

13.0 Stay to the left after a short singletrack downhill and then cross the next intersection.

13.3 Power up a short steep climb and come out onto Miller Heights Road. Turn right onto Miller Heights Road.

13.6 The entrance to the CCT is clearly marked with a crosswalk and a trail marker. Turn left onto the trail.

14.1 Follow the Oak Marr Golf Course fence line to the right.

14.7 Turn right onto the paved CCT and continue following the golf course fence line. The CCT is paved again. At this point all of the singletrack portions of the ride are behind us. From now on we ride on the road (3.2 miles and on a combination of paved and doubletrack gravel paths).

14.9 Turn left onto Jermantown Road and follow the trail along the sidewalk for a short distance. At the corner of Elmendorf Road, cross Jermantown and continue in the same direction on Jermantown Road. Jermantown becomes Blake at mile 16.2 and then Picket after crossing Fairfax Boulevard.

15.3 Cross Chain Bridge Road.

16.6 Cross Route 66.

17.3 7-Eleven to the left—perfect place to replenish and get some water.

17.6 Cross Fairfax/Arlington Boulevard.

17.9 Turn left into Pickett Park and then left into the parking lot. The CCT picks up at the far right corner on the backside of a small baseball field. Turn right onto the CCT. We will now follow the trail as it paral-

The CCT can be a busy place on weekends; still, there's plenty of it to go around.

lels and crosses Accotink Creek for virtually 20 miles, along the way riding past Lake Accotink.

18.6 Turn right onto the gravel doubletrack to continue on the CCT.

19.0 Cross Barkley Drive and enter Sally Ormsby Park.

19.5 Cross Prosperity Avenue.

19.8 Stay to the right at this intersection. The path is now paved.

20.3 Cross Woodburn Road. Make a quick right into the CCT and then a quick left to continue on the CCT.

21.2 Stay right at this intersection.

21.4 The CCT curves over to the right. You can start to hear the Capital Beltway traffic. This section of the CCT will run near the nation's busiest thoroughfare.

22.1 The trail comes out from the Little River Turnpike Beltway under-passes under a set of power lines. Continue following the trail to the left as it curves around the outfield of the baseball field to the left. When it reaches the pavement, turn left to head into the tree cover.

22.4 As the road curves to the right, the CCT picks up straight ahead.

22.6 Continue following the trail to the right to cross the creek, and then immediately after crossing the creek turn to the left.

22.8 Turn left to go over a bridge and then right immediately after you cross it. You are now in Wakefield Park (see Ride 12, Wakefield Park).

22.9 You have the option of continuing straight at this intersection to remain on the CCT or following the path to the left toward the Audrey Moore Rec Center. I'll take you that way since there is water and restrooms available in case you need them.

23.1 After turning left, follow the trail to the right as it follows the edge of the tennis courts. Come out into the parking area and head straight to the rec center beyond the skate park to the right. When you reach the rec center, continue following the parking area to the left and pick up the CCT again at the far end. Turn right onto the CCT at mile marker 23.6. After turning right you'll go over a small bridge. To the left is the Wakefield area commonly known as "The Bowl," a small playground of intertwined singletrack trails. Continue on the double-track and come out into the athletic fields parking area. The trail picks up at the opposite far corner of the parking lot to the right.

23.9 Enter the CCT and go over the small arched bridge and continue following the paved path to the right.

24.1 Stay to the left and then to the right to go under Braddock Road.

24.6 Continue straight at this intersection and follow the signs to the Lake Accotink Marina. You are now on the Lake Accotink Trail.

25.7 Stay to the right at this intersection.

26.3 Pass the marina and turn right onto the road and head toward the dam and the railroad overpass.

26.5 The road will curve to the left and head under the railroad viaduct. Follow it into the parking area to the right; the CCT continues at the far end to the right.

28.0 Continue following the CCT to the right. You'll pass several baseball fields to the left.

28.5 Ride under Old Keene Mill Road. The trail turns to gravel.

28.7 Continue following the trail to the left.

29.5 Continue straight past two intersections and on the third one follow the path to the right up a steep climb to Hunter Village Road. Cross Hunter Village and continue in the same general direction on the path along the road.

30.2 As Hunter Village Drive curves to the right you'll reach a crosswalk; use it to cross the road. Climb up the ramp and cross Rolling Road. Immediately after crossing turn right and ride along the sidewalk that parallels Rolling Road for a short distance.

30.4 Turn left onto the CCT. You'll be riding along the backside of some town houses.

30.6 Turn right along the Fairfax County Parkway.

30.8 At the light, turn left to cross the Fairfax County Parkway and then right onto Hooes Road immediately after you cross.

30.9 Turn left onto the CCT. Thankfully it is right before the ominous climb you see up ahead.

31.1 The trail will turn sharply to the right.

31.2 After crossing the creek, turn left and up to continue on the CCT.

31.3 After a steep climb follow the trail to the left.

31.5 Stay left at this intersection, go over the small bridge, and continue following the Pohick Creek. You'll now ride parallel to and cross Pohick Creek several times before we finish.

32.8 After a short creek crossing, turn right and then go through the creek again. You'll see a house up high to the right as you ride under the power lines. Continue straight through the next intersection.

33.1 Cross the creek again. This crossing seems to be the deepest of all of the ones we've encountered thus far.

33.3 Continue straight following the creek.

33.9 Shortly before you reach the underpass for Pohick Road, turn left and shoot straight up to continue on the CCT. Once you reach Pohick Road, turn right to go over the overpass. The CCT will now parallel Pohick Road for a short distance.

34.1 Turn left to cross Pohick Road. Then, immediately after crossing, turn left again to stay on the CCT. The trail will actually follow the sidewalk as it heads toward Creekside View Lane.

34.2 Turn right to continue on the CCT.

34.4 Continue to the left.

35.1 Cross Bluebonnet Drive and then turn right at the T intersection to cross Laurel Crest Drive.

35.4 Cross Paper Birch Drive and hop onto White Spruce Way to cross over Silverbrook Road. You can now see the old Lorton Penitentiary up ahead. After you cross Silverbrook Road, continue straight toward Lorton's "other" gated community, Spring Hill. The trail entrance is to the left as you reach the community gates.

35.5 Enter the CCT again and follow it as it circles the old penitentiary to the left.

36.0 Stay to the left and continue following the perimeter of the penitentiary. As you reach the last tower, veer right to continue on the CCT. The trail is marked with paint on the pavement and continues down the hill to the left. (Ride 9, Laurel Hill, begins on the parking area to the left.)

36.4 Continue straight and go over the bridge that spans Giles Run. After crossing the bridge, you'll see the Giles Run Meadow Trail trailhead to the left.

36.6 Stay left at this intersection.

36.8 The Barret House parking area is to the right. Continue straight under the arched bridge.

37.0 Turn left onto the road and head down to the stop sign to cross Lorton Road. Use caution at this intersection. The CCT continues on the other side of the road. Immediately after crossing the road, stay to the right. To the left is the entrance to the Laurel Hill trails. Continue following the trail southwest as it parallels Lorton Road until you reach OX Road (Route 123).

37.5 Turn left onto Route 123. The Lorton Workhouse Arts Center will be to your left.

37.9 Turn left to enter the Occoquan Regional Park. The CCT runs parallel to the road shortly after you enter the park. Follow it to the bottom.

39.0 The ride is complete.

RIDE INFORMATION

Local Events and Attractions
The CCT bisects Fairfax County from north to south, beginning at Great Falls and ending in Occoquan Regional Park.

Great Falls Park – Falls Walk: A great way to learn about Great Falls from the Rangers at **Great Falls Park:** Visit www.nps.gov/grfa for additional information and event schedules

Local Fairfax County events: www.fairfaxcounty.gov

Lorton Workhouse Arts Center: www.lortonarts.org/calendar.php

Historic Occoquan: www.occoquan.org

Restaurants
Cock & Bowl: 302 Poplar Alley, Occoquan, VA 22125; (703) 494-1180; www.cockandbowl.com

Restrooms
Available at Occoquan Regional Park, Lake Accotink Park, Wakefield Park, Oak Marr Park, Colvin Run Mill Park, and Great Falls National Park. Portable restrooms are available seasonally at Byron Avenue Park, Eakin Community Park, and Thaiss Park.

This is a shuttle ride, unless you really want to make it an out-and-back and double the distance. A couple of things to confirm before you start: have plenty of water and make absolutely sure that each driver in the shuttle chain has their respective vehicle keys—trust me on this one.

Fountainhead Regional Park

This ride will take you through one of the region's most successful off-road cycling projects. Originally conceived by a band of riders from MORE in early 1994, and redesigned with the International Mountain Biking Organization (IMBA) in 2010–12, the new Fountainhead trail is challenging, fun, and an incredibly rewarding system of trails. The once straight and steep climbs and downhills that crossed the park have been replaced with challenging switchbacks and screaming berms. Fountainhead is a glorious playground in which to take your mountain biking skills to the next level.

Fountainhead Regional Park is an easy trail to follow. As part of the new design, the trail has been adequately marked, and all intersections are clear and easy to understand. The trail is unidirectional to avoid any collisions and is mountain bike specific, so you will be unlikely to run into any other trail users. Do watch your speed though, and ride within your abilities.

Fountainhead is also a closely monitored trail. When conditions are not favorable for riding, the trail gates are closed and access to the system is denied. Do not bypass the gates; if the trail is closed, please respect the closure and come back another day. Bypassing the gates only threatens access to other users. I highly recommend you check the Fountainhead Project Facebook page (www.facebook .com/thefountainheadproject) for daily updates on trail conditions and closures. You can also call the Fountainhead ride line (703-250-9124) to make sure the trail is open before you head out.

Start: Fountainhead Regional Park parking area, mountain bike trail entrance

Length: 8.2 miles

Approximate riding time: 1.5–3 hours

Best bike: Mountain bike

Terrain and trail surface: Singletrack dirt trails built specifically for mountain biking. Fast and technical with various trail features and man-made obstacles, including berms, ledges, and drop-offs.

Traffic and hazards: Trail obstacles and other users; Fountainhead is a mountain bike specific trail

Things to see: Historic Occoquan, Historic Clifton

Getting there: From the Capital Beltway (I-495), take exit 54 for Braddock Road W. Continue on Braddock Road for approximately 1.5 miles and turn left onto Burke Lake Road. Turn left onto OX Road, VA 123. Turn right onto Henderson Road, VA 643, and then left onto Hampton Road, VA 647. The park entrance will be approximately 1.5 miles to the left. GPS: 38.724367,-77.330382

Fees: None

THE RIDE

When I included Fountainhead Regional Park in my first book, I wrote, "The Fountainhead Regional Park Mountain Bike Trail was opened in the spring of 1997. Before then, bicycles were not permitted on any of the trails within the park. The Fountainhead Regional Park Mountain Bike Trail represents an important opportunity and major breakthrough in the Washington metropolitan area. It was planned by the Northern Virginia Regional Park Authority (NVRPA) in close collaboration with the Mid-Atlantic Off-Road Enthusiasts (MORE) and initially funded, in large part, by REI (Recreational Equipment, Incorporated). This flagship mountain bike trail project was designed specifically for mountain bikers and will serve as a real litmus test for other park officials who are interested in constructing and maintaining mountain-bike-specific trail ways at their parks."

Suffice to say; I think the litmus test proved to be a success. Since it was opened, the trails at Fountainhead have evolved considerably, and after a period of transformation are better than ever. The original loop, which was roughly around 4.5 miles, has nearly doubled in length, and the trails are far better than what was originally laid out. Today, with the help of the International Mounting Biking Association (IMBA) and careful planning, the trails

> ## Bike Shops
>
> **The Bike Lane:** 8416 Old Keene Mill Rd., Springfield, VA 22152; (703) 440-8701; www.thebikelane.com
> **Olde Town Bicycles:** 14477 Potomac Mills Rd., Woodbridge, VA 22192; (703) 491-5700; www.oldetowne bicycles.com
> **Village Skis & Bikes:** 12383 Dillingham Sq., Woodbridge, VA 22192; (703) 730-0303; www.vsbsports.com

You May Run into Larry (My Other Brother) Cautilli

Larry's quest for fitness led him to buy a bike in early 1985. Then, a few years later he added another, a mountain bike. It was with that mountain bike that Larry began racking up the miles. "It became an addiction," Larry said. "The more I rode, the more I wanted to ride. I really can't pinpoint what one thing I love about cycling, but if I had to, it is just being on the bike."

PHOTO COURTESY LARRY CAUTILLI

That fix to just "be on the bike" has become our benefit. In early 1996 when MORE was beginning to work on the first loops at Fountainhead, Larry used most of his 200 hours of "use or lose" leave to manually work on the trails. Over the years he has seen the loops evolve. Most recently, due in large part to Larry's dedication, the trails at Fountainhead have been transformed into a regional mountain biking destination.

Larry loves to ride Gambrill State Park in Frederick and the Frederick Watershed, but you'll undoubtedly find him spinning the trails at Wakefield and now, more than ever, over the fruits of his efforts at Fountainhead. If you see him, say hello and make sure you thank him for a job well done; he certainly deserves it.

are an off-road cyclist's dream. Tight switchbacks, rock outcroppings, banked turns, and fast descents are but a few of the features that have been recently incorporated into the improved trail design. Drainage issues and a variety of troublesome erosion problems have been addressed, and the entrance and exit to the trail have been divided so that there is no longer a "two-way" traffic trail. The entire loop continues to be a directional loop, which ensures that you'll never run into a rider going in the opposite direction; this makes riding the new downhill and banked turns extremely fun.

Additional improvements have also been made at key intersections. Additionally, a new boardwalk and bridge leads riders to a new exit trail, and midway through the ride you can hang out and play around in a technical section that was designed to improve your handling skills.

Initially there was a little bit of an uproar when announcements were made that Fountainhead would receive a face-lift. Some riders felt that the goal of the New Fountainhead Project was to "dumb down" the trails and take away its challenging sections. On the contrary, the new Fountainhead continues to be a challenging trail that has been made longer. Of particular pride to me is that the original name of Shock-a-Billy Hill has been retained. Back during the first Fountainhead project, one of the sponsors for the trail was FAT City Cycles, a custom frame builder from Massachusetts, and makers of one of my first "real" mountain bikes. My relationship with Chris Chance and his company helped us secure a Shock-a-Billy frameset to raffle off during one of several events promoted by MORE in support of the project. Having that prize helped MORE to raise the funds necessary for the project. In exchange, my friend Valerie Dosland, and a MORE board member, suggested to FAT that we would name one of the trails after their bike. They agreed to the deal, so we coined the steepest part of the trail (at the time) Shock-a-Billy Hill. As you close out the ride, you'll come to an intersection giving you the option of riding old Shock-a-Billy (SOB) or the new improved version (SAB).

Before heading out to Fountainhead, I highly suggest you check the trail's status. Despite its excellent design, and all precautions made to ensure it remains sustainable, Fountainhead is often closed due to wet or muddy conditions or, as it happened recently during a rather severe storm, for downed trees along the path. Park managers and project leads have set up a Facebook page (www.facebook.com/thefountainheadproject) where they promptly post trail conditions, and a ride line (703-250-9124) is also available to obtain more information.

Fountainhead continues to be a showpiece for the Mid-Atlantic region. From its early ambitious beginning to its successful redesign, Fountainhead is certainly bound to bring a smile to your face.

MILES & DIRECTIONS

0.0 Enter the trail system through the main trail gate and get ready for a quick taste of what the next 8 miles will be like.

1.2 Stay to the left to go on the Blue Trail and to continue to the remaining loops. The Green Trail is the exit trail. If you feel you are in over your head, follow the Green Trail over the bridge and back to the parking area.

1.8 This is an easy/difficult split. The trail to the right has a trail feature with a steep exit; to the left is an easier path. Both trails connect less than 100 yards ahead.

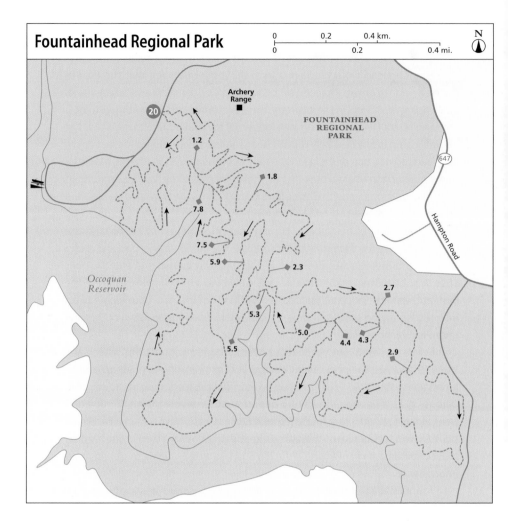

Fountainhead Regional Park

0   0.2   0.4 km.
0   0.2   0.4 mi.

N

Archery Range

FOUNTAINHEAD REGIONAL PARK

20

1.2

1.8

7.8

7.5

5.9

2.3

2.7

Occoquan Reservoir

5.3

5.0

4.4   4.3

5.5

2.9

647

Hampton Road

2.3   Arrive back to the picnic tables. The trail continues to the left. You can use this point as a bail-out point by following the trail to the right of the picnic tables. Both paths are clearly marked. This was the original location of Fountainhead's "skills area." The only thing that remains from that is a long skinny log you can practice your balance on. Continue to the left to join the black loop.

2.7   You reach one of Fountainhead's "bypass points." You can continue to the left or bail out to the right.

2.9   Bypass point.

4.3   Stay to the left.

4.4   Bypass point. Over to the left is my personal favorite section of Fountainhead.

A rider enjoys the new trails at Fountainhead.

5.0 Stay to the left.

5.3 Back at the picnic tables, continue to the left, following the signs to the parking lot.

5.5 Stay to the right to remain on the main loop. You can bypass the next section to the left.

5.9 You've reached the new "features area" of Fountainhead. You can bypass this by following the trail to the left, or hang out and play.

7.5 Stay left to follow the new Shock-a-Billy (SAB) Hill. To the right is old Shock-a-Billy (SOB). The left fork is longer and more fun. I suspect that in the future SOB will be closed to avoid erosion issues.

7.8 Stay to the left at the bottom of SAB and ride over the boardwalk that will take you over the new exit bridge and trail.

8.2 The loop is complete.

RIDE INFORMATION

Local Events and Attractions
Historic Occoquan: www.occoquan.org
Historic Clifton: www.clifton-va.com

Restaurants
Cock & Bowl: 302 Poplar Alley, Occoquan, VA 22125; (703) 494-1180; www.cockandbowl.com

The Main Street Pub: 7140 Main St., Historic Clifton, VA 20124; (703) 266-6307; www.themainstreetpub.net

Glory Days Grill: 9526 Old Keene Mill Rd., Burke, VA 22015; (703) 866-1911; www.glorydaysgrill.com

Restrooms
Restrooms are available adjacent to the main Fountainhead parking area.

Fairland

Nestled along the border of Montgomery County and Prince George's County is this little gem of a park. One of the rides will meander through a unique and diverse ecosystem, while the other will take you around one of Maryland's most controversial and newest highway projects, the Inter County Connector (ICC).

Start: Parking lot adjacent to soccer field #5—*not* the main parking area

Length: Off-road loop 6.6 miles, road loop 6.4 miles

Approximate riding time: 1–2 hours

Best bike: Mountain bike for the off-road loop, any bike for the road loop

Terrain and trail surface: Mostly singletrack trails on the off-road loop, all paved paths on the road loop

Traffic and hazards: Natural obstacles on the off-road loop, other trail users. Minor traffic issues on the road loop. Use caution at road intersections and crossings.

Things to see: Local neighborhoods, the new ICC, wildlife along the small lake

Getting there: From the Capital Beltway (I-495) take I-95 north to exit 33B and merge onto MD 198 west toward Burtonsville. Continue for 1.4 miles and turn left onto Old Gunpowder Road. After 2 miles turn right onto Greencastle Road and then right again onto Chelsea Park Lane. Enter the first parking area to your right and head toward field #5. GPS: 39.082006,-76.929515

Fees: None

THE RIDE

It's hard to believe how far Fairland has come since I first laid knobby wheels on it in the mid '90s. My wife and I were fresh out of the Army and had just

You May Run into Austin Steo, www.trailconservancy.org

I first met Austin back in the mid 1990s. Our good friend Dan Hudson (now with the International Mountain Biking Association—IMBA) thought it would be a good idea for us to meet, especially since the trails at Fairland Regional Park were in need of some help. I remember riding with Austin through Fairland and him always envisioning how the trail would work best. "This section should be routed over there," he used to say. Or, "This creek crossing would be better if . . . " Austin was always envisioning a "better" way for the trail to flow. That vision and all of his hard work eventually led him to spearhead the effort to create the network of trails highlighted on this ride. To this day Austin continues to be involved with Fairland in some capacity, but now has his hand in other projects as well. "While driving to Cedarville State Park to meet some friends for a ride, I noticed a gated, underused park," he once told me. "I later explored it and saw a huge potential for trails. At that time I had just joined the MORE board and went down the long path of initiating a new trail system. Now when I see a full parking lot at Rosaryville State Park (see Ride 31), it brings a smile to my face." His love for mountain biking has even taken him further, and now Austin is the executive director of the Trail Conservancy (www .trailconservancy.org), a nonprofit organization whose mission is to provide assistance in developing, building, and maintaining natural-surface trails using sustainable design principles. He's still hard at work and involved in several other trail building projects in the region, including a project in Emmitsburg, Maryland (see Ride 23, Frederick Road Ride), as well as other trails in Montgomery County. If you do run into Austin, say hi, and ask him how he would have built that particular section of trail up ahead.

PHOTO COURTESEY AUSTIN STEO

bought a home in Burtonsville, Maryland. I generally packed the gear and bike and headed north to Patapsco Valley State Park for my regular mountain bike dosages, but more often than not time kept me from making the trip. So one day I ventured out of the house in search of suburban trail opportunities. A quick glance at an area map showed that Fairland Regional Park was just around the corner, so I headed out to explore. Back then there was a network of trails that crossed the park, nothing to write home about, but at least there were trails. For the most part, they followed the grade and were often in pretty bad shape. There were also some other trails nearby, which unfortunately were graded over by the construction of the Inter County Connector road project. That said, the park was so close to the house, and the trailhead was just a stone's throw away, that I didn't complain. Plus, bikes were allowed, which was a luxury back in those days.

Roughly at the same time that I moved to Burtonsville I was introduced to my friend Austin Steo. Austin lived opposite from me on the other side of Fairland, and we would often meet somewhere in the middle to spin our bikes through the woods. Back then I had just finished my first book and was heavily involved with the Mid-Atlantic Off-Road Enthusiasts (MORE), a local mountain bike social and advocacy group that has grown to become a force in our region, as well as one of the most successful IMBA-affiliated clubs in the states. It was during those rides that Austin and I (well, mostly Austin) talked about the potential Fairland offered, and how the trails could be rerouted and rebuilt to make them much more fun. On several occasions we left the bikes at home and simply walked through the woods, envisioning what the place "could" become.

Bike Shops

Laurel Bicycle Center: 14805 Baltimore Ave., Laurel, MD 20707; (301) 490-7744; www.bicyclefun.com
REI: 9801 Rhode Island Ave., College Park, MD 20740; (301) 982-9681; www.rei.com

Austin acted on all those brainstorming sessions and reconnaissance outings, and as I phased out from MORE, he phased in. Austin became the club's Maryland Advocacy Director. That's when he began working with the Fairland Park managers on a plan to improve the trails and overall riding experience within the park. Slowly but surely he cut and built the ribbon that now exists in the park. With the help of Austin's volunteer army—and the backing of MORE—the trails at Fairland were transformed from just a few "unplanned" miles to a fun and twisty network consisting of nearly 8 miles of trails. His job hasn't ended there though; today there are additional plans to add even more singletrack to the system, and chances are that by the time you read this chapter there will be a few additional miles of freshly cut ribbon at Fairland.

Fairland is not all dirt though. The park is a very unique destination since it is the only bi-county (Montgomery and Prince George's) park in the Maryland National Capitol Park and Planning Commission. The majority of the land on the Montgomery County side of the park remains undeveloped, and it's where the majority of the off-road trails are. On the Prince George's County side, there is an extensive athletic complex that includes an aquatic and sports center, several athletic fields, and playgrounds. Next to it there is a privately owned ice skating rink, the Gardens Ice House. The Prince George's County side also has a small pond and a series of paved bike paths that connect with the Montgomery County side. Ride 2, The Capital Crescent Trail and Rock Creek Park, makes use of these paths and also takes us past some newly built bike routes along the Inter County Connector (ICC), one of the region's most controversial highway projects. Proponents of the ICC argued that construction of the highway, which connects Gaithersburg in Montgomery County and Laurel in Prince George's County, would improve traffic flow. Opponents, on the other hand, argued that building the connector would not improve traffic dramatically and in turn would damage the environment and disrupt established communities along its path. Ultimately supporters of the project won the battle and the ICC was built, partially adjacent to this ride.

Fairland is a relatively "unknown" park when it comes to being a cycling destination, but these new trails—along with those slated to be built in the near future—will certainly put it on the map. I predict this park will evolve to become yet another valuable biking destination for the region.

MILES & DIRECTIONS

Most riders generally start at the main lot by the restrooms, but that parking lot generally gets crowded, so we'll go to the opposite end of the park by the soccer field (#5).

MTB loop:

0.0 Head down the paved trail toward the softball field. Stay to the left at the first intersection so the field is on your right.

0.1 Notice the singletrack to the right, you'll ride that . . .

0.4 Stay to the left at this intersection.

0.5 Turn right onto the short connector trail across from the main paved trail bench and then immediately right onto the main singletrack trail. You will be heading back in the direction you started from, but now on the dirt path.

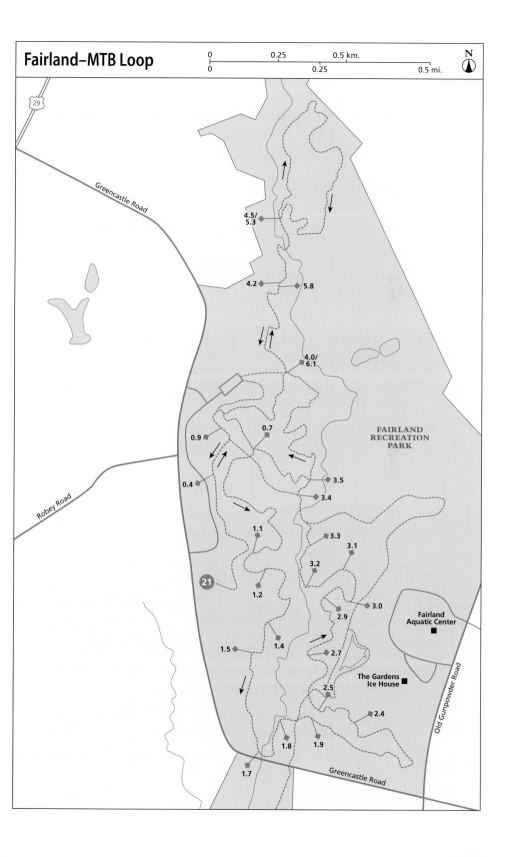

Fairland–MTB Loop

0   0.25   0.5 km.

0   0.25   0.5 mi.

N

US 29

Greencastle Road

4.5/
5.3

4.2   5.8

4.0/
6.1

0.9   0.7

0.4

3.5

3.4

1.1

3.3

3.1

3.2

1.2

3.0

2.9

Fairland
Aquatic Center

21

1.5   1.4

2.7

2.5

The Gardens
Ice House

2.4

1.8   1.9

1.7

Greencastle Road

Robey Road

Old Gunpowder Road

FAIRLAND
RECREATION
PARK

0.7 Turn right at this intersection to follow the Crows Foot Trail and cross over the paved path.

1.1 Continue following the trail to the left. The paved path is to the right. This is the spot noted on marker 0.1.

1.2 Continue straight at this trail intersection.

1.4 Continue to the left; the trail to the right heads up to the softball field near the start of our ride.

1.5 Ride over the wooden boardwalk and continue straight on the trail beyond.

1.7 Turn left onto Greencastle Road then make an immediate left back onto the trail.

1.8 Stay to the right at this intersection.

1.9 Continue on the singletrack trail over the paved path and the subsequent fire road.

2.4 Continue to the left at this intersection and continue following the trail as it curves away from the paved path.

2.5 Continue straight and then over the paved path.

2.7 Stay to the right at this intersection.

2.9 Stay to the right at the next two intersections.

3.0 Turn left at this intersection.

3.1 Stay left after crossing the small wood bridge, and then straight at the next intersection.

3.2 Turn right and ride parallel to the stream on your left.

3.3 Continue following the stream to the left and then turn left onto the paved trail to go over the wood bridge.

3.4 Immediately after crossing the bridge, take a right onto the dirt trail.

3.5 Continue to the right at this intersection and then immediately bear to the left to go over another small wood bridge.

4.0 Turn right at this intersection and follow the light blue blazes of the Holly Trail—the trail will bear slightly to the left.

The Holly Trail will test your root handling abilities.

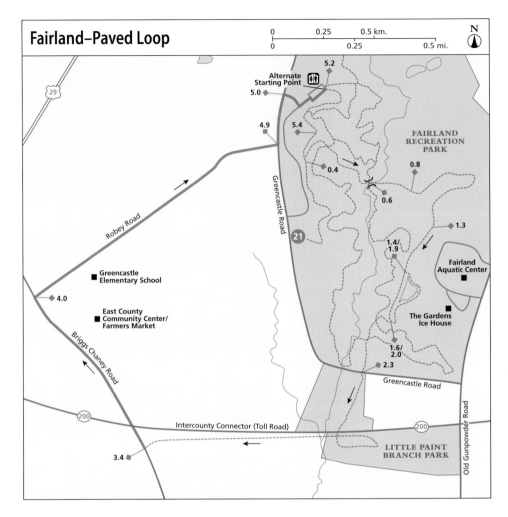

Fairland–Paved Loop

0   0.25   0.5 km.

0   0.25   0.5 mi.

N

Alternate Starting Point

FAIRLAND RECREATION PARK

Greencastle Road

Robey Road

Greencastle Elementary School

East County Community Center/ Farmers Market

Briggs Chaney Road

Fairland Aquatic Center

The Gardens Ice House

Greencastle Road

Intercounty Connector (Toll Road)

LITTLE PAINT BRANCH PARK

Old Gunpowder Road

4.2 After a short climb follow the fork to the right and descend straight and down to a tight right-hand berm turn and a stream crossing. Cross the stream and follow the trail up to the left past some ruins.

4.5 Reach the entrance to the Holly Trail loop. You can go either direction here, but I prefer the clockwise loop. You'll have a short steeper climb at the beginning and a more enjoyable downhill on the backside. This section has several feeder trails, so just make sure you follow the light blue blazes.

5.3 You're back at the entrance of the Holly Trail loop. Turn left to return to the creek and backtrack your way to the park. Continue following the light blue blazes.

5.8 Continue straight to the intersection of Holly Trail with Crows Foot Trail. You can also turn left at this point and ride the loop again in the opposite direction.

6.1 Turn right and head to the paved trail and then turn left onto the paved path. This is basically the same spot where we started our off-road portion of the ride. Continue on the paved path back to your vehicle.

6.6 Complete the loop.

Paved loop:

0.0 Head down the paved trail toward the softball field. Stay to the left at the first intersection so the field is on your right.

0.4 Turn right to continue on the paved path; watch your speed as you head down toward the bridge.

0.6 Continue over the wood bridge.

0.8 Welcome to Prince George's County!

1.3 Continue straight past this small community center bridge.

1.4 Continue straight; we will circle the pond to the left and double back on the same path again.

1.6 Turn left and circle the pond. The pond is generally busy with animal activity. Don't be surprised if you see groundhogs, ducks, and other wildlife.

1.9 Turn left after going over the bridge and ride over the same section of path you just rode.

2.0 Turn right.

2.3 Carefully cross over Greencastle Road.

2.6 Turn left to go toward Briggs Channey Road. The gate is generally closed but unlocked; pull to open it and then close it. You are now riding along one of Maryland's newest roads and the source of years of controversy for this area: the Inter County Connector.

3.4 Turn right onto Briggs Channey Road and continue riding on the sidewalk until you reach Robey Road.

4.0 Cross Robey Road and turn right on the bike path that runs along it. Stay on Robey until you reach Greencastle Road.

4.9 Turn left onto Greencastle Road. Alternatively you can cross straight into Fairland Park and then right to head back toward your vehicle.

5.0 Turn right into the main entrance for Fairland Regional Park and then turn left at the stop sign. Continue into the main parking area to the right. The paved trail picks up again at the far end of the parking lot to the right of the restrooms.

5.2 Enter the paved trail (Little Branch Trail) and follow it to the right. The main entrance to the off-road loops will be to your left.

5.4 Stay to the right and follow the path back to your vehicle.

6.0 Complete the loop.

RIDE INFORMATION

Local Events and Attractions
Briggs Channey-Greencastle Farmers and Artisans' Market: www.bcg market.org
Dutch Country Farmers Market: www.burtonsvilledutchmarket.com

Restaurants
Old Hickory Grille: 15420 Old Columbia Pike, Burtonsville, MD 20866; (301) 421-0204; www.oldhickorygrille.com
Pasta Plus: 209 Gorman Ave., Laurel, MD 20707; (301) 498-5100; www.pasta plusrestaurant.com

Restrooms
Restrooms are available in the main parking lot on the Montgomery County side of the park and in the sports complex on the Prince George's side.

Cabin John Regional Park

Located in Montgomery County, Maryland, Cabin John Regional Park is a great destination for any local mountain biker who can't get away to more remote locations. It's also great for the visitor looking for a quick ride close to the urban landscape. Cabin John offers a variety of rolling trails that descend and run parallel to Cabin John Creek and within the vicinity of I-270 and the Capital Beltway. Its proximity to the Beltway; Rockville, Maryland; and the conveniences of Montgomery Mall make it the ideal urban getaway.

Start: Pauline Addie Betz Tennis Center

Length: 7.1 miles

Approximate riding time: 1–2 hours

Best bike: Mountain bike

Terrain and trail surface: Off-road trails, mostly singletrack

Traffic and hazards: Other trail users and off-road hazards

Things to see: Miniature Railroad in the Park, Montgomery Mall, Downtown Bethesda is only minutes away

Getting there: From the Capital Beltway (I-495) take the 270 Spur North. Take exit 1 onto Democracy Boulevard and turn left. The Pauline Addie Betz Tennis Center will be on your right approximately 0.5 mile after you exit. If you reach Seven Locks Road, you've gone too far. GPS: 39.033119,-77.149901

Fees: None

THE RIDE

Say the phrase Captain John several times. Continue saying it long enough, and you'll begin to notice that *captain* slurs into *cabin*. At least that's what local folklore suggests. Rumor has it that the area was named after the famed

British explorer Captain John Smith, although there is no evidence to back this up. Folklore also suggests that the area was named for either one of two hermits that lived along the banks of the creek or after a pirate who buried his treasures along the creek.

The first man kept to himself and hunted along the valley, where he lived in a cabin. Others in the area referred to him as "John of the Cabin." Eventually, when the area was developed, the name evolved into Cabin John. The second was a commoner, an English settler named John who came to the colonies with his fiancée to escape the wrath of her nobleman father. On the trip to the colonies, his fiancée fell ill and ultimately died in Alexandria shortly after their arrival. Out of fear that her father would make the journey to claim her body for interment at the family plot in England, John had her buried in an unmarked grave in Alexandria where he could visit and grieve for her. John followed the river valley and ultimately settled in a cabin in the area that is now Cabin John. Again, locals referred to him as "John of the Cabin."

The last legend suggests that a pirate captain named John sailed upriver to Little Falls and then traveled inland to the area near the creek. There he buried his treasures to hide his riches from his enemies, killing the men who helped him, so that they would never speak of the location or return to rob him.

I personally prefer the legend of Captain John Smith the Explorer, who certainly spent lots of time exploring the area, and whose adventures helped shape the colonies. After settling in Jamestown, Virginia, in the winter of 1607, Captain Smith survived an ambush by Native Americans. He was captured and taken as prisoner to the chief of the tribal confederacy, Chief Powhatan. Impressed by Smith's confidence and determination, Powhatan interviewed his captive to learn more about his travels and allowed Smith to participate in a ritual, a test to determine his worth and courage. Painfully unaware of his fate, Smith endured and passed all of the challenges placed upon him. With the help of Pocahontas, Powhatan's 11-year-old daughter, Smith survived and was made a subordinate chief of the tribe. After four weeks of captivity, Smith left the tribe in friendship and returned to Jamestown.

As a result of unrest, lack of supplies, and dissent within the colony, Smith left Jamestown again to explore and map the lands of the Chesapeake

Bike Shops

Revolution Cycles: 1066 Rockville Pike, Rockville, MD 20852; (301) 424-0990; www.revolutioncycles.com
Big Wheel Bikes: 9931 Falls Rd., Potomac, MD 20854; (301) 299-1660; www.bigwheelbikes.com
Fresh Bikes: 7626 Old Georgetown Rd., Bethesda, MD 20814; (301) 312-6159; www.freshbikescycling.com
Performance Bikes: 1667 Rockville Pike, Congressional Plaza, Rockville, MD 20852; (301) 468-0808; www.performancebike.com

You May Run into David Scull

I honestly I can't remember when I first met Dave exactly, but I do remember that it was during a local county meeting where I spoke on behalf of mountain bikers seeking access to a trail in Montgomery County—so, it had to have been about 1993. Dave introduced himself as a cycling advocate, and together we spent some time talking about the issues that concerned cyclists in the region. Later, Dave, a DNR representative, and I walked the woods in what is now Schaeffer Farms and flagged some of the initial trails that would eventually be built there. We've ridden

David Scull has been a tireless advocate for mountain bikers in the mid-Atlantic region.

together on countless occasions, and I've had the pleasure of taking him back home to Peru to ride the trails of my "original neck of the woods." Dave is a gentleman and an articulate diplomat. He's built trails with the rest of us, and wielded a McLeod on more occasions than many can count, but it's his off the trail efforts that have set him aside. He's spent countless hours reaching out to local park managers and politicians "educating" them on the merits and benefits of off-road cycling. He's even taken a few on a ride around area trails, including here at Cabin John, his neighborhood loop. Through his efforts, the off-road cycling community has created and maintained relationships with area politicians. While intangible, these have been critical in getting access to, and permission to build miles of trails in the region. You'll often find Dave and his wife Nancy riding Cabin John and other trails in the Montgomery county region. He'll be easy to spot, since he's the self-proclaimed "oldest mountain biker alive." If you ever have the pleasure to meet him, give him a pat on the back for all the efforts he's made to ensure we all have off-road places to ride.

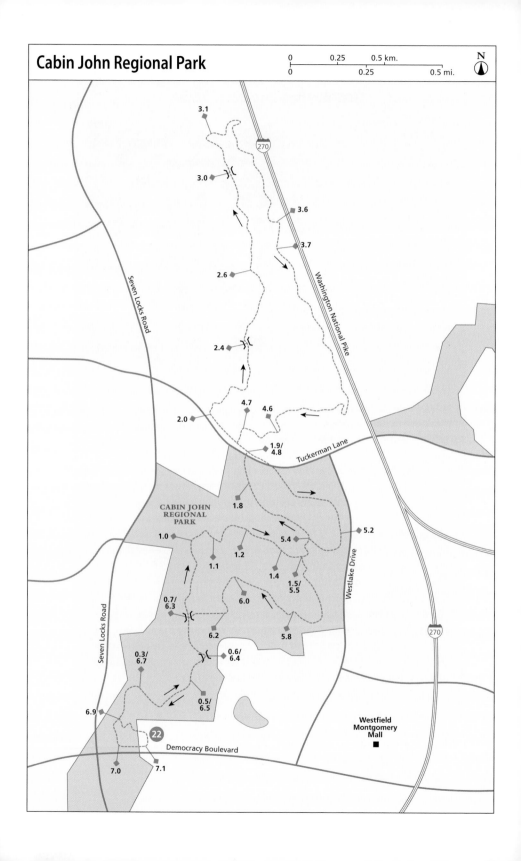

Cabin John Regional Park

0   0.25   0.5 km.

0   0.25   0.5 mi.

N

3.1

270

3.0

3.6

3.7

2.6

2.4

Washington National Pike

Seven Locks Road

2.0

4.7

4.6

1.9/
4.8

Tuckerman Lane

1.8

CABIN JOHN
REGIONAL
PARK

1.0

5.4

5.2

1.2

1.1

Westlake Drive

1.4

1.5/
5.5

0.7/
6.3

6.0

6.2

5.8

0.3/
6.7

0.6/
6.4

Seven Locks Road

270

6.9

0.5/
6.5

22

Democracy Boulevard

Westfield
Montgomery
Mall

7.0   7.1

Bay Region. Because of his efforts and mapping endeavors, the early colonists were able to more easily expand their settlements and survive in the new lands. References to "Captain John's Run" (or Creek) that date back as far as the early 1700s would suggest that he traveled through here, and perhaps that is how the area near the creek was named Captain John, and eventually slurred into Cabin John. However uncertain, this is the most "romantic" legend that suggests how the area got its name, and one that many residents in the area subscribe to.

MILES & DIRECTIONS

The ride starts at the Pauline Addie Betz Tennis Center off Democracy Boulevard, Montgomery County, Maryland. If you are facing the tennis center, the trailhead will be on the left side of the parking area and is marked by a 6x6 timber post. Restrooms are available in the tennis center if you ask nicely. In this ride I detail a little-known loop through the park. The more common ride will take you along the Cabin John Trail as it parallels the creek from the main park to River Road. If you prefer to do the out-and-back, simply follow the blue blazes to the trail's terminus shortly after crossing River Road.

0.0   Enter the trail from the parking area.

0.1   Turn right as you reach Cabin John Creek.

0.3   Turn left at this intersection.

0.5   Stay to the left at this intersection.

0.6   Go over the small wood bridge and then immediately bear left to head up on the trail. The trail is blazed blue.

0.7   Stay left and continue following the trail as it parallels the creek.

1.0   Turn right and follow the trail as it climbs away from the creek.

1.1   Turn left to ride on Diamond Circle.

1.2   Stay to the right and then follow the trail to the left. The trail to the right will simply take you up to the athletic field. Continue following the blue blazes. Come out into a clearing and stay to the right to continue on the Cabin John Trail and then immediately bear to the left.

1.4   Stay to the left again and cross under the power lines.

1.5   Immediately after crossing the power lines, stay to the left.

1.8   Continue right at this intersection, and continue following the trail as it parallels the creek.

1.9 Bear left to reach Tuckerman Lane. We'll take the right fork on the way back. Use caution when crossing Tuckerman Lane. Turn left to head in the direction of the scout gate and access point to the campground. Continue riding northwest on Tuckerman past the gate.

2.0 The trailhead to the north section of the Cabin John Trail is to the right and marked with a 6x6 post similar to the one we encountered at the beginning of the ride.

2.4 After crossing the bridge, stay to the right. The majority of branches from the main trail are short access points.

2.6 Continue following the trail to the right as it parallels Cabin John Creek.

3.0 After going over a short wood bridge, turn right at this intersection. The left fork will take you to the north terminus of the Cabin John Trail at Goya Drive.

3.1 Cross Cabin John Creek. At the immediate T intersection, turn left and follow the trail as it climbs toward I-270. The trail will then turn right and south as it parallels the highway. You can hear it but can barely see it through the trees.

3.6 Turn left at this intersection and again left at the subsequent fork in the trail. The right fork will head down a steep hill while the left will follow a more forgiving path.

3.7 Stay to the left again.

4.6 Stay to the right and then left at the next fork. The left fork follows the low side while the right fork will climb up and then descend a steep section of technical rocks.

4.7 Stay to the left once again to come out on Campground Road. To the left is Tuckerman Lane and the access gate mentioned on mile 1.9. Head left to it, cross Tuckerman Lane, and left again to head back to the trail on the opposite side from which we popped out on mile 1.9.

4.8 Turn right onto the Cabin John Trail and then immediately left to climb up on the Cabin John Trail as it parallels Tuckerman Lane for a short distance until you exit into the Cabin John Train Station Parking area. Follow the road toward the left as it passes the Cabin John Station, Porky the litter eater, and then bear right through a second parking area (mile 5.1).

Cabin John is a popular urban destination.

5.2 When the parking area ends, you'll see the trailhead marked by a large 6x6 timber. Enter it.

5.4 Turn left at this intersection. We will be doubling back on some of the initial trails we rode thin. This is the intersection we first saw at mile 1.5. Cross under the power lines and then turn left into the trail on the opposite side.

5.5 Come out into the parking area for the Shirley Povich Field and turn left to head toward the Cabin John Ice Rink. (Restrooms are available here.)

5.7 Turn right and follow the signs toward fields 5, 6, and 7 and then bear right to continue following the "restricted access" paved road.

5.8 Directly across from the tennis courts turn left onto the gravel path and then immediately right to enter the singletrack.

6.0 Turn left and then left to join the Goose Neck Loop.

6.2 Turn left at this intersection and then, after a quick downhill, right. Continue to follow the blue blazes.

6.3 Turn left and go over the small wood bridge and then bear to the left.

6.5 Turn right and then quickly left to go over the small bridge. Shortly after continue to the right. Do *not* ride on the Tulip Tree Trail—bikes are not permitted there.

6.7 After crossing the field, turn right. If you continue straight, you'll reach the back of the tennis center.

6.9 Stay to the right, continuing to follow the creek trail.

7.0 Turn left onto the sidewalk that parallels Democracy Boulevard.

7.1 Turn left into the tennis center parking lot to complete the loop.

RIDE INFORMATION

Local Events and Attractions

Cabin John Mall on 11325 Seven Lock Rd. has free children's entertainment, crafts, and more on the 1st and 3rd Friday each month at 10:30 a.m, in the Cabin John Mall Atrium.

Rockville Farmers Market:

Every Wed, June through September, from 11 a.m. to 2 p.m. in the Rockville Town Center, East Montgomery Avenue.

Every Sat, May through November, from 9 a.m. to 1 p.m. in the Rockville Town Center on the corner of Route 28 and Monroe Street.

City of Rockville: www.rockvillemd.gov

Restaurants

Momo Taro Sushi: 11325 Seven Locks Rd., Potomac, MD 20854; (301) 983-1868

Wild Tomato: 7945 MacArthur Blvd., Cabin John, MD 20818; (301) 229-0680

Restrooms

Available in the main park areas and in the Pauline Addie Betz Tennis Center.

Frederick Road Ride – The Covered Bridges

This ride will take you through some of Frederick County's most picturesque roads, including through three of only eight remaining covered bridges in the state of Maryland. Along the way you'll ride past the town of Emmitsburg, Mount Saint Mary's University, and the town of Thurmont.

Start: Lewiston Elementary School

Length: 33.2 miles

Approximate riding time: 2–3 hours

Best bike: Road bike

Terrain and trail surface: Paved country roads

Traffic and hazards: Traffic

Things to see: Three of Maryland's eight remaining covered bridges, Mount Saint Mary's University, the National Shrine of Saint Elizabeth Ann Seton, Fallen Firefighters' Memorial, Gettysburg National Park, Cunningham Falls State Park, and the town of Emmitsburg

Getting there: From the Capital Beltway take I-270 north toward Frederick. Drive for 30 miles and merge onto Route 15 north. In approximately 10 miles turn right onto Fish Hatchery Road and then left onto Hessong Bridge Road. Lewistown Elementary will be to your right. GPS: 39.539429,-77.415848

Fees: None

THE RIDE

Chances are you won't run into Meryl Streep or Clint Eastwood by the bridges of Frederick County, but you will definitely get to see three of only eight remaining historic covered bridges in the state of Maryland. As many as 52 of these structures spanned creeks across the state, but neglect, progress, and other natural circumstances have slowly claimed the others. We'll ride through three bridges in the county that are listed in the National Park Service's National Register of Historic Places: the Utica Mills, Loy's Station, and Roddy Road covered bridges.

The first of the bridges will come quickly—only 1.5 miles after starting the ride we'll reach the Utica Mills Bridge. The 101-foot bridge was originally one of two 250-foot spans that crossed the Monocacy River via Devilbliss Road in the county, and the only one to survive the great 1889 Jamestown Flood. After the flood, in 1891, the bridge was dismantled and rebuilt as a 101-foot span over Fishing Creek on Utica Road, where it stands today. Because the bridge is composed of the original lumber and trusses that were part of the Devilbliss Road Span, its build date is registered as 1843. Since it was moved in 1891, the bridge has seen considerable maintenance. It was damaged twice by oversize vehicles, most recently in 2006, and has had to be reinforced and repaired because of termite damage. Today the bridge stands as a testament of the county's historic past and was listed on the National Register of Historic Places on June 23, 1978.

Bike Shops

Frederick Bike Doctor: 5732 Buckeystown Pike, Frederick, MD 21704; (301) 620-8868; www.bikedoctorfrederick.com
The Bicycle Escape: 7280-E Wormans Mill Rd., Frederick, MD 21701; (301) 663-0007; www.thebicycleescape.com

We'll ride for an additional 7 miles before reaching the second bridge of the ride, the Loy's Station Bridge. Also added to the National Register of Historic Places on June 23, 1978, the Loy's bridge has had a considerable amount of history pass over it. Originally built in 1849 to cross Owens Creek, the bridge measured approximately 90 feet. Known by the railroad station of the same name, the bridge survived the Civil War, and it is believed that none other than Gen. George Meade crossed its surface on July of 1863 while pursuing Confederate forces retreating from the Battle of Gettysburg.

The bridge was modified in 1930 when a concrete pier and steel beams were added below its decking to provide more support for the structure. The construction project divided the bridge into two 45-foot spans. The bridge was almost lost to arson in June 1991 when a pickup truck was set on fire as part of an insurance fraud scheme. Fearing the loss of the bridge, local residents and the Frederick County Covered Bridge Preservation Society rallied and succeeded to save it. It took a little over three years for the bridge to be rebuilt, and on July 4, 1994, the bridge was reopened to traffic amidst celebration from the area's residents.

You May Run into Jason Ashmore (@crashmore)

I met Jason through my involvement with the Mid-Atlantic Off-Road Enthusiasts (MORE) over a decade ago. Back then I was the webmaster for MORE and put considerable amount of time into managing the website and membership application process. I had been doing that for a long time and was in need of some help (aka I was burning out), which is when Jason stepped up and took the process and pressure away from me. We became good friends as I passed the baton and have gone on many rides together, including a trip to the west to ride Colorado's trails. He started biking to help eliminate a smoking vice. The funny thing is that he didn't know he was replacing one vice with another (albeit a healthy one). "I just love the freedom and sense of accomplishment I get when I ride," he told me. "That feeling hasn't changed since I was a kid. I'm proudest of finishing the Shenandoah Mountain 100 (SM100), something I wouldn't have been able to do a decade ago." Off the bike Jason has created a valuable resource for cyclists in the area, the LORO community (www.logoffrideon.com). LORO offers an extensive trail and rides database and a real-time trail conditions reporting tool. LORO is also a community where riders share information and plan cycling outings. Jason was the one who introduced this ride to me. He also spent a considerable amount of his time tagging along with me and helping me document many of the rides in the book; he was critical in helping me complete it. For that I'm incredibly grateful. Stop by www.logoffrideon.com and say hi. Better yet, make a contribution to the community by participating in its forums.

Before reaching the third and final bridge of the ride, we'll bike through the small town of Emmitsburg and Mount Saint Mary's University, the oldest independent Catholic university in the United States. Also known as "The Mount," the university was founded in 1808 by French Father John Dubois. In 1805 Father Dubois placed the cornerstone on a modest parcel of land to build a church, Saint-Mary's-on-the-Hill, and later a school. Today, The Mount encompasses a campus that is nearly 1,400 acres and includes five residence halls, three apartment buildings, and several academic halls and athletic facilities. The campus

Frequency Road Ride–The Covered Bridges

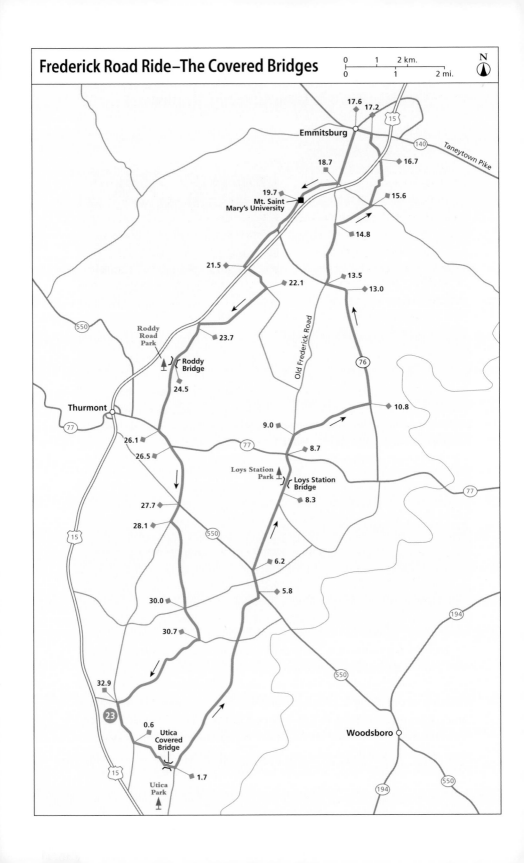

also includes the National Shrine of Grotto Lourdes, a popular pilgrimage site to which Catholics and tourists from all over the world visit annually. The shrine is the oldest known replica of the famed Sanctuary of Our Lady Lourdes in France.

After riding through the university campus, you'll cross Route 15, a busy Frederick thoroughfare, before making your way to the last of the three covered bridges, the 40-foot Roddy Road Bridge, the smallest covered bridge still standing in the state of Maryland. There is no record of when the bridge was constructed, but common belief in the county is that it went up during the same period as Utica and Loy's Station, around 1850. The bridge is unique in that it is the only one that is built using a single kingpost truss. Just like the Utica and Loy's Bridges, Roddy Bridge was added to the National Register of Historic Places on June 23, 1978. Although no record exists, it is believed that Confederate soldiers used the bridge on their way to their ill-fated campaign at the Battle of Gettysburg, the turning point of the American Civil War, and the battle in which the North and South suffered the most casualties.

Following the bridge we'll ride through the small town of Thurmont before making our way back to the Lewiston Elementary School parking area. Thurmont was originally a railroad town built to accommodate the Western Maryland Railway, which connected Baltimore with other Maryland towns to the west. Thurmont is the gateway to the Catoctin Mountains, and its closest neighbor is Camp David, the presidential retreat. Thurmont is also near Cunningham Falls State Park and Catoctin Mountain Park.

MILES & DIRECTIONS

0.0 Start from the Lewiston Elementary School parking area. Turn left to head south on Hessong Bridge Road.

0.6 Turn left onto Utica Road.

1.5 Go through the Utica Covered Bridge, the first of three covered bridges you'll encounter on this ride.

1.7 Turn left onto Old Frederick Road.

5.8 Continue straight and head north on Creagerstown Road.

6.2 Veer right and continue on Old Frederick Road. Follow the sign toward Loy's Station Park.

8.3 Loy's Station Park. Great place for a rest, there is a porta-potty available here. You'll cross the second covered bridge of the ride.

8.7 Cross Rocky Ridge Road. Use caution here.

Narrow, twisty roads are part of the norm in this country ride.

9.0 Turn right onto Appolds Road.

10.8 Turn left onto Motters Station Road and continue north.

13.0 Continue following the road to the left. In the distance you can see Mount St. Mary's University.

13.5 Turn right and head northeast on Old Frederick Road.

14.8 Turn right onto Dry Bridge Road. Keep your eyes peeled for some llamas to the left.

15.6 Turn left onto Keysville Road and then immediate right onto Creamery Road.

16.7 Cross Route 15—use caution.

17.2 Turn left onto East Main Street. Welcome to Emmitsburg.

17.6 Turn left onto South Seton Avenue. Watch for the National Shrine of Saint Elizabeth Ann Seton to your left followed by FEMA's headquarters.

18.7 Turn right onto Old Emmitsburg Road. There is a gas station on the corner with access to a restroom. Chubby's BBQ is across Route 15 to the right.

Best Bike Rides Washington, DC

19.7 Reach Mount Saint Mary's University. You are now on St. Anthony Road.

21.5 Cross Route 15.

22.1 Turn right onto Old Kiln Road.

23.7 Turn left on Roddy Road. Then continue to the right to remain on Roddy Road.

24.5 Continue through our third and final covered bridge.

26.1 Turn left onto East Main Street.

26.5 Continue straight to Jimtown Road.

27.7 Continue straight to Hessong Bridge Road.

28.1 Turn left onto Layman Road.

30.0 Turn right onto Blacks Mill Road and make an immediate left onto Wilhide Road.

30.7 Turn right onto Angelberger Road.

32.9 Turn left onto Hessong Bridge Road.

33.2 Loop is complete.

RIDE INFORMATION

Local Events and Attractions
Frederick County, MD, offers an array of visitor attractions and is easily accessible from Washington, DC; www.visitfrederick.org/events

Restaurants
California Tortilla: 1700 Kingfisher Dr., Ste. 15, Frederick, MD 21701; (301) 631-1996
Chubby's BBQ: 16430A Old Frederick Rd., Emmitsburg, MD 21727; (301) 447-3322
The Carriage House Inn (formal): 200 S. Seton Ave., Emmitsburg, MD 21727; (301) 447-2366; http://carriagehouseinn.info

Restrooms
There is a porta-potty at Loy's Station Park.

Agricultural Greenbelt

*The Greenbelt loop starts out through some of the community's planned neigh-
borhoods before heading into the rolling roads in and around the US Department
of Agriculture's Agricultural Research Center and the National Wildlife Refuge. It's
hard to believe, but at some points in this ride you'll think you are in rural Maryland
or in Pennsylvania's farm country, and not within minutes of the Capital Beltway.*

Start: Buddy Attick Park in Greenbelt, Maryland

Length: 20.2 miles/1.4 miles kids loop

Approximate riding time: 2 hours

Best bike: Road bike

Terrain and trail surface: Paved country roads

Traffic and hazards: Vehicular traffic

Things to see: Patuxent National Wildlife Refuge

Getting there: From the Capital Beltway (I-495) take exit 23 for MD 201/
Kenilworth Avenue toward Bladensburg/Greenbelt. Turn right onto MD
201 N/Kenilworth Avenue and then take the first right onto Crescent
Road. The entrance to Buddy Attick Park will be immediately to your
right. GPS: 39.005112,-76.890306

Fees: None

THE RIDE

The Greenbelt loop was one of the very first "road" rides I was introduced
to by my fellow roadie friends here in the DC region. This ride will take you
through a series of roads (including one of my favorites) that run through the
USDA's Agricultural Research Station, the world's largest agricultural research
complex. To get to them, however, we must first ride from Greenbelt Lake and
Buddy Attick Park, and through some of Greenbelt's local neighborhood roads.

The lake, like so many of the others I mention in this book, is a man-made body of water created to control flooding and protect water quality. Unlike the others, however, Greenbelt Lake was built in conjunction with a new planned community as part of FDR's New Deal.

The 23-acre lake was created in the late 1930s and was virtually built by hand. Wanting to provide work for as many unemployed workers as it could, the federal government required that the land be cleared manually. It took nearly 200 workers one year to remove brush and trees and to build the 22-foot dam on the east side that would hold its waters. Originally the lake was designed to have a boathouse for boat rentals and a sandy beach so that local residents could enjoy its water, but that never materialized in the end. That was a good thing, as it was found out later that the lake's waters were contaminated and posed a health hazard.

Creation of the lake also coincided with the building of Greenbelt. The city was one of the first planned communities built by the federal government, and every aspect of its physical construction was planned and modeled after English garden cities of the 19th century. Interior paths and walkways connected courtyards and "mega blocks" that offered residents the ability to reach the center of the community without having to cross a busy road. Its major arteries followed the natural contour of the land and used the surrounding green space as a buffer, hence the name Greenbelt. Greenbelt, Maryland, was one of four planned communities slated to be built. Two others were built in Ohio and Wisconsin; the final fourth slated to rise in New Jersey never broke ground.

Bike Shops

Family Bike Shop: 1286 MD 3 South, Ste. #13, Crofton, MD 21114; (410) 721-8244; www.familybikeshop.com
Proteus Bicycles: 9217 Baltimore Ave., College Park, MD 20740; (301) 441-2928; http://proteusbicycles.com

Greenbelt was not only a physical experiment in community building but also a social one. The initial group of nearly 900 residents who came to live in the community was selected from a large pool of applicants. The criteria to be considered for habitation was based on income and the willingness of applicants to participate in community-related activities. The first residents, most of whom were in their 30s, formed a town government—the first of its kind in the state of Maryland. They also founded a community newspaper, which is still in publication today. Over the years Greenbelt has expanded and grown; however, its social cooperative spirit has remained alive and active.

The ride will begin from the small park surrounding Greenbelt Lake and named after longtime Greenbelt resident Albert "Buddy" Attick. Buddy was instrumental in the development and building of the city and was a longtime

Where to Eat: Andy's Picks

As I mention in my acknowledgments section, it is virtually impossible to set out on an endeavor such as this one without the help of numerous individuals. Case in point: where to eat in and around Greenbelt. Although I have visited the area often and have dined in several of its establishments, my good friend Andy Carruthers (see Ride 11, Arlington and the Pentagon) is a longtime resident of the planned community and knows it better than most. When it came time for me to list a couple of places to eat, I humbly asked him for his suggestions. I would be remiss if I did not share his eloquent response:

"Greenbelt: not really, but I'm picky. In my hidden 'hood, **The New Deal Cafe** is a Lebanese restaurant/'coffee house'/community living room/live music venue in the historic little town plaza of Old Greenbelt. It just won top local music venue for the entire DC area according to WTOP's website visitor contest (this is not a scientific survey), but the music is often very good, the beer fresh, and the cover charge is ZERO. During the day, if you like hummus and hippies, it has its charm. Prices are low by DC standards, "high-ish" by parsimonious Greenbelt standards. You'll want to leave your GOP T-shirts home, though, as this is a sacred spot for local leftists. Beer and wine. Crème brulée rocks. *Mui* veggie options.

"In nearby Beltsville on Route 1 (Ikea exit), probably less than a mile north of the Beltway, is **Sardi's Chicken.** O.M.G. Peruvian/Greek. No kidding. Known most for shockingly good rotisserie chicken, sweet plantains, and fried yucca in copious portions. Move down the menu for *churrasco de pollo* and really good lamb or pork gyros, etc., plus a fun array of Peruvian chow including an unglamorous-but-affordable edition of *ceviche mixto*. It's inexpensive, friendly, and has some delightful chicken art all over the place. The joint hums at lunch and dinnertime. It is the epitome of the anti-chain. Yum. No alcohol. Warning: Tour de France-size portions here.

"Finally, driving south to the East Hyattsville/Bladensburg area (some might call it SE Edmonston) is a taqueria that *Washingtonian Magazine* said was the best in the region. No frills. Meat-intensive. Family-friendly, cafeteria seating, and *español*-only on the TVs. Sometimes a little noisy, but never unwelcoming: **La Placita.** The three different kinds of pork rinds are enough to make a vegan waiver (which is good, because after breakfast, other than steamed cactus, a vegan's gonna starve here. Except that starting late afternoon, they sometimes have a vendor who sells all kinds of fresh fruit and corn on the cob with sour cream, and corn chowder with "limon"). It's a little tricky to find, just look for the mariachi band on the roof (seriously), well worth the visit. Some picnic tables outdoors. Nuttin' fancy. Super yum. No alcohol. This place opens at 0-dark-30 and closes pretty late. The Latin bakery next door is enticing in the unlikely event you have any room left in your gut after La Placita."

Greenbelt employee where he served as director of public works for over two decades. We will continue via Crescent Road, one of the original main arteries of the planned community, before heading into one of its neighborhoods and then into the Henry Wallace Beltsville Agricultural Research Center (BARC), a unit of the USDA's Research Service. The BARC is the largest agricultural research complex in the world. As you ride its roads you'll pass by facilities that study everything from air quality to genomics and urban entomology. The area where the facility stands has remained unchanged for years, and most of the roads cross several fields where the quality and utilization of agricultural products are closely monitored.

The BARC was founded in 1910 when the USDA purchased a 475-acre parcel of land to turn into a research facility. The land was originally owned by Thomas Snowden (see Ride 27, The North Tract) in the 18th century, who then passed it down to his daughter. Snowden's daughter married John Herbert of Walnut Grange, Virginia, and they established a home in the area. Unlike much of the land in the North Tract, which was changed and altered for military use, this tract of land has remained unchanged. Except for the evident development and agricultural activity, not much is different. As you ride through the roads of the facility before making your way back to the starting point, you'll get a sense of what it may have been like in the 18th and 19th centuries, and you'll understand why this area is so popular with cyclists.

MILES & DIRECTIONS

0.0 Start from the dedication plaque at the entrance of Buddy Attick Park. Exit the parking lot and turn right onto Crescent Road.

0.3 Turn left onto Green Hill Road.

0.7 Turn left onto Research Road.

1.0 Go through the gate to enter the USDA's Agricultural Research Service Facility (ARS). You are entering a federal installation, so please stay on the roads and obey all posted signs.

1.9 Turn left onto Beaver Dam Road.

3.0 Turn right onto Edmonston Road. There is a nice wide shoulder on this road. Use caution when riding on this road since there is traffic.

3.3 Continue straight through Powder Mill Road.

4.0 Turn right onto Odell Road.

5.1 Stay to the right and continue on Odell Road.

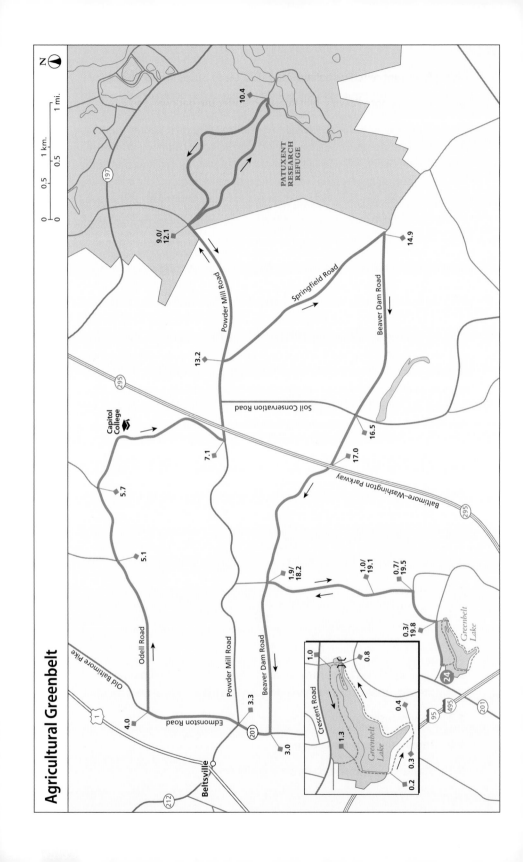

Agricultural Greenbelt

5.7   Turn right onto Springfield Road.

7.1   Turn left onto Powder Mill Road. Go under the parkway and continue straight to the National Wildlife Visitor Center.

9.0   Turn right onto Scarlet Tanager Loop and into the Patuxent National Wildlife Refuge. The gates close promptly at 4:30 p.m.

10.4   As you reach the visitor center, turn left before entering the parking area for the visitor center and then make another left to enter the exit road that parallels the road you just came in on. Restrooms are available here.

12.1   Turn left onto Powder Mill Road.

13.2   Turn left onto Springfield Road and ride toward the three [water] towers.

14.9   Turn right onto Beaver Dam Road.

16.5   Cross Soil Conservation Road.

17.0   You'll ride under the Baltimore Washington Parkway.

18.2   Turn left onto Research Road.

19.1   Go through the gate to exit the USDA ARS Facility.

19.5   Turn right onto Green Hill Road.

19.8   Turn right onto Crescent Road.

20.2   Turn left into the Buddy Attick Park and complete the loop.

The kids loop:

Greenbelt Lake has a nice wide, groomed trail along its perimeter that is perfect for walking and for biking with young kids.

0.0   Start at the entrance to the Buddy Attick Park sign and the wide gravel trail behind the restrooms. Pedal down a short hill and then make a right at the first intersection to follow the trail over the dam and around the lake in a counterclockwise direction.

0.2   Stay to the left.

0.3   Stay to the left.

0.4   Stay to the left.

0.8   Turn left to go over the bridge and then make an immediate left to enter a small peninsula overlooking the lake. This is a minor side trip to a spot with benches where kids can play for a little while. On your way out turn left again.

1.0   Turn left again to continue riding around the lake.

1.3   Turn right to head back up to the parking lot.

1.4   Complete the loop.

RIDE INFORMATION

Local Events and Attractions
Greenbelt Patch: www.greenbelt.patch.com
The College Park Area Bicycle Coalition website lists upcoming events and activities in the community: www.cpabc.org
Until recently, the **USDA ARS** hosted a summer field day, but it has been discontinued for lack of funding. Check with them regularly though as it may pop up again.

Restaurants
The New Deal Cafe: 113 Centerway, Roosevelt Center, Greenbelt, MD 20770; (301) 474-5642; www.newdealcafe.com
Sardi's Chicken: 10433 Baltimore Ave., Beltsville, MD 20705; (301) 595-3222; www.sardischicken.com
Taqueria La Placita: 5020 Edmonston Rd., Hyattsville, MD 20781; (301) 277-4477

> ## Greenbelt's Pledge
> *The strength of Greenbelt is diverse people living together in a spirit of cooperation. We celebrate people of many cultures, faiths, and races living together. By sharing together all are enriched.*
>
> *We pledge to foster a community which is respectful, safe, and fair for all people.*

Restrooms
Restrooms are available in Buddy Attick Park and at the Patuxent National Wildlife Refuge.

Montgomery County Back Roads

If you choose to do only one road ride in the book, choose this one. Seriously. This is a favorite of many area cyclists. The ride winds through western Montgomery County's back roads and will offer you a glimpse into an area of the region that has seen very little development over the years. Residents value this and actively fight urban development projects so that the areas where they live retain their country character.

Start: Start in front of the restrooms behind the tennis courts on the parking lot at the corner of Germantown Park Drive and Schaffer Farms Road for fields C, D, and E

Length: 28.7 miles

Approximate riding time: 2–3 hours

Best bike: Road bike

Terrain and trail surface: Paved country roads

Traffic and hazards: Vehicle traffic

Things to see: Black Rock Mill, Lewis Farm Orchards

Getting there: From the Capital Beltway (I-495) take I-270 north toward Frederick. Take exit 15B to merge onto MD 118 S toward Germantown. In approximately 4 miles turn right onto Germantown Park Drive. Shortly before you reach the traffic circle, turn left into the parking area for field E. GPS: 39.149832,-77.312164

Fees: None

THE RIDE

Welcome to Montgomery County, Maryland! This ride will take us through the western portion of one of the most affluent counties in the United States. You'll understand why as you ride through miles of country roads dotted with large homes and exquisite farm land, as well as some of the least-traveled roads in the region. This area of Montgomery County has managed to retain its country feel and fend off the tentacles of urban development.

We can trace Montgomery County's history way back to when its forested lands were populated by tribes of Native Americans, including the Senecas. The first settlers arrived in the area in the mid-1700s. Those settlers had their work cut out for them. Back then, only a few wagon roads and Indian trails crossed the land, and very little land was ripe for agriculture. But the perseverance of the hardy settlers transformed the area into a rich crop-producing locale. Early crops included corn and the almighty tobacco, which was traded and shipped to Georgetown—which was part of the county back then—for distribution throughout the colonies.

As the capital city flourished, DC began to expand, and many of its affluent residents built homes in nearby Chevy Chase and Bethesda, but the western part of the county remained unchanged. Farms and agriculture continued to be the driving economic force, and small towns and communities like Poolesville and Dickerson remained untouched by the fast pace of growth in nearby vicinities. Over the years residents have continued active resistance to urban sprawl, and this portion of the county has managed to retain much of its initial character.

Bike Shops

Germantown Cycles Bike Shop: 12615 Wisteria Dr., Germantown, MD 20874; (240) 404-0695; www.germantowncycles.com
Gaithersburg Bicycles: 811 Russell Ave. #C, Gaithersburg, MD 20879; (301) 948-6126; www.gaithersburgbicycles.com

That said, it has not been completely immune to growth. Back when I first moved to the county in the mid-1980s, the area near Clopper Road and Route 118, very near where our ride starts, was virtually undeveloped. Today several communities have taken shape, and the Germantown Soccer Complex has sprouted in what was once precious farmland. Schaffer Road, where our ride starts, used to be a desolate, one-lane enclave. Today, it is filled with single-family homes and "speed" cameras to deter law breakers from speeding down its lanes.

Several development projects are currently in dispute. Closer to Rockville, but very near to where the Route 28 Corridor starts, there are plans to build a Johns Hopkins University mega complex of buildings. The site, described as the "four pentagons," is on hold pending a court day to resolve the dispute with residents and the owners of Belward Farm.

Farther west, where our ride takes place, proposals to build another Potomac River crossing to augment and alleviate the traffic that bottlenecks at the American Legion Bridge—which was the last bridge built over the

Peach Tree Road. I wonder where they came up with that name?

Potomac River, constructed in 1962—have been going on for years. Dialogues between the offices of the governors of both Maryland and Virginia have again started, in an effort to link both Montgomery and Fairfax Counties. A new crossing to alleviate traffic congestion is one of the few transportation options left for residents in the heavily populated areas of Gaithersburg and North Potomac. But there have been two other options presented. The second is to extend the new Inter County Connector (ICC) for approximately 15 or 11 miles via Darnestown and Seneca. The third option would be to extend the Route 28 Corridor, through which we ride in this loop, all the way to Virginia's 7100 (the Fairfax County Parkway). The latter is the one opposed the most by residents of the area, since it would destroy the character of the communities that exist around the proposed route.

As you ride these roads, you'll understand why the residents of western Montgomery County oppose further development. For the sake of this loop, let's hope no superhighway is built in this area, because it would simply destroy the scenic beauty that so many have fought so hard to preserve.

MILES & DIRECTIONS

0.0 Head north out of the parking area and turn left, then go three quarters of the way around the circle and continue on Schaffer Road to the south.

2.3 The Montgomery County Model Airpark is to the left. You may hear some of the RC planes buzzing above.

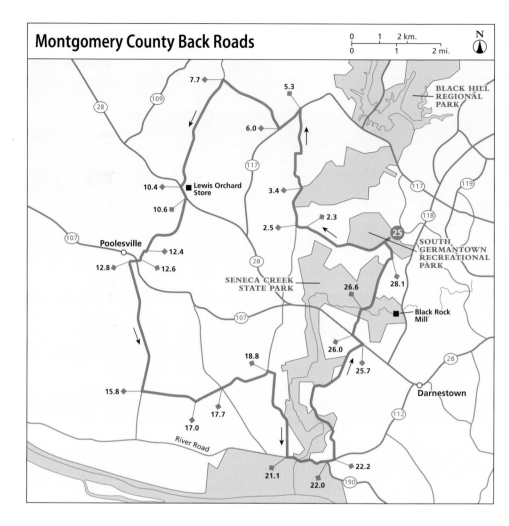

Montgomery County Back Roads

2.5 Turn right onto White Ground Road.

3.4 Turn left onto Old Bucklodge Lane.

5.3 Turn left onto Bucklodge Road. Use caution here since there is traffic on this road.

6.0 Turn right onto White Store Road.

7.7 Turn left onto Peach Tree Road. You'll soon see where this road gets its name.

10.4 Turn left onto Darnestown Road (MD 28). The Lewis Orchard store is at this intersection. Make note of where it is and come back to get some Million Dollar Pickles; trust me. Tell them we sent you.

10.6 Turn right onto Cattail Road.

12.4 Turn left onto Kohlhoss Road and continue through the neighborhood. You are now in Poolesville.

12.6 Turn right onto Wooton Avenue and cross Fisher Road.

12.8 Turn left onto Hughes Road. Hopefully by the time you read this the now-defunct Shelby's grocery store will have been replaced by something else. There is a CVS at the opposite end of the plaza.

15.8 Turn left onto Sugarland Road.

17.0 Turn left to continue on Sugarland Road.

17.7 Continue straight on Sugarland; cross Partnership.

18.8 Continue bearing to the left on Sugarland as it follows the perimeter of Homestead Farms. If you're lucky, strawberries will be in bloom; you can smell them in the air. This is a pick-your-own place. Turn right onto Montevideo Road.

21.1 Turn left onto River Road (MD 190). There is a designated bike lane on the right shoulder. Still, use caution since River Road is a heavily used thoroughfare.

22.0 Continue straight at this intersection to get on Seneca Road. River Road bears to the right.

22.2 Turn left onto Berryville Road.

25.7 Turn left onto Darnestown Road.

26.0 Turn right onto Black Rock Road.

26.6 Reach Black Rock Mill. If you look closely to the right before crossing the bridge and to the left after crossing the bridge, you'll see the trailheads for the Seneca Ridge Trail. The first one takes you toward Seneca Creek State Park while the second toward Schaffer Farms. That trail is detailed elsewhere in the book. Get ready for a short but steep climb out of the Seneca Creek.

28.1 Turn left onto Burdette Lane.

28.5 Turn right onto Schaffer Road.

28.6 Turn right at the circle and then right again to enter the parking area.

28.7 The loop is complete.

The Montgomery County back roads are a popular destination for cyclists in the DC region.

RIDE INFORMATION

Local Events and Attractions

Lewis Farm Orchards (local produce): 18901 Peach Tree Rd., Dickerson, MD 20842; (301) 349-4101; www.lewisorchardfarmmarket.com

Homestead Farms (pick your own blackberries, peaches): 15604 Sugarland Rd., Poolesville, MD 20837; www.homestead-farm.net

Restaurants

La Mexicana: 13016 Middlebrook Rd., Germantown, MD 20704; (301) 972-0500; www.lamexicanaonline.com

Restrooms

Restrooms are available in the parking area for fields C, D, and E at the beginning of the ride.

Sugarloaf Mountain Base Loop

This is a great country loop. The ride will take you around the base of Sugarloaf Mountain, a "monadnock," or isolated hill that rises abruptly from the gently level surrounding area, on some nice gravel, dirt, and paved roads. Although we hit several dirt roads, the ride is suitable for a sturdy road bike and makes for an excellent loop.

Start: Parking area at the intersection of Sugarloaf Road and Comus Road. If parking is unavailable here, you can drive up the mountain and use one of the lots available higher up.

Length: 12.5 miles (7.1-mile mountain bike loop)

Approximate riding time: 1.5–2 hours

Best bike: Road/cross bike

Terrain and trail surface: Unpaved and paved country roads

Traffic and hazards: Traffic

Things to see: Sugarloaf Mountain

Getting there: From the Capital Beltway (I-495) take route I-270 north to the Hyattstown exit, circle under I-270 and continue on Route 109 to Comus, then right onto Comus Road to the Sugarloaf Mountain entrance. GPS: 39.251464,-77.393489

Fees: None

THE RIDE

I was first introduced to Sugarloaf Mountain shortly after arriving in the area back in the summer of 1985. At that time my interest in cycling was curbed a little. I had just arrived in this country and had to focus on other things, school and work to name a few. My bike was unable to make the trip with me, and the prospect of purchasing another was bleak. I found a job working for a publisher of equestrian magazines based out of Gaithersburg, Maryland. Being a starving student, I also worked on weekends, and typically that meant heading to the boss's polo farm only 2 miles or so from the mountain in Dickerson, Maryland. In addition to endless polo field mowing and weed whacking, I was occasionally tasked with exercising the horses (to my serious displeasure, as I have never been a horse guy, especially since I was bit by one when I was very young). Those outings often included rides to and around the trails of the mountain.

Years later, long after my last day of work on the farm, I returned . . . this time with my mountain bike. Once again I explored the trails around the mountain, albeit aboard a different steed. Eventually I documented a ride around its base and published it as part of my previous book, *Mountain Biking the Washington, DC/Baltimore Area.* The loop I detailed here is virtually the same as the one I did then, but this time around I opted to ride it in a clockwise direction. I previously recommended not doing it on your road bike because you would be riding on several dirt and gravel roads. Since then I've changed my mind, and have often headed out there and do this very loop on my trusted steel Hampsten. That's not to say you should; if you don't want to subject your pricey speed machine to the undulations of a dirt ride, then I suggest you opt for knobby tires instead, but you'll suffer a bit on the paved portions. If you really must ride your mountain bike, then I suggest you do the yellow loop instead, a challenging 7-mile ride around the base of the mountain on singletrack trails. Bear in mind, though, that access to mountain bikes is limited and only permitted between Memorial Day and Labor Day Mon through Fri.

Bike Shops

Germantown Cycles Bike Shop:
12615 Wisteria Dr., Germantown, MD 20874; (240) 404-0695; www.german towncycles.com
Gaithersburg Bicycles: 811 Russell Ave. #C, Gaithersburg, MD 20879; (301) 948-6126; www.gaithersburg bicycles.com

Named for its shape by early settlers, Sugarloaf Mountain is what is called a monadnock, meaning a hill or mountain that has remained standing high above the surface while the plains and land around it have eroded away. That process took nature nearly 14 million years to create, and today the mountain stands at nearly 1,300 feet and more than 800 feet above the Monocacy Valley.

During its more recent history, the beginning of the 20th century to be precise, Sugarloaf and the area around it was purchased by Gordon Strong, a Chicago businessman who sought to make the mountain a driver's retreat and destination—an "automobile objective." To that end, he commissioned famed architect

Casualty by Popular Demand

In 1993, under the staff supervision of the Stronghold Corporation, groups of off-road cyclists, hikers, and Boy Scouts worked together to create a trail system that combined both forest roads and challenging singletrack. The result was a fantastic network of trails ideal for mountain biking, hiking, and horseback riding. Unfortunately, the trail's popularity was far more than its narrow, twisting pathways could bear, as hundreds of cyclists and other users crowded its course every weekend. The Stronghold Corporation reassessed the trail's design and concluded that, with parking spilling into nearby towns and the trail's capacity overextended, limited access was the only answer. Currently, the Saddleback Trail (blazed yellow) is open to cyclists only from June through Oct, Mon through Fri. It is not open to bikes on weekends at any time of the year. While this may appear unfair and inconvenient to some, remember that Sugarloaf Mountain is a privately owned resource. Thankfully, the Stronghold Corporation is generous enough to allow the Saddleback Trail to remain open to cyclists at certain times.

Frank Lloyd Wright in 1924 to design, as he put it, "a structure on the summit of Sugar Loaf Mountain that would serve as an objective for short motor trips and that would enhance the enjoyment of views from the mountaintop." That plan never materialized, though in 1947, Strong created the Stronghold Incorporated to manage the land and the trust that would maintain it as a retreat where one could appreciate its natural beauty. Since his death in 1954, the Stronghold Corporation has maintained that vision and continues to manage the 3,250 acres of land on and around the mountain.

MILES & DIRECTIONS

0.0 Start from the parking area at the intersection of Sugarloaf Mountain Road and Comus Road. There is a small parking area with limited spaces in front of the Stronghold area. Head south on Sugarloaf Road.

0.4 Turn right onto Mount Ephraim Road. You'll remain on this road for a little over 4 miles.

0.8 Stay to the left at this intersection. To the right will take you back to the parking area.

4.6 Turn right onto Park Mill Road.

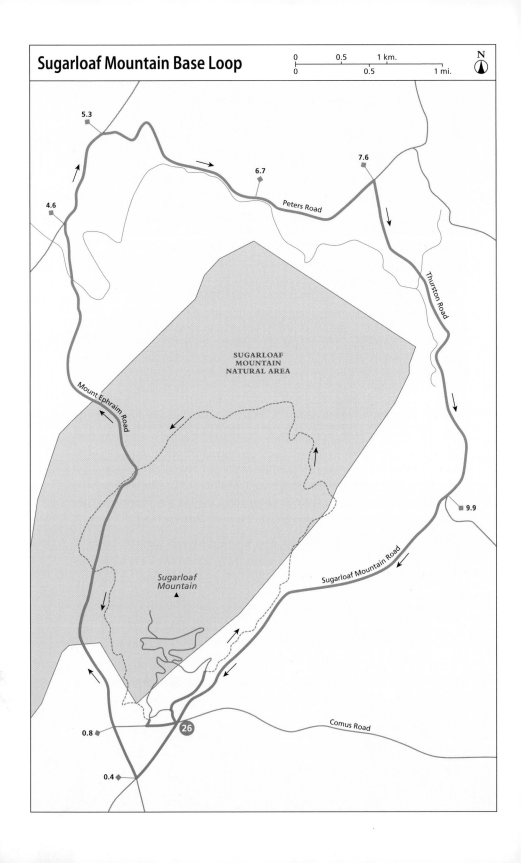

Sugarloaf Mountain Base Loop

0   0.5   1 km.
0   0.5   1 mi.

N

5.3

7.6

6.7

Peters Road

4.6

Thurston Road

SUGARLOAF
MOUNTAIN
NATURAL AREA

Mount Ephraim Road

9.9

Sugarloaf
Mountain
▲

Sugarloaf Mountain Road

26

Comus Road

0.8

0.4

5.3   Turn right onto Peters. Stay on Peters for approximately 2.3 miles.

6.7   A local watering hole; $5 if you swing and jump in.

7.6   Make a sharp right onto Thurston Road.

9.9   Turn right onto Sugarloaf Mountain Road and continue straight until you reach the parking area.

12.5   The loop is complete.

Mountain bike loop:

Mountain bikes are permitted on the Yellow Trail only, between Memorial Day and Labor Day, Mon through Fri.

     Start from the same spot and turn right onto Sugarloaf Mountain Drive (the road that will take you to the mountain summit). The Yellow trailhead is less than 0.5 mile to the right. Enter the trail and follow the yellow blazes in a counterclockwise direction for approximately 7 miles until you reach Sugarloaf Mountain Drive again, turn right and then left on Comus Road, then head back to the starting point. The Yellow Trail is well blazed and easy to follow.

RIDE INFORMATION

Local Events and Attractions

For information and links about local events and attractions near Sugarloaf Mountain, visit www.fredericktourism.org.

Sugarloaf Mountain Vineyard: 18125 Comus Rd. (1 mile west on Comus Rd. from the start of the ride), Dickerson, MD 20842; Vineyard (301) 605-0130, Fax (301) 605-0163; www.smvwinery.com

Restaurants

Brewer's Alley: 124 N. Market St., Frederick, MD 21701; (301) 631-0089; www .brewers-alley.com

Growlers Brew Pub: 227 E. Diamond Ave., Gaithersbutg, MD 20877; (301) 519-9400; www.growlersbrew.com

Restrooms

Porta-potties are available on the mountain. Go before you go.

The North Tract

This is a ride I covered in my previous book. I'm updating it to include a slightly different version of the Mountain Bike loop, as well as a quick "documentation" of the road "out and back ride." In theory you could do the road ride as a loop, but access beyond the bridge that crosses the little Patuxent River on the southeast side of the tract, and access beyond Lake Allen on the north, have been restricted because deteriorating road surfaces between these two points make it unsafe. Do ask at the contact station though; hopefully, they have reopened the wildlife loop completely by the time you read this.

Start: Contact Station Parking Area

Length: 6.7-mile MTB loop/13.8-mile out-and-back road ride

Approximate riding time: 1–1.5 hours for either ride

Best bike: Mountain bike or cross bike for the MTB Loop, road bike for the out-and-back

Terrain and trail surface: Gravel roads/paved road

Traffic and hazards: Very few, traffic is minimal on the out-and-back. Spray yourself with insect repellent in the summertime—the mosquitoes are relentless.

Things to see: Wildlife viewing area, historic Laurel

Getting there: From the Capital Beltway (I-495) take I-95 north toward Baltimore. Take exit 33A for Route 198 E. Continue on Route 198 for approximately 5 miles and turn right onto Bald Eagle Drive. Continue on Bald Eagle until you reach the Contact Station. GPS: 39.077709,-76.771431

Fees: None. You must register at the Contact Station before entering the trails. The North Tract Visitor Contact Station and grounds are open every day 8 a.m. to 4 p.m. except for federal holidays. The North Tract has extended summer hours, Fri and Sat June through Aug, 8 a.m. to 7:30 p.m.

THE RIDE

Both of the rides detailed here will take you through a tract of land that the Department of the Interior has designated to support and promote wildlife and has specifically set it up for research, conservation, and wildlife education. The off-road loop is a perfect introduction to mountain biking and offers novice riders a chance to spin through wide old roads with very little elevation change through an area that has remained unchanged for quite some time. This is the perfect ride to bring your kids along. Meanwhile, the out-and-back road option gives riders a relatively safe road section to put in some miles, all while enjoying the isolation that the North Tract offers.

The Patuxent Research Refuge was established in 1936 by executive order of President Franklin Delano Roosevelt, making it the nation's first wildlife research station. The refuge extends for 12,000 acres across the Patuxent River Valley, between Baltimore and Washington. It is divided into three main tracts. The North Tract, where these rides take place, is open to the public for hunting, fishing, wildlife observation, hiking, bicycling, and horseback riding. The South Tract is the site of the National Wildlife Visitor Center (see Ride 24, Agricultural Greenbelt), and one of the largest science and environmental education centers in the Department of the Interior. Finally, the Central Tract is designated for research and the protection of wildlife; it is closed to the public.

> ### Bike Shops
>
> **Crofton Bike Doctor:** 1312 Main Chapel Way, Gambrills, MD 21054; (410) 451-6901; www.croftonbikedoctor.com
>
> **Family Bike Shop:** 1286 MD 3 South, Ste. #13, Crofton, MD 21114; (410) 721-8244; www.familybikeshop.com

When you enter the North Tract, you are required to check in at the Contact Station. Why? Because the North Tract was used by the US Army as a training facility for more than 75 years, and although the area has been cleared of unexploded ordnance, managers don't want you to veer off the paths and accidently find something they may have missed. And the North Tract is a research facility and continues to be used as such.

Native Americans once occupied this area, and the name Patuxent is a Native American word that means "running over loose stones." The refuge was later settled by Europeans who built small farms and mills. More recently, the US Army managed the land, prior to its being transferred to the Department of the Interior. Family cemeteries are all that remain of the early European settlers. Within the cemeteries—one of which we'll ride past—you may notice the name Snowden. Like their neighbors to the north in Howard County, the Carrols and

The North Tract

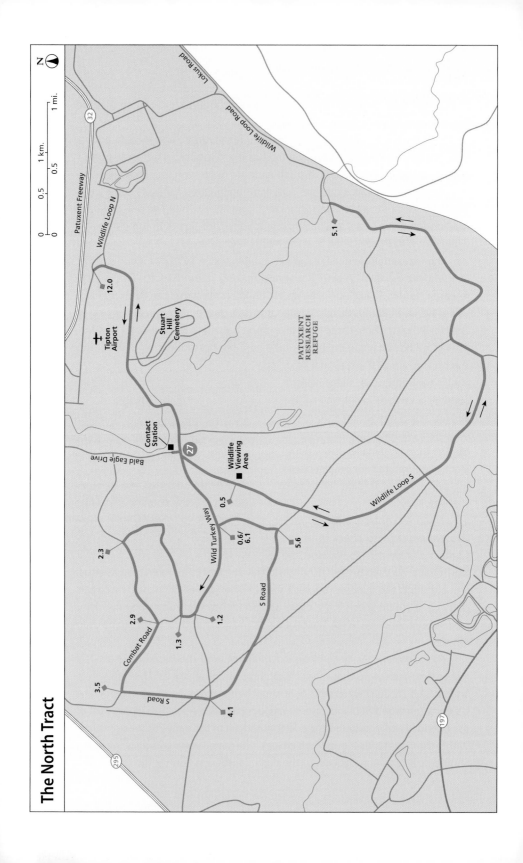

the Ellicotts, the Snowdens had much to do with the growth of Laurel and the surrounding areas.

The Snowdens settled in this area in the late 1600s, when King Charles II granted Richard Snowden nearly 2,000 acres. Richard Snowden would eventually own more than 16,000 acres of land along the banks of the Patuxent River, which locally is known as Snowden River because of the extensive tracts of land he owned along both banks. Birmingham Manor, seat for the Snowden family, was a thriving plantation. Its current location is on the east side of the Baltimore-Washington Parkway, opposite the Laurel Airport. In its prosperous days, the plantation had 24 tobacco barns all in a row. Unfortunately, a fire destroyed the Snowden home in 1891, and the surrounding outbuildings were demolished in 1953 to create the northbound lanes of the Baltimore-Washington Parkway. However, rubble from the old home and two wells are still present next to the Snowden Cemetery.

Adjacent to the refuge and Birmingham Manor is Fort Meade, originally built in 1917, and known as Fort Leonard Wood. By 1941, the Army had absorbed much of what was Birmingham Manor and many of its old structures. Many of these have since been removed, but some foundations still stand. In an effort to regain its past history and to document and preserve the historic richness, the Patuxent Historic Research Project was established in 1991. Rick McGill and Brian Alexander, volunteer researchers, are predominantly responsible for the preservation of these cemeteries and buildings. The Patuxent visitor center and the Patuxent Research Refuge website both have additional information on the history of the North Tract, the Snowden family, and other families who were instrumental in shaping the state of Maryland.

MILES & DIRECTIONS

Mountain bike loop:

0.0 Check in at the Contact Station and then ride your bike around the back of the building to access the wildlife loop. We'll begin measuring shortly before exiting the parking area by the small yard behind the Contact Station. Exit the parking area and turn right onto the Wildlife Loop. As the Wildlife Loop curves to the left, continue straight onto the gravel road. You can't miss it—this is Wild Turkey Way.

0.6 Continue to the right to remain on Wild Turkey. We'll return on the road to the left.

1.2 Bear right and follow the sign to enter Sweet Gum Lane.

A few structures along the ride show their age. Areas around the base of the mountain have retained their "charm" over the years.

1.3 Turn right onto Whip-Poor-Will Way.

2.3 Continue following Whip-Poor-Will Way to the left.

2.9 Turn right onto Sweetgum Lane.

3.5 Turn left and continue on Sweetgum Lane.

4.1 Turn left at this intersection and then follow South Road to the right. You can take Wild Turkey to the left for approximately 1 mile to the site of the Snowden Cemetery.

5.6 Turn left onto Kingfisher.

6.1 Turn right onto Wild Turkey and backtrack to the Contact Station.

6.7 Continue straight onto the Wildlife Loop and then left back into the Contact Station.

Out-and-back (road):

0.0 Check in at the Contact Station and then ride your bike around the back of the building to access the wildlife loop. We'll begin measuring shortly before exiting the parking area by the small yard behind the Contact Station. Exit the parking area and turn right onto the Wildlife Loop. Continue following the pavement to the left. Do not enter the dirt road to the right. You'll stay on the paved road for the next 5 miles.

0.5 The wildlife viewing area is to your left.

5.1 Make a U turn on the bridge and head back in the same direction you came.

Best Bike Rides Washington, DC

10.2 The Contact Station is to your left. You can finish your ride here if you want; we'll add a couple more miles to the ride here.

12.0 Shortly after the entrance to the Lake Allen loop make a U turn and head back along the same way you came to the Contact Station.

13.8 Turn right into the Contact Station parking area, and the loop is complete.

RIDE INFORMATION

Local Events and Attractions
North Tract Programs: www.fws.gov/northeast/patuxent/ntedu.html
Laurel Maryland: www.cityoflaurel.org/content/events

Restaurants
Pasta Plus: 209 Gorman Ave., Laurel, MD 20707; (301) 498-5100; www.pasta plusrestaurant.com
Red Hot and Blue: 677 Main St., Laurel, MD 20707; (301) 953-1943; www.red hotandblue.com

Restrooms
Restrooms are available at the Contact Station.

Upper Rock Creek and Montgomery County

This ride will explore the northernmost portions of the Rock Creek to Lake Needwood and then back down to the start along one of the region's hidden treasures, the Matthew Henson Trail. Combine this ride with the Capitol Crescent Trail Loop to make it an epic ride.

Start: Winding Creek Park, Wheaton, Maryland

Length: 18.1 miles

Approximate riding time: 1.5–3 hours

Best bike: Road bike

Terrain and trail surface: Paved bike trails and paved roads

Traffic and hazards: Other trail users and vehicle traffic

Things to see: Lake Needwood

Getting there: From the Capital Beltway (I-495) take exit 31A for Georgia Avenue North toward Silver Spring/Wheaton. After approximately 1.5 miles turn left onto Veirs Mill Road and continue on for 2.3 miles to Randolph Road. Turn left onto Randolph and then right onto Dewey Road. Winding Creek Park will be to your left as Dewey veers right and becomes Edgebrook Road. Park in front of the playground. GPS: 39.057675,-77.092073

Fees: None

THE RIDE

Along this ride we'll head north to the genesis of the Rock Creek Trail at Lake Needwood, and then head back to the beginning of our ride via the Matthew Henson Trail, a local community path that is a gem in the region.

I talked about the creation of Rock Creek Park in Ride 2, The Capital Crescent Trail and Rock Creek Park, one that you can also access from the starting point of this ride, and which, if you combine the two, can add up to a healthy and scenic long day in the saddle. Originally envisioned to serve just as a 100-acre getaway for the president in the mid-1800s, Rock Creek grew to become a 2,000-plus-acre national treasure and one of the first established National Parks in the nation.

We'll head north along the banks of the Rock Creek to Lake Needwood, a reservoir created to tame the mighty Rock Creek and provide flood control and protection for residents along the banks of the creek to the south. Lake Needwood also serves as a filter to ensure that water quality in Rock Creek is maintained by trapping sediment and storm runoff. Over the years that sediment has been dredged from the lake to ensure that water quality is maintained.

Strong rains over time have forced the evacuation of nearby residents from the reservoir for fear that the earthen dam, which was built in 1965, would collapse and cause catastrophic floods downstream. The latest evacuation took place in the summer of 2006, when over 2,000 residents had to be evacuated for fear that the dam would collapse. At that point the lake was more than 25 feet above its normal level. Fortunately for the residents downstream, the collapse didn't occur. Part of the reason that the lake reached such high levels was because it had not been dredged in nearly 2 decades.

When the lake was initially built, it was expected that dredging of its floor would take place every 5 years.

Bike Shops

Revolution Cycles: 1066 Rockville Pike, Rockville, MD 20852; (301) 424-0990; www.revolutioncycles.com
REI: 1701 Rockville Pike, Rockville, MD 20852; (301) 230-7670; www.rei.com

Initially, park staff accomplished this task, but the practice was discontinued in 1990 as a result of constantly failing park equipment. For nearly 20 years the reservoir accumulated runoff sediment, and not until late 2010 did park officials plan for the dredging process to begin anew. The process to remove 20 years of accumulated sediment was finally completed in the winter of 2011, returning the lake, and the peace of mind of residents, to its original levels.

Our ride will continue on new sections of trail built along Georgia Avenue, the Inter County Connector (ICC), and Layhill Road before joining up with the Matthew Henson Trail. Named after the famous Marylander explorer, who blazed a trail to the geographic North Pole in 1909, the Matthew Henson Trail is a relatively new path along the Turkey Branch Stream. We will follow the trail westward back toward the starting point of the ride, along the way riding on long boardwalk trail sections that hover above the forest ground. We will pass by tall oaks and newly planted trees to replace those lost during trail construction.

Unbelievably, it took nearly a decade to complete the trail, primarily because of strong opposition by residents and environmentalists in the area who feared that the trail would devastate parkland, threaten endangered species of plants, and bring all kinds of "unpleasant and criminal activities" to their backyards and homes. Even the Sierra Club opposed its construction and at one point set up information booths during a parks and planning meeting in late 2001 that escalated to near violence. The result is undeniable. The Matthew Henson Trail is a wonderful addition to the Rock Creek Stream Valley and the Turkey Branch. It offers a safe alternative for users and residents to link up with the Rock Creek Trail and a chance for local residents to enjoy the Matthew Henson Park, which until the trail's existence was underappreciated.

Proponents of the trail envision it extending well beyond its terminus in Silver Spring at Alderton Road to the south and connecting it with the Sligo Creek Trail.

MILES & DIRECTIONS

0.0 The ride starts from the Winding Creek Park parking area. Enter the trail between the playground and gazebo and ride toward the basketball courts. Head northwest on the Heron Trail, cross over the small bridge, and turn immediately right into the Rock Creek Trail.

0.8 Go over a small bridge and continue following the trail to the right. The trail will shortly cross the access road to the Parklawn Community Garden.

1.4 Go over the bridge that spans Veirs Mill Road.

3.3 Cross Baltimore Road.

3.5 Go under Norbeck Road and continue straight on the Rock Creek Trail.

4.6 Cross Southlawn Lane.

5.3 Reach Lake Needwood. Turn right at the parking area and head up and to the right to the stop sign. Turn right and follow Beach Road around the lake to the Needwood Road Entrance. To the left are Picnic Area 1 (restrooms) and the Lake Needwood Snack Bar.

5.8 Continue straight.

6.3 Continue straight. Restrooms are available to the left at Picnic Areas 2 and 3.

6.6 Turn right onto Needwood Road. Use caution on this short section of road.

Upper Rock Creek and Montgomery County

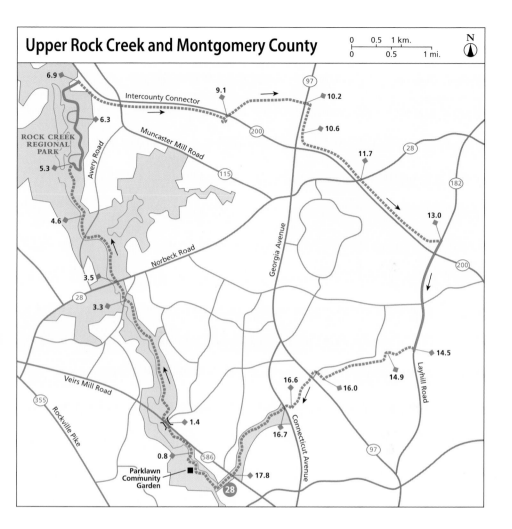

6.9 After a short climb the bike route will pick up again on the right side. Turn right and follow the trail east as it parallels the Inter County Connector (ICC).

9.1 When you come out of the ICC trail, turn right onto Emory Lane to go over the ICC.

10.2 Cross Georgia Avenue to pick up the path on the opposite side of Georgia Avenue.

10.6 Follow the path as it curves to the left. We will follow this trail until it reaches Layhill Road.

11.7 Cross Norbeck Road.

Crossing one of the many bridges on this ride. The paved trails along this ride are all well-kept and maintained.

13.0 Turn right onto Layhill Road. There is a designated bike lane on Layhill.

14.5 When you reach the intersection with Middlevale Lane, make a sharp right (almost U turn) to pick up the Matthew Henson Trail. We'll follow the Matthew Henson Trail all the way back to Winding Creek Park.

14.9 Continue to the left to stay on the Matthew Henson Trail.

16.0 The trail will come out onto Georgia Avenue. Follow the sidewalk to cross Hewitt Road, and then turn left to cross Georgia Avenue. The trail continues on the other side.

16.6 Turn right to continue on the trail and to ride under Connecticut Ave.

16.7 Continue straight.

17.8 Use caution as you cross Veirs Mill Road. The trail picks up on the other side along Edgebrook Road.

18.1 The loop is complete.

Local Events and Attractions

Montgomery County Parks: www.montgomeryparks.org

Restaurants

Azucar Restaurant Bar and Grill: 14418 Layhill Rd., Silver Spring, MD 20906; (301) 438-3293; www.azucarrestaurant.net

Sole D'Italia Restaurant: 14324 Layhill Rd., Silver Spring, MD 20906; (301) 598-6660; www.soleditaliapizza.com

Restrooms

A porta-potty is available at the start of the ride in Winding Creek Park. Restrooms and drinking water are also available in Lake Needwood in Picnic Areas 1, 2, and 3. A snack bar, open in season, is also available in Lake Needwood.

National Harbor

This ride will take you over the newly built Woodrow Wilson Bridge to one of Maryland's newest and most thriving attractions: National Harbor. Along the way we'll ride along both banks of the Potomac where the river begins its journey to the Chesapeake Bay.

Start: Bell Haven Marina

Length: 8.1 miles

Approximate riding time: 1–2 hours, longer if you hang out at National Harbor

Best bike: Any bike

Terrain and trail surface: Paved bike paths and a short section of roads while you explore National Harbor

Traffic and hazards: Other trail users and vehicle traffic in National Harbor

Things to see: Sweeping views of the Potomac, the Bike Deck over the Woodrow Wilson Bridge, National Harbor, and the Awakening

Getting there: From Virginia: Take the Capital Beltway (I-495) to exit 1 headed south on Richmond Highway, Route 1. Once on Route 1, stay in the right lane to take the exit for Fort Hunt Road. Follow Fort Hunt Road for 1.1 miles and turn left onto Belle View Boulevard. At the end of Belle View Boulevard, turn left onto the George Washington Parkway. Turn right into the Belle Haven Marina and then immediately left toward the parking areas.

From MD: Take the local lanes of the Capital Beltway (I-495) over the Woodrow Wilson and take the first exit toward Mt. Vernon. Merge onto Church Street and then make an immediate right onto Washington Street. Cross the Washington Street Deck (bridge over I-495) and you'll be on the George Washington (GW) Parkway. Drive 1.25 miles and turn left into Bell Haven Marina. Immediately turn left again toward the parking areas. GPS: 38.779146,-77.051883

Fees: None

THE RIDE

Just three short years ago, this ride and its destination in Prince George's County, Maryland, would have been impossible: Largely in part because the old Wilson bridge did not include a cycling path, but also because the destination itself, National Harbor, didn't exist. Both projects were in the making for several years. The construction of the new Wilson Bridge was a necessity for the region. Traffic along the old span linking Maryland and Virginia over the Potomac River in the vicinity of Old Town Alexandria often slowed down to a painful crawl, and it was a source of constant frustration for area residents and an ever-increasing number of commuters. In addition, the nearly 40-year-old span was in disrepair, and because of the added traffic using its spans, it was considered a safety hazard.

The bridge, which was originally built between 1958 and 1961 at a cost of nearly $15 million wasn't supposed to carry the traffic it ultimately did over the years. Its original main function was to connect the communities of Alexandria, Virginia, and Oxon Hill, Maryland, but with the completion of the Capital Beltway and the exponential growth of the region, the bridge was quickly outgrown. In 1975 the I-95 Corridor was slated to run through the city, but opposition to the project forced the Interstate Highway Commission to utilize the portion of the Beltway that included the Wilson Bridge, further increasing its use.

By the mid '80s it was evident that the exiting six-lane bridge needed to be replaced. Studies were conducted to come up with alternatives, among those proposals for a tunnel and a tunnel/bridge project. But these alternatives proved to be too expensive. Ultimately the 12-lane bridge with an additional 20 feet of main span clearance and with a dedicated pedestrian and bicycle lane was approved. The bridge was part of an overall Beltway improvement project that is continuing to this day and has cost nearly $2.5 billion.

Construction on the bridge was initiated in early 2000 and included various stages, the first of which was dredging the Potomac to make room

Bike Shops

Spokes Etc.: 1506 Belle View Blvd., Alexandria, VA 22307; (703) 765-8005; www.spokesetc.com
Big Wheel Bikes: 2 Prince St., Alexandria, VA 22314; (703) 739-2300; www .bigwheelbikes.com

A New Maryland Destination

The completion of the Wilson Bridge and the corresponding bike lane and park deck on the Maryland side coincided with the opening of National Harbor, making a ride across the new spans of the bridge for recreational purposes much more worthwhile. As National Harbor has evolved, so have the opportunities for recreation. Not only can you get to the waterfront destination by bike, but you can also hop on one of the many water taxis that depart from the shores of the Potomac on Virginia's side. Once at the Harbor you can enjoy several activities. During the warm summer months, you can even enjoy free Friday night movies. Saturday mornings until early afternoon the Harbor hosts a farmer's market, and in the evenings you can enjoy the Pops on the Potomac concert series. Sundays are family movie nights. If all that doesn't interest you, you can always just go to the harbor and enjoy a quick bite to eat in one of the many restaurants located there; most have outdoor seating. Or you can do as I often do: just grab a sandwich and head over to one of the piers for some fine waterside dining, no wait required.

for a channel to build the first, southbound six-lane span. The plan called for this effort to be completed first so that traffic from the existing bridge could be diverted to the new span. The plan was to demolish the original bridge. The first of the twin spans was open to traffic in 2006 and the second in 2008, culminating nearly a decade of construction.

Roughly at the same time, and with the anticipation of the culmination of the bridge project, officials in Maryland were advocating for the creation of a new resort-like waterfront project in an undeveloped tract of prime real estate land along the Potomac River and within view of Alexandria and the new bridge. The new multiuse development project would be anchored by a hotel and convention center. Plans were set to build hotels, waterfront homes, and other amenities, allowing the area to financially compete with other waterfront communities in the area, including Alexandria, Georgetown, and even Baltimore's Inner Harbor to the north. Proponents in Maryland saw it as an opportunity to bring development and investment to an area that had been otherwise historically ignored. With an anticipated cost of over $2 billion, nearly as much as the Wilson Bridge project itself, construction began in 2007 and the area was opened to the public in 2008.

The project was not all smooth sailing; it has had its setbacks. The Sierra Club opposed it early on because of environmental concerns but failed to stop

National Harbor

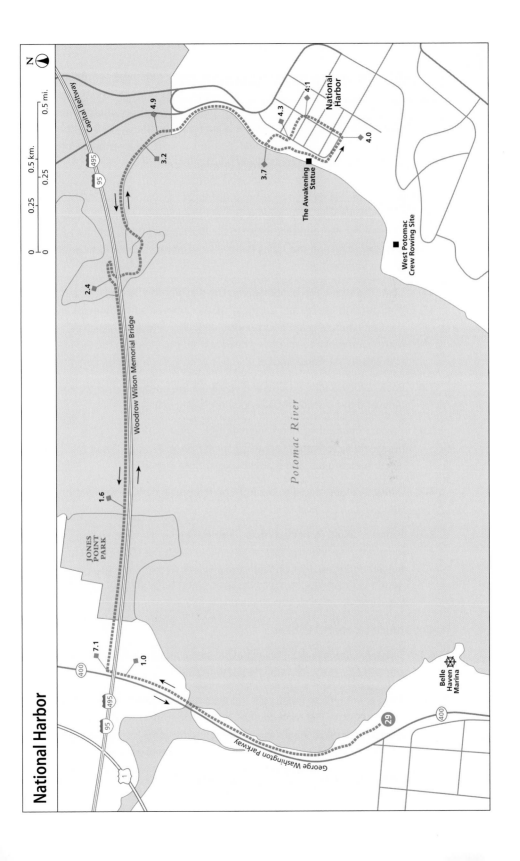

N

0   0.25   0.5 km.
0   0.25   0.5 mi.

Capital Beltway

4.9

3.2

4.3

4.1

4.0

National Harbor

3.7

The Awakening Statue

2.4

West Potomac Crew Rowing Site

Woodrow Wilson Memorial Bridge

Potomac River

1.6

JONES POINT PARK

7.1

1.0

Belle Haven Marina

George Washington Parkway

its development, and in 2008 the site was linked to the discharge of untreated sewage into the Potomac. Ultimately the hurdles were overcome and the mistakes corrected. Today, National Harbor is a new thriving destination for residents and tourists in the region. The site is anchored by the Gaylord National Resort and Convention Center, and when opened, unveiled the restored statue of "The Awakening" on its main plaza and beach.

MILES & DIRECTIONS

0.0 Start on the Mount Vernon Trail in the Bell Haven Marina in front of the restrooms and the Jones Point Historic Marker. Head north on the Mount Vernon Trail.

1.0 Cross the street and continue over the Washington Street Deck. Do not turn right at the first "cardinal" marker. Immediately after crossing the Deck (basically the bridge over I-495) and before you reach St. Mary's Cemetery, turn right to head toward Maryland on the Woodrow Wilson Memorial Bridge.

1.6 Look closely on the ground and you'll see the border marker for Virginia and the District of Columbia. You are now in DC.

2.4 You've crossed the bridge and reached a small park area on the bridge deck dedicated to the history of Prince George's County, worth hanging out and reading some of the markers.

3.2 Continue straight and to the right on the gravel path toward National Harbor.

3.7 You've reached National Harbor. Dismount your bike and walk toward the Awakening Statue. When you reach the statue, walk to the left and then right on Waterfront Street. At this point you can mount your bike again. Follow Waterfront as it curves up and to the left.

4.0 Turn left onto Fleet Street.

4.1 Turn left onto American Way. There is a cool little park on this street and you also get a nice view of the Woodrow Wilson Bridge in the distance.

4.3 Turn right onto Waterfront Street, and at the stop sign turn left to go down the ramp that will take you down to National Harbor. Walk your bike on the ramp and then head toward the gravel path and bike rack you passed when you immediately arrived to National Harbor. Lock your bike and go for a walk. Seriously . . .

The Awakening was relocated from Haines Point (see Ride 5) and now serves as the centerpiece for National Harbor.

After enjoying National Harbor for a while work your way back toward Belle Haven along the same route you came on.

4.9 Continue left to go up to the bridge. The right path will take you toward Oxon Hill Road and the Potomac Heritage Trail. There is a clear and useful map at this intersection.

7.1 Turn left onto the Washington Street Deck to head south to the Mount Vernon Trail.

8.1 The loop is complete.

RIDE INFORMATION

Local Events and Attractions
National Harbor: www.nationalharbor.com

Restaurants
There are lots of restaurants in National Harbor, both formal and casual. When cycling through there, these are my favorites.
Pot Belly: 146 National Plaza, Oxon Hill, MD 20745; (301) 686-1160; www.pot belly.com. Pick up a sandwich and go eat on one of the piers—best views of the river.
Cadillac Ranch: 186 Fleet St., Oxon Hill, MD 20745; (301) 839-1100; www .cadillacranchgroup.com

Restrooms
Restrooms are available at the beginning of the ride in Bell Haven Marina and throughout National Harbor.

Avalon and Rockburn

Over the years the Avalon area of Patapsco Valley State Park has become a regional favorite for mountain biking in the Washington, DC region. And now, with the addition of the Rockburn Mountain Bike Skills Park located in the adjacent Rockburn Branch Regional Park, the area is truly an off-road cycling destination that will keep you coming back for more. This ride will take you through what I think are some of the best trails in Patapsco Valley State Park. The loop I've chosen here is demanding yet incredibly fun and rewarding. I've chosen to combine Patapsco with a small portion of Rockburn Branch Regional Park because of the presence of the new skills park, a popular area with a pump track where you'll often find families enjoying hours of cycling fun. The area can also serve as a staging point for you and your group.

Start: Rockburn Branch Regional Park

Length: 12.9-mile loop; Patapsco does have over 20 miles of trails to augment this ride

Approximate riding time: 2–3 hours

Best bike: Mountain bike

Terrain and trail surface: Mostly singletrack, a section of road and paved bike path

Traffic and hazards: Other trail users

When to ride: This is a great year-round ride and most enjoyable during weekdays or when the weather turns a little cooler. The spring and summer months see a great deal of trail users.

Things to see: The Thomas Viaduct

Getting there: From the Capital Beltway (I-495) take exit 27 to merge onto I-95 North toward Baltimore and continue north for 17 miles to exit 43B for MD 100 West toward Ellicott City. Take exit 4 to merge onto

MD 103 West/Meadowridge Road. Continue straight for approximately 1 mile and turn right onto Ilchester Road. Then turn left onto Landing Road. The park entrance will be approximately 1.5 miles to the right. Continue following the park road all the way until it ends by the power lines and the traffic circle. The Rockburn skills park is up to the right, and the entrance to the trail and ride is along the traffic circle to the left. GPS: 39.219354,-76.759458

Fees: None at Rockburn; if you drive in into Pataspco Valley State Park, there are nominal fees for Maryland residents and out-of-state visitors.

THE RIDE

In Celtic mythology the word Avalon refers to an island paradise, and this portion of the Patapsco Valley State Park is aptly named. Situated between two major metropolitan areas (Baltimore and Washington, DC), this area of Patapsco offers cyclists myriad off-road opportunities. Simply known as "Avalon" by mountain bikers in the area, this corner of Patapsco is quite possibly one of the region's most popular playgrounds. Avalon's terrain is often severe and always challenging—conditions that serious off-roaders crave.

Very little remains of what this area used to look like in the early 19th century, and today, you would have to look hard to find the remnants of the village of Avalon as you ride the trails of Patapsco. A devastating flood in 1868 destroyed virtually all of the structures in the area, leaving only one house standing, which today serves as the River of History and Conservation Visitor Center, a 185-year-old structure that has stood the test of time.

Bike Shops

Princeton Sports: 10730 Little Patuxent Pkwy., Columbia, MD 21044; (410) 995-1894; www.princetonsports.com
Race Pace Bicycles: 8450 Baltimore National Pike, Ellicott City, MD 21043; (410) 461-7878; www.racepace bicycles.com

The park is rich with history, but unfortunately, because of the great flood of 1886, many of the historic structures were washed away. Today, you really have to look hard for signs of the past within the park. Some remnants are clearly visible though. Notable historic landmarks in the park include the Swinging Bridge, which you will cross at mile marker 9.4. Although not the original bridge, previous bridges spanned this area to allow residents of the Orange Grove Mill town to cross the Patapsco to work in the Orange Grove Flower Mill. The mill burned in the early 20th century, but bits and pieces

You May Run into Jonathan Seibold

PHOTO COURTESY JONATHAN SEIBOLD

I first met Jonathan on a group ride on a cold winter day at Rosaryville State Park in Maryland shortly after the park trails had been finished and opened to bikes. It was one of those times when I wasn't physically at my best, and I knew I was slowing him and the group down. But he made no big deal about it, and instead he patiently encouraged me on. The pleasure of being out riding in the woods with friends was augmented by his eagerness to push on and help me finish the ride. This is one of the things I love best about mountain biking: the sense of camaraderie and community that you feel when you're out with a group of friends just enjoying the solitude of the woods, and something that Jonathan and that group of friends reemphasized for me that day.

Jonathan doesn't think it's a big deal, but the encouragement he provided me is something he does every day via his shop, The Family Bike Shop in Crofton. "Running my shop and getting people into riding is awesome," he told me. "I like when kids learn how to ride for the first time. And getting adults that haven't ridden in years back onto a bike is a great feeling; it beats working for a living."

Even though Patapsco is not that close to the shop, Jonathan says it's his favorite place to ride and chances are that's where you'll run into him. "Mountain biking has always been my favorite, ever since I started riding," he added. "I like all the people that I have met and the new people I continue to meet out on the trails. Riding allows me to check out for a while without really having to go anywhere. I always feel refreshed after a ride."

remain. The mill was five stories high and extended from the railroad tracks to the bridge's abutment, and its ruins are still there.

Farther north from the Swinging Bridge are the remains of Bloede's Dam. The dam, which was fully operational by 1907, was meant to provide electricity to nearby towns. It functioned until it was decommissioned in 1924, and later, due to severe storm damage from Hurricane Agnes in 1972, the dam was gutted. Built of reinforced concrete, it was the first of its kind and was the first to house a hydroelectric plant under its causeway.

As you ride along on the orange trail, you will pass by some very prominent ruins. These were homes that belonged to residents of the area, likely people who worked in the mill below by the bridge. They also served as homes for the many young men who were part of the Civilian Conservation Corps (CCC). Those folks worked and transformed the area into the park we know today—Maryland's first state park. Known as Roosevelt's Tree Army, the CCC was composed of thousands of young men who had nowhere else to go. Because of the Great Depression, jobs were nonexistent, and Roosevelt created the CCC to plant trees, build trails, picnic areas, campsites, and various other structures in parks around the country. Patapsco was one of these places, and the majority of the structures that are standing today are a result of those mid-20th-century efforts. Guided by the Army and the National Park Service, the young men would earn $30 per month, of which they kept $5 and sent the rest home to their struggling families. During the day they would work on the parks and in the evenings they would attend school. Many later joined the military and served in WWII in defense of our nation, as part of "the greatest generation," the ones who truly reshaped our nation.

Most recently, the park trails have been worked on and maintained by an army of local volunteers. Several trails, including the ones in the orange grove, have been rerouted to withstand the daily use by numerous park visitors. The proximity of Patapsco to two major metropolitan areas raises some concerns regarding overuse. Hundreds of cyclists, hikers, and equestrians crowd this trail system on any given weekend, making trail maintenance a very serious issue, not to mention a serious challenge. To maintain access to this priceless off-road habitat, make sure you get involved with local clubs, organizations, park officials, and other trail users to preserve the integrity of the area.

The loop I provide here is one of my personal favorites and the one I generally ride when I come to Patapsco. If you want to add a few miles to this route, you can also ride the Rockburn Branch loop. Although I don't detail it here, it is very easy to follow. You can also park alongside Landing Road (though I don't recommend it), in the Park & Ride off route I-195, or in the park itself to begin your ride. With more than 20 miles of singletrack and a seemingly endless network of trails winding up and down the river valley, this section of Patapsco Valley State Park is a do-it-yourselfer's paradise. My route is simply a recommendation to get you acquainted with the trails, and although I think it hits the best trails, there are many more I simply could not list. I highly encourage you to get a park map from the visitor's center and head out into the woods. You can spend an entire day exploring this incredibly valuable natural resource from the seat of your bike.

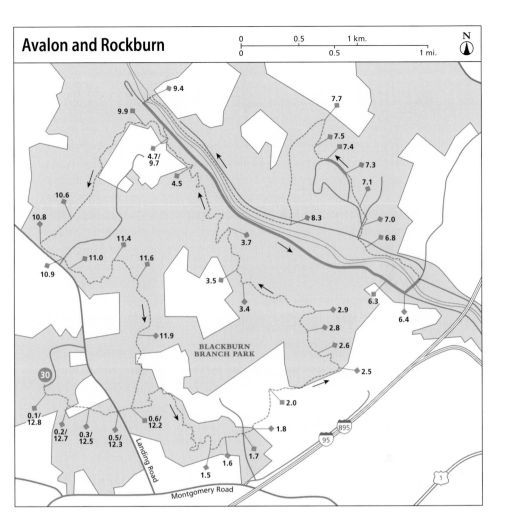

MILES & DIRECTIONS

0.0 From the far parking lot, ride down to the small traffic circle. Use the trailhead to your left adjacent to the paved path that leads toward the athletic fields. As soon as you enter the trail, turn to the left.

0.1 As you come down the short hill and cross the small creek, turn right. Follow the fence line as it curves to the left.

0.2 Continue following the fence line to the left.

0.3 Stay to the left and follow the trail as it continues under the power lines.

0.5   Cross Landing Road and enter the Morning Choice Trail of Patapsco Valley State Park. Shortly after entering the trail, turn right.

0.6   Turn left into the singletrack trail. If you reach an open field, you've gone too far. This trail is a narrow and twisty path that will bypass an often muddy and troublesome area of the park.

1.5   Continue to the left at this T intersection.

1.6   Stay to the left again.

1.7   Cross the private road and continue straight on the trail on the opposite side.

1.8   Turn left onto the main trail and prepare for a nice downhill. Use caution since this is a two-way trail.

2.0   The trail curves to the right.

2.4   Continue following the trail to the right and then as it curves up and to the left. Your first climb starts here.

2.5   Turn left and follow the purple blazes. The trail to the right is a shortcut to the intersection at mile marker 2.9.

2.6   Stay to the right after crossing the small ground-level bridge; the climb will get a little steeper here.

2.8   Turn right at this intersection.

2.9   Turn left onto the yellow-blazed Morning Choice Trail. The trail will climb for a short time and then come out to the perimeter of the field. At dusk there are often multiple deer on the fields.

3.4   The trail turns back into the woods. As soon as you enter the tree cover, you'll turn right to follow the connector trail to the orange-blazed Ridge Trail. To the left the yellow trail continues back toward the intersection for mile marker 11.0 (you can cut the ride considerably here if you choose).

3.5   Turn left at this intersection. You'll now be on the orange loop as it descends (mostly) to the Patapsco River.

3.7   Stay to the left; to the right is the hiking-only Valley View Trail—years ago that trail was open to bikes. It was a glorious time.

4.5   Stay to the left to continue on the orange trail.

4.7 Stay to the right and continue down the doubletrack to the road. Our return trip will take us up the path to the left. This is another bail-out point if you choose to head back. When you reach the road, turn right.

6.3 The Avalon Area is to the left. Restrooms and water are available here.

6.4 Turn left onto Gun Road to go over the bridge that spans the Patapsco River. Immediately after crossing the bridge, turn left onto the singletrack trail that parallels the river.

6.8 Come out of the trail and head through the parking area and go under the tunnel that crosses the railroad tracks toward the upper and lower Glen Artney areas.

7.0 At this point you have three options. You can climb up on the road to the left, continue straight and turn left to climb up on the trail adjacent to the restrooms, or take the Soapstone Trail, slightly ahead to the left as you ride on the right fork. We'll take the Soapstone Trail to the top. Either option will be a grueling category 4 climb to the top, but it's worth it, trust me . . .

7.1 Continue straight through this intersection and then follow the trail to the left to join the road, one final push on this climb. The trail to the right is one of the options I outlined at mile 7.0.

7.3 Turn right on the pavement. Had you taken the road climb, this is where you would end up.

7.4 Continue on the road to the split and follow it to the right through the small parking area. Go through the gate and continue on the doubletrack as it climbs slightly to the left. The trail will be blazed red.

7.5 Continue straight on the path following the red blazes. The trail to the left is hiking only.

7.7 Turn left onto the Vineyard Trail and enjoy one of the best singletrack descents in the region.

8.3 Turn right onto the paved path.

9.4 Turn left and walk over the hanging bridge. As soon as you cross the bridge, turn left onto the road.

Riders will always have a smile on their face when they exit the Vineyard Trail; quite possibly one of the most fun singletrack descents in the DC/Baltimore area.

9.6 Turn right onto the dirt path as it climbs into the tree cover. This is the same point where we exited on marker 4.7.

9.7 Make a sharp right and continue on the orange trail.

9.9 Stay left at this intersection and follow the blue blazes.

10.6 Continue to the right at this intersection.

10.8 Turn left at the trail sign shortly before you reach Landing Road. Follow the trail as it slightly climbs and rides parallel to Landing Road.

10.9 Cross the road and continue on the trail straight across.

11.0 Continue straight.

11.4 Turn right at this intersection. You are now on the yellow loop. Stay right again to follow the red blazes.

11.6 Stay to the right again and continue following the yellow blazes.

11.9 Stay to the left. The fork to the right will ultimately take you to the same place, but it is a longer route.

12.2 Continue to the right. At this point you are doubletracking back on the trail you came in on and heading back to Rockburn Branch Park.

12.3 Cross Landing Road and enter Rockburn Branch Park.

12.5 Turn left at the second turn that enters the tree cover.

12.7 Continue following the trail and fence line to the right and then swing left to cross the creek.

12.8 Follow the trail to the right and out into the parking area.

12.9 Complete the loop.

RIDE INFORMATION

Local Events and Attractions
Howard County, Maryland: www.visithowardcounty.com
Patapsco Valley State Park: www.dnr.state.md.us/publiclands/central/patapsco.asp

Restaurants
Frisco Grille: 6695 Dobbin Rd., Columbia, MD 21045; (410) 312-4907; www.friscogrille.com

Restrooms
Restrooms are available as you enter Rockburn Branch Park and at Patapsco Valley State Park in the Avalon area. Porta-potties are also available by the west-side pavilion in Rockburn Branch Park.

Rosaryville State Park

Avalon's little sister. Nestled just outside the Beltway in Southern Maryland is Rosaryville State Park. Conceived in partnership by the Mid-Atlantic Off-Road Enthusiasts (MORE) and Maryland's Department of Natural Resources (DNR), Rosaryville is one of the region's newest off-road destinations. The ride is similar to Patapsco, but with less of the "extreme" portion. There is a single 8-mile single-track perimeter loop that circumnavigates the park with a short inner extension technical loop that's bound to please the most demanding riders.

Start: Rosaryville State Park Parking lot

Length: 8.3/9.8 miles

Approximate riding time: 1–2 hours

Best bike: Mountain bike

Terrain and trail surface: Mostly singletrack trails

Traffic and hazards: Other trail users, including runners and the occasional equestrian group

Things to see: Mount Airy Mansion

Getting there: From the Capital Beltway (I-495) take exit 11A for MD 4 South/Pennsylvania Avenue toward Upper Marlboro. Continue for approximately 2 miles and take the MD 223/Woodyard Road exit toward Clinton/Melwood Road and then make an immediate left onto Marlboro Pike. Marlboro Pike will become Osborne Road. Turn right onto US 301 South and then right again onto West Marlton Avenue (the park entrance). Turn right at the first intersection (pay your fee) and continue into the parking area to your right. GPS: 38.78091,-76.802641

Fees: Honor system chargeable at all times

Rosaryville State Park is a relatively new riding destination in the Washington, DC region. Not long ago off-road cyclists had very few options to ride in southern Maryland, Cedarville State Forest being one of them. Riders often had to make the trek across the Beltway to neighboring Virginia or farther north in Maryland to find quality singletrack, but that all changed in 2000 when MORE member Austin Steo (see Ride 21, Fairland ride, for more about Austin's vision and passion for cycling) spied a small sign and locked gate at an undeveloped area of Rosaryville State Park. Austin was on his way to ride Cedarville with a group of friends when he noticed the tract of land, and later, after inspecting some topographic maps of the area, he came to the realization that they could be the perfect location for a system of trails. Excited about the prospect (he borrowed my GPS), Austin headed out to do an initial survey of what was out there and returned wide-eyed as to the incredible potential the area offered. Soon after his discovery he started making a few calls and wound up in contact with the Rosaryville Conservancy and members of the Maryland Department of Natural Resources, to whom he pitched the idea of building new sustainable trails and offered to put together a proposal to do so.

Bike Shops

Bike Doctor: 3200 Leonardtown Rd., Waldorf, MD 20601; (301) 932-9980; www.bikedoctorwaldorf.com
Family Bike Shop: 1286 MD 3 South, Ste. #13, Crofton, MD 21114; (410) 721-8244; www.familybikeshop.com

The Conservancy and DNR were intrigued and allowed Austin to proceed. Since Rosaryville was a little out of the way for him, Austin recruited another MORE member, Todd Brooks, to aid him in the effort. After a brief meeting the two set out to explore and survey Rosaryville even further and determined that the potential for a 9-mile perimeter loop existed in the park. With two people excited about the prospect of new trails in the area, the project began to gain steam. Todd and Austin then took Dan Hudson of IMBA and his wife, Karen Garnett, out to the park to show them what they had found, and Dan recommended they involve IMBA's trail building guru, Rich Edwards, to advise and help with the planning. The involvement of Rich Edwards was critical in the development of the trails. By this time Austin had become MORE's Maryland advocacy director and had managed to help the club secure $75,000 in grants from the state of Maryland toward the development of trails in the region. Part of that money went into the building of trails at Rosaryville and the funding needed to have IMBA's Trail Solutions Crew provide their expertise and mechanized equipment to bench cut and build new trail. During the peak of

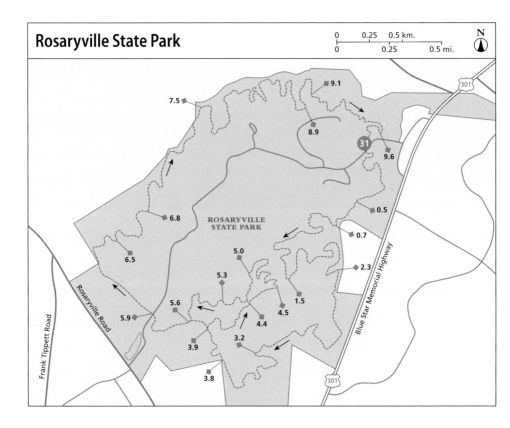

Rosaryville State Park

construction, volunteers and IMBA's crew were building about 800 feet of trail per day.

The first build day was scheduled for November 12, 2002, and was attended by myriad volunteers who included not only MORE members but also DNR representatives and members of the Rosaryville Conservancy, including avid equestrians. After nearly 3 years of work, the trail was completed in 2005, and today it has become an incredibly popular destination for cyclists in the region.

The perimeter loop runs for a little over 8 miles and offers cyclists of all levels a challenging and fun experience. The trails take complete advantage of the lay of the land and follow its contours in a natural and exciting fashion. Fast downhills, challenging climbs, and fun and twisty singletrack make for a ride that you'll want to head back to over and over. After the trail's completion an extension was added to the loop, also documented here, but for some reason it has seen very little use over time, a testament, perhaps, to how well built and enjoyable the perimeter loop is. As you ride Rosaryville, please bear in mind that unlike Fountainhead, this is a two-way trail, and encountering other riders coming at you in the opposite direction is a real possibility. Please ride within your limits.

MILES & DIRECTIONS

0.0   As you drive into the trail parking area, you'll see a trailhead to your left. After you park, make your way back to that entrance. It is where we'll start the ride. The majority of the ride is clearly marked with white trail markers and very easy to follow.

0.5   Continue straight through this intersection.

0.7   Cross the creek; continue to the right.

1.5   Stay to the left at this intersection.

2.3   Stay left at this intersection and then left again at the T intersection to cross the creek.

3.2   Continue to the left.

3.8   Continue straight.

3.9   At this point you can continue to the left on the perimeter loop or take a right to do a quick side loop to add a little mileage to your ride. We'll go right to give you this option and eventually come out on the perimeter loop about 100 yards farther down the trail.

4.4   Follow the trail to the left and then immediately to the right at the three-way intersection.

4.5   Turn left as the trail reaches the power lines. Continue left again.

5.0   Stay to the right and continue through the next intersection.

5.1   Continue straight through this intersection. No more than 10 yards up to the left is the intersection we just rode through at mile 4.4.

5.3   Stay to the left.

5.6/4.1   Stay to the left and then to the right again at this intersection. Less than 100 yards to the left is the intersection we passed at marker 3.9. You have effectively added 1.7 miles to your ride. If you chose NOT to ride the optional loop, you are now at mile marker 4.1. Continue to follow the second set of numbers from now on.

5.9/4.4   Cross the park road to continue on the perimeter loop.

The author riding one of the wood features at Rosaryville State Park. PHOTO JASON ASHMORE

6.5/5.0 Continue to the left as you ride over a small bridge.

6.8/5.3 Either fork will take you to the same place. Your choice.

7.5/6.0 Continue straight through this intersection.

8.9/7.4 Stay to the left to continue on the perimeter trail.

9.1/7.6 Continue straight through this intersection.

9.3/7.8 Stay to the left at this intersection; to the right is a shortcut to the parking area.

9.6/8.1 Stay to the right.

9.8/8.3 The trail comes out into the parking area; your loop is complete.

RIDE INFORMATION

Local Events and Attractions
Upper Marlboro: http://uppermarlboromd.gov
Mount Airy Mansion: www.mountairymansion.org

Restaurants
Olde Towne Inn: 14745 Main St., Upper Marlboro, MD 20772; (301) 627-1400; www.otitherestaurant.com
Moms Thai Kitchen: 14710 Main St., Upper Marlboro, MD 20772; (301) 627-0011; www.momsthaikitchen.com

Restrooms
A porta-potty is available in the main parking area.

Schaeffer Farms

The trails at Schaeffer Farms are a perfect example of mountain bike advocacy at work. In this ride you'll be rolling across the fruits of hard work and efforts of a handful of dedicated mountain bikers. The trail system at Schaeffer is a gem in the region, miles of twisty and fun singletrack cross the landscape to give you an oasis of dirt.

Start: Schaeffer Farms parking area

Length: Up to 18 miles, more if you add the Seneca Ridge Trail into the mix. The loop detailed here is 10.0 miles.

Approximate riding time: 1–2 hours

Best bike: Mountain bike

Terrain and trail surface: Mostly singletrack

Traffic and hazards: Trail features and obstacles and other trail users

Things to see: Schaeffer is a great example of a piedmont trail. Through the ride you'll cross and ride by local farms.

Getting there: From the Capital Beltway (495) take I-270 north toward Frederick. Take exit 15B to merge onto MD 118 South toward Germantown. In approximately 4 miles turn right onto Germantown Park Drive and then left onto Schaeffer Road. The entrance to the Schaeffer Farms Trail system will be 0.5 mile to the left as the road curves right. Watch your speed along Germantown Park Road and Schaeffer Road; Montgomery County has speed cameras installed on both of these streets. GPS: 39.142809,-77.310448

Fees: None

THE RIDE

Schaeffer Farms, near Germantown (northern Montgomery County), is within the boundaries of Seneca Creek State Park. This area is part of a stream valley that extends for approximately 12 miles along Seneca Creek. The trails at Schaeffer are located on a portion of land leased by the county to local farmers, who use it to grow corn and a variety of other vegetables.

For some time, an adjacent tract of land of nearly 2,000 acres lay undeveloped and overgrown. Today, the white-blazed trail (unofficially the Scull loop) and the longer yellow-blazed trail (unofficially the Magill loop) are complete. Several new trails have been added since the main loops were completed, including a connector trail blazed green (unofficially Hurson Heights) that ties both loops together, a red-blazed extension loop, and several bisecting trails in the white and yellow loops blazed orange. In total there are nearly 18 miles of trails at Schaeffer Farms. Add to that the Seneca Ridge Trail, which begins from the white loop and the connecting Hoyles Mill Trail, and you could feasibly ride over 40 miles of singletrack in one day. It's no surprise why Schaeffer is an integral part of the MoCo epic, an organized and supported autumn event that takes riders through several Montgomery County Parks and reaches nearly 70 miles in length.

Originally the trails were meant to be mountain bike only, much like those at Fountainhead Regional Park in neighboring Virginia, but in 1994 State Senator Brian Frosh helped the Mid-Atlantic Off-Road Enthusiasts (MORE) persuade the Maryland Department of Natural Resources to honor their promise that Schaeffer would remain multiuse.

MORE has always worked with land managers to ensure that other users also enjoy the trails built by cyclists. The club advocates and practices responsible riding and abides by an unwritten creed to respectfully share the trail with other users. Their efforts in educating riders across the region have been instrumental in ensuring the fostering of lasting relationships with other users. What was once an uncommon site today is the norm: equestrians, hikers, and cyclists all working together to build trails that can be enjoyed by all.

Bike Shops

Germantown Cycles Bike Shop: 12615 Wisteria Dr., Germantown, MD 20874; (240) 404-0695; www.germantowncycles.com

Gaithersburg Bicycles: 811 Russell Ave. #C, Gaithersburg, MD 20879; (301) 948-6126; www.gaithersburgbicycles.com

The additions of the green and orange trails were made possible not only by the efforts of volunteers but also by the help of Maryland's leaders in the state's Capitol. In the early 2000s the chair of the House Environmental Matters Committee, State Congressman John Hurson, invited representatives of

You May Run into Denis Chazelle (@MoCoEpic)

As you ride through the shaded portions of Schaeffer Farms, you'll likely chance by Denis, and more than likely he'll just be passing through during one of his epic rides. See, Denis loves long-distance cycling and has completed (actually finished 2nd) in one of the most demanding races on the planet, the Tour Divide. Denis finished the 2,750-mile self-supported mountain bike race along the Continental Divide, from Antelope Wells, New Mexico, to Banff, Canada, in 23 days and 9 hours, virtually riding through heat, rain, and snow for nearly 16 hours a day. It's a grueling race that includes over 200,000 feet of climbing (imagine riding up Everest seven times) and crosses some inhospitable territory, including deserts with extreme weather changes. "I always liked to be outside and to travel long distance," he told me. "A bike is the best way to accomplish that."

His love for long-distance cycling led him to launch an event that is quickly becoming one of the most popular in the region, the MoCo Epic (Montgomery County Epic). As Denis rode the Montgomery County trails and dirt roads, he realized that he could link them all together to create one "epic" ride and felt the need to share his routes with the rest of us. So, in 2009 he and a group of friends set out to ride what would become the first MoCo Epic in 2010.

Today, the annual event draws nearly 700 riders who choose from one of four epic rides (25-, 35-, 50-, and 65-mile loops) along some of Montgomery County's best parks and trails.

"It's very easy to forget that you're in the middle of a suburban area with close to a million people," he told me. "I've been cycling all of my life, and these are some of my favorite trails."

The ride is supported along the way by several aid stations provided by local area businesses and bike shops and volunteers, and all proceeds benefit the local Mountain Bike Club, the Mid-Atlantic Off-Road Enthusiasts (MORE). So, if you're up to it, and want to experience an incredible adventure, join Denis for a short ride through MoCo's trails.

the Maryland Department of Natural Resource to his office in Annapolis. Their meeting resulted in the approval of several extensions in the system, including one of the best additions to the park, the green trail that connects the yellow and white loops. Unofficially named Hurson Heights, the trail offers riders additional options previously unavailable. Riders can now take the white loop to the yellow via the green trail and return to the starting point of their ride without riding a trail twice, something that couldn't be done before. The new trails have further improved the quality of the Schaeffer Farms and made it a local favorite.

MILES & DIRECTIONS

The trails at Schaeffer Farms are well marked and blazed. Each intersection is numbered and has a trail map so you can easily locate yourself within the system. I have offered you my personal favorite "guided" route, but I think you would be best served by exploring the landscape on your own and designing your own favorite loop. There are two main trails at Schaeffer Farms—I have "unofficially" named each after the men responsible the creation of this system, Dave Scull and Dave Magill.

The white "Scull" loop is a 4-mile belt that will give you a good idea of what the rest of the system is like. From the white loop you can access the longer yellow loop (in two places), ride the new orange connector trails, the green trail, and access the Seneca Ridge Trail (Ride 33). The orange connectors split the white loop in two places, allowing you to ride a figure 8 if you choose.

The yellow "Magill" loop is longer but very much like the shorter white loop. You can access the yellow loop shortly after starting the white loop if you are riding it counterclockwise or via the green connector trail about 1 mile into the white loop, if you are riding clockwise.

From the yellow loop you can also access another short orange extension, the lightly used red loop, and the blue connector "open field trail," which often serves as a bail-out out from the yellow loop.

My personal preference, and the ride I detail here, begins with the white loop, then the yellow loop, and returns again to the white loop via the green connector trail. My ride generally skips the two orange bisecting trails in the white loop, unless I still have the legs for them. I encourage you to study the map as you enter the system or at every intersection and decide along the way what is best for you. Once you familiarize yourself with the system, you are bound to find your favorite.

(#) denotes the intersection number as marked on the official Schaeffer Farms map and on the trail signs along the trail.

0.0 (1) From the parking area, enter the trail system and turn left onto the white loop. I like heading in a clockwise direction since you get to hit a couple of very nice downhill sections and get to ride most of the white trail before entering the yellow loop.

0.7 (2) Stay left to continue on the white loop and then right over the small bridge. The orange trail will split the white loop in half.

0.9 (3) Stay to the left; the orange connector continues to the right.

1.8 (5) Stay to the left to continue on the white loop. To the right is the orange connector.

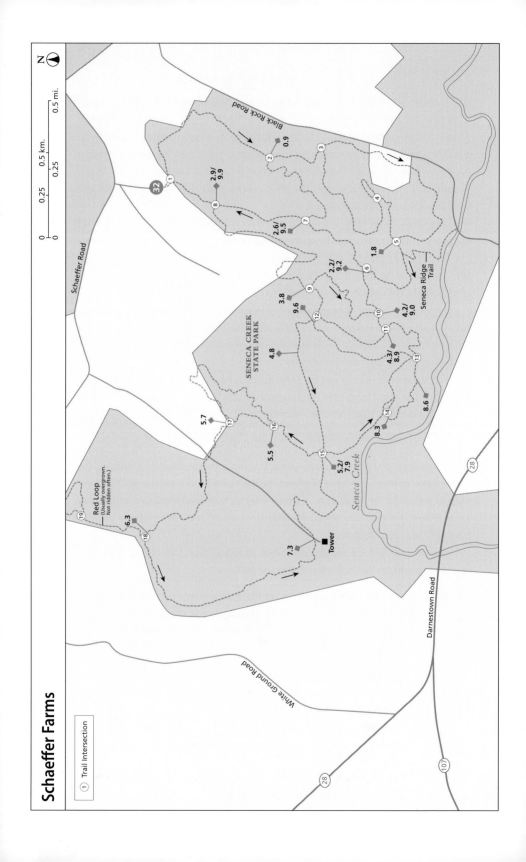

Schaeffer Farms

○1 Trail Intersection

Schaeffer Road

Black Rock Road

32

0.9

2.9/
9.9

2.6/
9.5

1.8

2.2/
9.2

Seneca Ridge
Trail

SENECA CREEK
STATE PARK

3.8

9.6

4.8

4.2/
9.0

4.3/
8.9

8.6

5.7

5.5

8.3

5.2/
7.9

Seneca Creek

Red Loop
(Usually overgrown.
Not ridden often.)

6.3

7.3

Tower

White Ground Road

Darnestown Road

28

28

107

N

0   0.25   0.5 km.

0   0.25   0.5 mi.

1.9   To the left is the entrance to the Seneca Ridge Trail (SRT); continue straight.

2.2 (6)   Stay to the right after crossing the creek. We will return from the green trail to the left when finishing the ride and double back along this short section of the white loop.

2.6 (7)   Stay to the left to continue on the white loop. To the right is the orange connector trail; taking it would take you to intersection #2, mile marker 0.7.

2.9 (8)   Turn left to enter the yellow loop. The parking area is 0.5 mile ahead to the right.

3.8 (9)   Stay to the left at this intersection to continue on the yellow trail.

4.2 (10)   Stay right to continue on the yellow loop. We'll ride the green trail on the way back.

4.3 (11)   Stay to the right.

4.6 (12)   Continue straight (to the right) to enter the blue open field trail.

4.8   Stay to the left on the doubletrack.

5.2 (15)   Turn right to get back on the yellow trail.

5.5 (16)   Stay to the left to stay on the yellow loop.

5.7 (17)   Stay to the left to continue on the yellow loop.

6.3 (18)   Stay to the left to continue on the yellow loop. To the right is the seldom-used red trail.

7.3   Cross the gravel road. The cell tower will be to your right.

7.9 (15)   Back at intersection 15, turn right to hop on the yellow trail and begin the return to the starting point.

8.3 (14)   Turn right and hop on the green trail. Continue following the green "Hurson Heights" trail all the way down to the white loop.

8.6   Stay to the right at this intersection to continue on the green trail; intersection 13 is about 20 yards to the left.

8.9 (11)   Stay to the right, you'll be riding the yellow/green trail. After a short uphill you'll turn right again to stay on the green trail.

9.0 (10)   Stay right on the green trail.

9.2 (6)   Turn left on the white trail. You'll double back along this portion of the white trail on the way back to your vehicle.

The trails at Schaeffer Farms run right through the middle of working farms.

9.5 (7) Continue straight to head back to the parking area, or, if you want to add a little extra mileage, turn right to ride the orange trail. The available trail maps will show you the way.

9.9 (8) Stay to the right.

10.0 (1) Back at the parking area, the loop is complete.

RIDE INFORMATION

Local Events and Attractions
Maryland Soccerplex: www.mdsoccerplex.org
Montgomery County, Maryland: www.visitmontgomery.com/events-calendar

Restaurants
La Mexicana: 13016 Middlebrook Rd., Germantown, MD 20704; (301) 972-0500; www.lamexicanaonline.com

Restrooms
A portable toilet is available in the parking area of Schaeffer Farms. Restrooms are also available in the parking area for fields C, D, and E at the corner of Schaeffer Road and Germantown Park Road adjacent to the playground and tennis courts.

Seneca Ridge Trail (SRT)

The Seneca Ridge Trail (SRT) is one of the region's new additions to the vast catalog of off-road riding destinations. This trail is pretty special, and bound to become a showpiece for the Maryland Department of Natural Resources. The 7-mile ribbon of singletrack connects Schaeffer's white loop with the Seneca Creek Park System, giving you the chance to ride nearly 20 miles of just singletrack. Add the loops at Schaeffer Farms and you could spin nearly 40 miles in classic East Coast ribbon.

Start: Schaeffer Farms parking area, entrance to the white loop

Length: 21.9 miles

Approximate riding time: 2–3 hours

Best bike: Mountain bike

Terrain and trail surface: Mostly singletrack

Traffic and hazards: Trail features and obstacles and other trail users

Things to see: Black Hill Mill

Getting there: From the Capital Beltway (I-495) take I-270 north toward Frederick. Take exit 15B to merge onto MD 118 South toward Germantown. In approximately 4 miles turn right onto Germantown Park Drive and then left onto Schaeffer Road. The entrance to the Schaeffer Farm Trail system will be 0.5 mile to the left as the road curves right. Watch your speed along Germantown Park Road and Schaeffer Road—Montgomery County has speed cameras installed on both of these streets. GPS: 39.142809,-77.310448

Fees: None

THE RIDE

Back in the mid-1990s when I was working on my first book, I had the plea-sure of heading out with good friend and local advocacy guru David Scull on

33

a flagging mission to Schaeffer Farms, a local tract of land that for the most part lay undeveloped and was only being used by local farmers. Much of the wooded lands around the farm eventually become the Schaeffer Farms mountain bike trail system (see Ride 32). That day we hung tape on what was to become the white loop in the park. Little did we know how far those first steps would take the mountain bike community and how important that park would become in the development of off-road cycling, not only in Montgomery County, Maryland, but in the region as a whole.

Fast-forward nearly 20 years and there are over 18 miles of singletrack trails in that park. And just recently, efforts to add more trails to the system have been successful. Thanks to the efforts of another friend, and also an advocacy and trails guru in our region, Dave Magill, there is a new strip of trail extending from the white loop at Schaeffer Farms to the already established trails at Clopper Lake. Our ride will take us along that trail and back so that we can ride both the white loop at Schaeffer and the perimeter trail at Clopper Lake.

The genesis of the Seneca Ridge Trail goes to the time when the Schaeffer Farms trails were being first put in but it never materialized. The hiker-only Seneca Greenway Trail was also being built at the same time, and unfortunately it was unfeasible to build a second multiuse trail alongside it, simply because the area along the north/west side of Seneca Creek was too narrow and could not support two trails. Furthermore, and despite the fact that there were several neighborhood-maintained trails along the south side of the creek, it was impossible to build a through-way because of the existence of a shotgun skeet shooting range along the banks of the creek that would have made safe passage via a trail impossible.

Bike Shops

Germantown Cycles Bike Shop: 12615 Wisteria Dr., Germantown, MD 20874; (240) 404-0695; www.germantowncycles.com
Gaithersburg Bicycles: 811 Russell Ave. #C, Gaithersburg, MD 20879; (301) 948-6126; www.gaithersburgbicycles.com

That all changed, however, when in 2008 the lease for the shooting range expired and the Maryland Department of Natural Resources decided not to renew it. That created the opportunity for the Seneca Ridge Trail (SRT) to be built. With the success of Schaeffer Farms behind them, the Mid-Atlantic Off-Road Enthusiasts (MORE) developed a proposal for DNR in which they outlined how to provide all the necessary funds and labor to build the new multiuse trail. DNR and the local area park managers liked what they saw and decided to approach other user groups to get their input, including equestrian and hiker organizations. After a couple of years of environmental studies and reviews, public meet-

You May Run into Dave Magill

Dave Magill is mostly responsible for the majority of the trail you'll be riding here. He's also responsible for several miles of other trail, including Schaeffer Farms and sections of Cabin John Regional Park. Now, he'll humble up and tell you otherwise. Truth is he's had help, but really, if it weren't for him, many of the trails mountain bikers enjoy in Montgomery County would not be available

PHOTO COURTESY OF DAVE MAGILL

today. Dave has lived in Rockville, Maryland, for nearly 20 years, and cycling for as long as he can remember. He rode solo in France for three weeks before taking some time off from cycling to care for his children. He discovered off-road cycling in 1993 when he moved to the DC area and loves the freedom cycling offers him. "It gives me a chance to clear my mind," he said, "to feel strong and happy, to enjoy the beauty of the great outdoors; it's what keeps me coming back."

He's put that love for cycling into good use. Along with his good friend Dave Scull (who drew on his incomparable contacts from many years of public service in state and county government), they have advocated to build miles of trails in Montgomery County. His first efforts were the loops that cyclists continue to enjoy at Schaeffer Farms. After a short hiatus he came back with a vengeance, and in 2000 led the expansion of Schaeffer and sold regional park managers on a vision that has continued to guide trail development in Montgomery County. Since then things have fallen into place and the Hoyles Mill Connector, the Seneca Ridge Trail, and the Seneca Bluffs Trail have become a reality. The vision for a trail (trails) to connect Montgomery County's park is also closer to happening. "I'm not sure what we'll get approved to build next year or so," he said, "but I am hoping for more." Let's hope so as well, because judging by his efforts thus far, the results should be highly enjoyable. If you run into Dave on the trail, make sure to say thanks; he certainly deserves it.

ings, and consultations, the SRT and a second trail, the Seneca Bluffs Trail, were approved, with MORE as the designated lead for its construction.

With the help of hundreds of volunteers from all user groups, MORE began the effort in earnest. By September 2011 the group completed the 6.25 miles of trail that connected the Schaeffer Farms white loop with Seneca Creek State Park, just in time for their annual fall picnic. The second trail, the Seneca Bluffs

Seneca Ridge Trail (SRT)

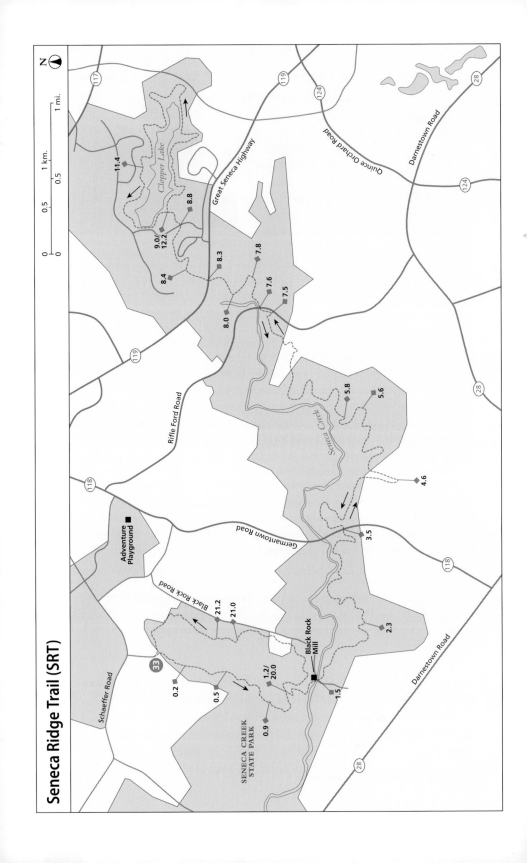

Trail, is currently under construction, and by the time you read this should have been completed and ready to ride (I'll provide an update on the book's companion site, www.bestridesdc.com, when it is completed).

The SRT has quickly become one of my favorite singletrack rides in the region. The flow of the trail is fantastic and built with the cross-country rider in mind. It utilizes the contours almost perfectly and is an absolute joy to ride. If you are a beginner to intermediate rider, you'll love it because it caters to your abilities. If you are an advanced rider, you'll simply adore it because it will give you an opportunity to find a rhythm you seldom can in other regional trails. You can certainly tell that great thought went into its development. During one of my last rides on the SRT, I got caught smack in the middle of a torrential downpour as I exited the Clopper Lake loop. By the time I reached Riffle Ford Road, the rain had stopped. I was astounded and amazed by how well the trail had drained in such a short period of time. As I made my way back to Schaeffer Farms, it was evident that the trail builders had taken this into account and ensured that the trail was properly aligned to allow water to run off its surface and to the stream below.

I do urge you to check ahead and plan accordingly so that you don't ride on wet trails, as they are more susceptible to damage. Despite the fact that the SRT has been built with this in mind, the trails at Clopper Lake and some sections of the white loop at Schaeffer don't drain as well and tend to degrade and erode much quicker, so please be cognizant of that.

MILES & DIRECTIONS

The ride starts from the Schaeffer Farm parking area. We will begin measuring by the gate where the tarmac meets the dirt. Turn left or right onto the Schaeffer white loop to reach the entrance to the SRT. For tracking purposes we'll go right and return from the left. Schaeffer Farms is clearly marked and trail maps are available at all major intersections to guide you.

0.0   Turn right to enter the Schaeffer white loop. Just follow the white blazes.

0.2   Stay to the left to stay on the white trail.

0.5   Continue straight to stay on the white trail. The trail to the left (orange) is also one of the newer additions to the Schaeffer Farms trail system. This trail bisects the white loop in two and adds a series of technical "whoops" to the ride. Stay on the white loop.

0.9   Stay to the left at this intersection slightly before the creek crossing. The green trail to the right connects with the longer yellow trail. This trail is awesome coming back in the opposite direction.

1.2 You've reached the intersection of the SRT. Turn right onto the SRT. You will pretty much ride straight (technically speaking) on the SRT for the next 7 miles.

1.5 Turn right onto Black Rock Road to cross the Seneca Creek and then turn left onto the SRT immediately after crossing the bridge. Black Rock Mill will be to your right. The Montgomery County Road loop takes you through this section.

2.3 Continue straight through this intersection. This is the first of several neighborhood connectors. As you continue on the SRT, you will encounter several more of these branch trails. From trail wear it is quite obvious which is the SRT and which are simply neighborhood connectors.

3.5 Cross Germantown Road (118). Use caution.

4.6 Continue straight through this intersection.

5.6 Stay to the left at this intersection.

5.8 Stay left past two intersections.

7.5 You've reached the end of the SRT. Cross Riffle Ford Road and turn left. Pass two trailheads to your right. These both lead into the yellow trail and are alternate entrances to Seneca Creek State Park. We will continue ahead and use the Seneca Creek Greenway Trail instead. If you choose, you can turn back at this point.

7.6 Turn right onto the gravel path immediately before the creek and ride parallel to the creek. The creek will be to your left. Go through the gate and then turn right onto the Seneca Creek Greenway Trail. The trail is blazed blue.

7.8 Stay to the left and follow the low trail. Cross the creek and then turn right onto the Greenway Trail. You will then turn left immediately. Both these intersections are well marked. Continue to follow the blue blazes.

8.0 Continue straight through this intersection. This is simply a disc golf access trail.

8.3 Go under Route 119 (Great Seneca Highway).

8.4 Turn right onto the boardwalk. The trail is now blazed white.

8.5 Stay to the left to remain on the white trail.

SRT builders went to great lengths to make this trail last. Creek crossings are "shored up" with modular concrete sections.

8.8 Cross Seneca Creek Road. The Mink Hollow Trail trailhead is directly opposite and clearly marked.

9.0 You can now see the lake to the left. Turn left at this intersection and then right to connect with the lake loop. The Mink Hollow Trail continues straight and will connect with the lake loop as well, but I want us to ride the entire lake loop.

9.2 Continue straight and to the left; to the right is the end of the Mink Hollow Trail. From now on we will basically stay to the left to ride around the lake in a counterclockwise direction. The trail will be blazed blue.

9.4 Stay straight through this intersection.

9.8 Turn left and go over a small bridge and then left at the next intersection to continue following the perimeter of the lake.

9.9 Stay to the right; the left fork is a dead end at the lake.

10.3 Turn left at this intersection and continue following the lake perimeter.

10.5 Stay to the right.

10.6 Turn left and follow the blue arrows over the bridge; stay left again.

10.9 Stay to the right; continue following the blue blazes.

11.0 Turn right to go over the small bridge and then turn left after crossing the bridge.

11.4 You've reached the Clopper Lake Boat Center. Restrooms are available here. Continue riding in front of the boat center; the trail continues to the right along the small traffic circle.

11.6 Stay to the right and continue straight as you enjoy the great view of the lake to the left.

12.2 Stay to the right to exit the Clopper Lake perimeter trail. At this point you will backtrack all the way back to Schaeffer Farms.

20.0 You're back at Schaffer's white loop. If you want, you can turn left and backtrack. We'll turn right to complete the white loop. Immediately after turning right, stay to the right. At this point simply follow the white blazes back to your vehicle.

21.0 Continue to the right to stay on the white loop. To the left is the orange trail we mentioned early on at mile marker 0.5.

21.2 Stay to the right.

21.9 Stay to the right to complete the loop.

RIDE INFORMATION

Local Events and Attractions
The MoCo Epic—annual epic ride in Montgomery County, Maryland: www.mocoepic.com

Restaurants
La Mexicana: 13016 Middlebrook Rd., Germantown, MD 20704; (301) 972-0500; www.lamexicanaonline.com

Restrooms
A portable toilet is available in the parking area of Schaeffer Farms. Restrooms are also available at Seneca Creek State Park and in the parking area at the corner of Schaeffer Road and Germantown Park Road adjacent to the playground and tennis courts.

Honorable Mentions

There are a few rides that I have not detailed in the book but which I think require at least an honorable mention. In most cases the rides included in this section are heavily documented and it would be redundant for me to include them again in this book, or they offer limited access or may be restricted at a moment's notice. In some cases the rides are also simple out-and-backs that are easy to follow. I will continue to explore these in the hopes of crafting complete loops to share with you in the future. Please visit the book's companion site, www.bestridesdc.com, for updates and info on these and all the routes in the book.

THE NATIONAL ARBORETUM—HM-A

The National Arboretum ride is well documented in dozens of publications and websites. You can squeeze out a 9- to 10-mile road loop within the research facilities. The Arboretum is open year-round, except for December 25, from 8 a.m. to 5 p.m. strict. Call before you go, (202) 245-2726, because they tend to close the facilities without warning on occasion. I have showed up at the gate twice only to be turned away twice. The roads within the facility are easy to follow and allow you to craft your own loop. For additional information visit the official Arboretum's site at www.usna.usda.gov.

SLIGO CREEK—HM-B

The Sligo Creek Trail is another regional bike trail that follows the Sligo Creek from central Montgomery County to the border of Prince George's County. The trail is simply an out-and-back from Wheaton Regional Park in Montgomery County to New Hampshire Avenue along the Prince George's County border. The trail is approximately 8.5 miles in length, well-marked, and easy to follow. For additional information and maps of the trail, visit the Montgomery County Parks website at www.montgomeryparks.org/.

N.W. BRANCH TRAIL—HM-C

The N.W. Branch Trail is another hard-surface trail that extends from the Capital Beltway in the southeastern portion of Montgomery County to Prince George's County and connects with the Anacostia Tributary Trail System. The N.W. Branch is actually two trails—the natural-surface portion of the trail north of the Beltway that is closed to bikes and the hard-surface trail mentioned here. This is another out-and-back trail that is well marked and easy to follow. You can combine it with the Sligo Creek Trail to create a longer ride. I will continue to explore ways to link these two trails together to offer a complete loop.

THE C&O CANAL—HM-D

The Canal is another heavily documented route that runs from Georgetown in DC to Cumberland, Maryland. Feasibly you could ride this path all the way to Pittsburgh, Pennsylvania. I do use the canal on a couple of rides in the book. If you are interested, the National Park Service website (www.nps.gov) offers comprehensive information on the Canal.

THE WASHINGTON AND OLD DOMINION TRAIL (W&OD)—HM-E

Certain sections of the W&OD (or "WOD," as local users like to call this trail) are highlighted in a few of the rides in the book, including the Loudoun County road loop, the CCT shuttle ride, and the Arlington Beltway. You can, if you want, ride the entire length of the CCT from Shirlington in Alexandria to Purcellville in Loudoun County. The paved trail extends for nearly 45 miles along the heartland of Virginia's countryside and offers a great challenge to any rider. For more information, maps, photos, and videos of the trail, visit The Northern Virginia Regional Park Authority's website at www.nvrpa.org/park/w_od_railroad and the Friends of the W&OD Trail website at www.wodfriends.his.com.

Nestled on Broad Street in Falls Church, right along the W&OD, is a small bike shop that has had a big impact with riders in the region, Bikenetic (www.bikenetic.com). The small shop has sponsored riders in various races and regional events and in the process has become a hub and meeting place for many. Their location helps, but their attitude has made them special and the reason more and more riders keep coming back through their doors. If you get a chance, stop by and say hi; they'll give you free advice and hook you up with whatever you need.

LAKE ACCOTINK MTB TRAILS—HM-F

Lake Accotink is a popular destination for mountain bikers in the region and generally an extension to the Wakefield trails detailed in the book. You can access the small network of trails from within the main gravel loop that circles the lake by the same name. From the small beach and merry-go-round, head up and over the dam to access the trails. Directions are available on the "Where to Ride" sections of both the LORO (www.logoffrideon.com) and MORE (www.more-mtb.org) forums.

FORT CIRCLE—HM-G

The Fort Circle Trail is one of the only trails within the District that offers singletrack paths. The trailhead is easily accessible from Branch Avenue in the district. The trail is a 7.5-mile out-and-back.

SKYLINE DRIVE—HM-H

Skyline is a regional (national) favorite and well-documented route extremely popular with road cyclists. This is not an easy ride. It is a 105-mile ride along the crest of Skyline Drive that offers breathtaking views of the Shenandoah Valley. For more info visit the National Park Service website at www.nps.gov.

Rides at a Glance

LESS THAN 10 MILES

Arlington and the Pentagon
Wakefield Park
Meadowood Recreation Area
Fountainhead Regional Park
Fairland
Cabin John Regional Park
The North Tract
National Harbor
Rosaryville State Park

10-20 MILES

Prince William Forest Park
Anacostia River Walk
The National Mall L'Enfant's Grand Avenue
The Four Bridges
The Tidal Basin and the Waterfront
The Alexandria Loop
Burke Lake Park
The Arlington Beltway
Laurel Hill
Arlandia
Elizabeth Furnace
Mount Vernon Loop
Agricultural Greenbelt
Sugarloaf Mountain Base Loop
Upper Rock Creek and Montgomery County
Avalon and Rockburn
Schaeffer Farms

MORE THAN 20 MILES

The Capital Crescent Trail and Rock Creek Park
Loudoun County Roads
Prince William Road Ride, Brentsville and Manassas Loops
The CCT, North to South
Frederick Road Ride – The Covered Bridges
Montgomery County Back Roads
Seneca Ridge Trail

Regional Bicycle Clubs and Advocacy Groups

Washington Area Bicycle Association (WABA): WABA is the national capital region's nonprofit bicycle advocacy and education membership association. Established in 1972, WABA's mission has been to create a healthy, more livable region by promoting bicycling for fun, fitness, and affordable transportation; advocating for better bicycling conditions and transportation choices for a healthier environment; and educating children and adults about safe bicycling. www.waba.org

Mid-Atlantic Off-Road Enthusiasts (MORE): MORE, founded in 1992, is a nonprofit organization representing thousands of area mountain bikers in the mid-Atlantic region. MORE volunteers maintain more than 250 miles of natural-surface trails in 25 state and county parks throughout the region. The club also leads hundreds of rides each year at local parks, ranging from beginner to advanced levels. www.more-mtb.org

Potomac Pedalers: The Potomac Pedalers is a nonprofit educational, recreational, and social organization and the largest cycling club in the Washington, DC region. Potomac Pedalers offers over 1,000 group rides each year covering the nation's capital and the surrounding countryside of Maryland and Virginia. www.potomacpedalers.org

Frederick Pedalers: The Frederick Pedalers Bicycle Club is a nonprofit organization run by volunteers that offers rides of all classes in and around the Frederick area. The Pedalers are primarily a road cycling club but occasionally have rides on the C&O towpath or other trails in the region. www.frederickpedalers.org

Babes on Bikes: Babes on Bikes is a group of women who enjoy bicycling and meet regularly to bike the paved trails and quiet roads in northern Virginia, Washington, DC, and Maryland. www.babesonbikes.org

Ride Index

Agricultural Greenbelt, 190

Alexandria Loop, 46

Anacostia River Walk, 1

Arlandia, 103

Arlington and the Pentagon, 87

Arlington Beltway, 62

Avalon and Rockburn, 227

Burke Lake Park, 56

C&O Canal, 258

Cabin John Regional Park, 175

Capital Crescent Trail and Rock Creek
    Park, 9

CCT, North to South, 146

Elizabeth Furnace, 113

Fairland, 165

Fort Circle, 259

Fountainhead Regional Park, 158

Four Bridges, 27

Frederick Road Ride – The Covered
    Bridges, 183

Lake Accotink MTB Trails, 258

Laurel Hill, 69

Loudoun County Roads, 118

Meadowood Recreation Area, 124

Montgomery County Back Roads, 197

Mount Vernon Loop, 129

National Arboretum, 257

National Harbor, 220

National Mall – L'Enfant's Grand
    Avenue, 18

North Tract, 208

N.W. Branch Trail, 257

Prince William Forest Park, 78

Prince William Road Ride, Brentsville
    and Manassas Loops, 137

Rosaryville State Park, 236

Schaeffer Farms, 242

Seneca Ridge Trail (SRT), 249

Skyline Drive, 259

Sligo Creek, 257

Sugarloaf Mountain Base loop, 203

Tidal Basin and the Waterfront, 36

Upper Rock Creek and Montgomery
    County, 214

Wakefield Park, 96

Washington and Old Dominion Trail
    (W&OD), 258

About the Author

Martin Fernandez is a native of Lima, Peru, who transplanted his roots in the Washington, DC metropolitan area in the mid-'80s. He has lived from northern Baltimore in Timonium to his current home in northern Virginia and several places in between the two, exploring all by bike. His love for cycling goes way back, but it really flourished when he was in the Army and stationed at Ft. Myer along the perimeter of Arlington National Cemetery. "Those early morning PT rides through Arlington National Cemetery and over the Memorial Bridge and into the Mall really cemented my love for the sport. Seeing the mist rise from the Potomac and riding along some of the most iconic monuments and memorials in the nation's capital with only my breath to keep me company made me appreciate and love the sites that this city and its surrounding areas have to offer. There is no greater pleasure than exploring your home aboard two wheels." That love for cycling prompted Martin to write his first cycling guide in the mid-'90s, *Mountain Biking the Washington, DC/Baltimore Area: An Atlas of Northern Virginia, Maryland, and DC's Greatest Off-Road Bicycle Rides*, also available through Falcon Press. You may run into Martin along the back roads and paths of Prince William County or on the trails at Fountainhead or Wakefield.

Come Ride With Us!

INTERNATIONAL MOUNTAIN BICYCLING ASSOCIATION

You've just purchased, or are about to purchase, the mountain bike of your dreams. Where will you take your new steed? Who will you ride with? Joining IMBA's network of chapters, clubs and patrols taps you into a friendly network of experienced mountain bikers. They host rides for all skill levels, build trails and get together before and after rides to share stories and plan the next adventure. Find a local group by visiting imba.com/near-you.

FIVE RECENT ACCOMPLISHMENTS

1) *Built incredible trails.* IMBA's trailbuilding pros teamed with volunteers around the nation to build sustainable, fun singletrack like the 32-mile system at Pennsylvania's Raystown Lake.

2) *Won grants to build or improve trails.* Your contributions to IMBA's Trail Building Fund were multiplied with six-figure grants of federal money for trail systems.

3) *Challenged anti-bike policies.* IMBA works closely with all of the federal land managing agencies and advises them on how to create bike opportunities and avoid policies that curtail trail access.

4) *Made your voice heard.* When anti-bike interests moved to try to close sections of the 2,500-mile Continental Divide trail to bikes, IMBA rallied its members and collected more than 7,000 comments supporting keeping the trail open to bikes.

5) *Put kids on bikes.* The seventh edition of National Take a Kid Mountain Biking Day put more than 20,000 children on bikes.

FIVE CURRENT GOALS

1) *Host regional bike summits.* We're boosting local trail development by hosting summits in distinct regions of the country, bringing trail advocates and regional land managers together.

2) *Build the next generation of trail systems* with innovative projects, including IMBA's sustainably built "flow trails" for gravity-assisted fun!

3) *Create "Gateway" trails* to bring new riders into the sport.

4) *Fight blanket bans against bikes* that unwisely suggest we don't belong in backcountry places.

5) *Strengthen its network* of IMBA-affiliated clubs with a powerful chapter program.

FOUR THINGS YOU CAN DO FOR YOUR SPORT

1) *Join IMBA.* Get involved with IMBA and take action close to home through your local IMBA-affiliated club. An organization is only as strong as its grassroots membership. IMBA needs your help in protecting and building great trails right here.

2) *Volunteer.* Join a trail crew day for the immensely satisfying experience of building a trail you'll ride for years to come. Ask us how.

3) *Speak up.* Tell land-use and elected officials how important it is to preserve mountain bike access. Visit IMBA's web site for action issues and talking points.

4) *Respect other trail users.* Bike bans result from conflict, real or perceived. By being good trail citizens, we can help end the argument that we don't belong on trails.

YOU BELONG WITH IMBA — JOIN

Join IMBA at www.imba.com or call 1-888-442-IMBA